# The Indoor Gardener's Companion

# The Indoor Gardener's Companion

by Dr. Dennis B. McConnell

Illustrated by Karen S. Brown

Service Communications, Ltd.

VAN NOSTRAND REINHOLD COMPANY
New York    Cincinnati    Toronto    London    Melbourne

Copyright © 1978 by Service Communications, Ltd.

Library of Congress Catalog Number 77-83700

Printed in the U.S.A.

Published in 1978 by Service Communications, Ltd. and
Van Nostrand Reinhold Company
A division of Litton Educational Publishing, Inc.
450 West 33rd Street, New York, NY 10001, U.S.A.

Van Nostrand Reinhold Limited
1410 Birchmount Road, Scarborough, Ontario M1P 2E7, Canada

Van Nostrand Reinhold Australia Pty. Limited
17 Queen Street, Mitcham, Victoria 3132, Australia

Van Nostrand Reinhold Company Limited
Molly Millars Lane, Wokingham, Berkshire, England

First edition
16  15  14  13  12  11  10  9  8  7  6  5  4  3  2  1

Library of Congress Cataloging in Publication Data
McConnell, Dennis B
        The indoor gardener's companion.


        1. House plants. I. Title.
SB419.M246        635.9'65        77-83700
ISBN 0-442-25267-6

# Contents

# PLANT DIRECTORY

## Common Name/Botanical Name Index

The recent publication of *Hortus III*—the standard cultivated plant reference book compiled and published by the Baily Hortorium at Cornell University—has changed the scientific names of a number of common indoor plants. To ensure that the information in this book be useful for many years to come, these name changes have been incorporated.

6

# INTRODUCTION

## From History . . .

Each year more people find enjoyment and pleasure in growing indoor plants. When I moved to Florida in 1970, one facet of the indoor plant industry, foliage plants, was estimated to be worth 18 million dollars. The estimated value now has increased to over 90 million dollars, and it is predicted that it will exceed 150 million dollars in the next decade. Production and sales have similarly increased in other states. Is this sudden and dramatic increase in the use of plant material just a passing fad or does it reflect a more basic human need?

People have grown plants inside buildings since the founding of early civilizations. Collecting and growing plants is an activity shared by people throughout history. During the early Middle Eastern civilizations, container-grown plants were used extensively, the Hanging Gardens of Babylon being the most notable example. Detailed records from any historical period show an intense interest in exotic, colorful, and attractive plants. Almost 3,500 years ago Thutmosis III of Egypt collected over 275 plants during his military campaigns in Syria, primarily for their aesthetic appeal. The arts and ruins of China, Greece, India, and Italy reveal the growing of potted plants.

The Romans are credited with the first greenhouses, built from transparent mica which allowed them to grow flowers throughout the year. However, only the financially secure could afford greenhouses and other facilities to grow the plants which were available. The pattern established by the Romans with only the wealthy and the aristocracy enjoying decorative plants remained unchanged for centuries.

From the fifteenth through the nineteenth century man's knowledge of the world grew enormously and plants were collected from all over the world and grown in botanical gardens. Two events occurred during the Victorian era which changed man's relationship with plants. Architectural styles changed, creating homes with windows large enough to allow ample light for growing plants indoors. The other change was the industrial revolution when the majority of Europe's population moved from the country to the city. Within a few generations, society had changed; most people who no longer spent their time outdoors in naturalistic settings were spending most of their time inside factories or offices, isolated from nature.

By 1860, Thomas Rochford and Sons, Limited, in England, were commercially growing ficus, ferns, and palms for sale as indoor plants. Photographs and drawings from the Victorian era vividly illustrate the popularity of these plants. The ability of plants to survive and flourish is demonstrated by the fact that they are still extensively used today to enhance our interior decors.

Use of indoor plants in the United States parallels that of England and Western Europe, but occurs at later dates because the population shift from rural to urban areas did not occur until the 1920's. However, as early as 1914, thousands of palms were exported from England to the United States for interior decorative purposes. Large-scale production of Boston ferns for use as indoor pot plants was started in Florida around the same time. During the late 20's and early 30's, the population shift from rural to urban areas continued and accelerated, with many people moving from small farms to major metropolitan areas. A major producer of indoor plants in Florida was founded in the 1930's and capitalized on selling inexpensive indoor plants to millions of Americans who had become permanent residents in a man-made environment of concrete and steel. Use of indoor plants in the United States continued to increase moderately through the late 40's. Demand for indoor plants increased dramatically during the 1950's and many new greenhouses and other plant growing areas were built. The late 60's and early 70's have seen tremendous expansion of greenhouses for commercial production of indoor plants. In California, Florida, and Texas where the majority of indoor plants are produced, there has been more than a 300% increase in greenhouses used for growing indoor plants since the 1950's. Some large companies have added more than 50 acres of greenhouses where they grow indoor plants.

# To Hobby . . .

A hobby is defined as an activity engaged in primarily for pleasure, and house plants provide pleasure for millions of Americans. For many indoor gardeners, the satisfaction of growing an attractive plant provides enough pleasure to make house plants a worthwhile hobby. They grow plants obtained from a friend or bought because they have special appeal. The current interest in house plants is demonstrated by the popularity of plants in the daily comic section of newspapers where cartoons depict characters concerned about their plants' health and care. In addition, almost all newspapers carry daily or weekly columns on growing and maintaining indoor plants.

Many indoor gardeners share their interest with other people by joining a garden club that emphasizes indoor plants. The meetings provide opportunities to discuss the latest techniques for best success with plants. Some indoor gardeners develop an intense interest in particular plants or plant families and specialize in growing ferns, bromeliads, succulents, or other plant types. These specialized interests provide opportunities to join national societies and communicate with people across the United States. National and international meetings of these societies provide opportunities to meet other plant growers with similar interests. Some national societies, such as the African Violet Society, are large enough to have local clubs which hold "plant shows" where you can display your prize varieties. (See Appendix for list of plant societies.)

Growing house plants as a hobby can even change your life! Several successful companies selling plants were founded by people who were growing plants as an avocation and soon found it their vocation.

Although many people grow and use plants to enhance their interior decor, too often creative uses of plants are overlooked. When you grow plants, you also can create with plants. Cuttings made when you prune and groom your plants can be used in floral and foliage arrangements. By using accessory pieces, you can create original centerpieces to accent your dining table or buffet when entertaining. Your artistic talents can be displayed in terrariums which can depict a variety of miniature scenes, from deserts to tropical rain forests. You can try your skill in miniature landscaping by grouping together small rooted cuttings that complement each other in dishgardens. The possibilities are unlimited and depend only on your imagination.

An interest in carpentry and construction is often reinforced by a plant collection as plants offer an excellent way to display your handicraft. Construction of plant stands, window greenhouses, small home greenhouses, or an indoor greenhouse with a self-contained light provides real satisfaction and allows you to grow more of the plants you prefer.

If your plant interests are cosmopolitan, you can spend many pleasant hours in nearby botanical gardens. Interest in house plants has stimulated trips to neighboring states or even foreign countries to visit world-famous botanical gardens. There you will find a variety of plants you may want to grow and you will be able to see plants larger than most of us can grow in our homes. Travel to foreign countries may mean an opportunity to collect new plants or to meet fellow plant enthusiasts.

Even if foreign travel is not feasible economically, by growing house plants you will have representatives from many foreign countries in your own home. Space and other considerations may limit you, but by careful selection even a small plant collection can represent several continents. You could have a sansevieria from Africa, a cast iron plant from China, a rubber tree from India, and a Boston fern from the Americas. Plants can provide opportunities to increase your knowledge and awareness of your local community and of the world you live in.

## Counterbalance to Concrete and Steel

America is changing, slowly in some areas, more rapidly in others. Densely populated areas sprawl for miles from our urban centers. Housing patterns are also changing with more and more Americans living in condominiums and townhouses. The shift from single family dwellings to multiple family residences has removed us a little further from natural surroundings. What can compensate for this separation from nature more effectively than bringing nature indoors with house plants? Man's most immediate environment is inside, and plants are the ideal way to create attractive, restful settings where we spend most time.

Growing plants indoors provides people with a welcome contrast from the pressures imposed on them by modern society. Observing the natural rhythms of plant growth makes us aware of the cyclic patterns of nature and creates a feeling of harmony with our environment.

The concept of using plants to reduce human tension and to make people feel more comfortable in their environment has been used in a large office building in West Germany. In construction of the building, partitions or walls between offices were eliminated; instead, large indoor plants are used to create a "living wall." Office morale has improved, production efficiency has increased, and sick leave taken by employees has decreased.

Perhaps the most familiar example of people's response to indoor plants can be found in shopping malls. People feel more at ease and spend longer periods of time in shopping malls with plants than in shopping malls without plants. Without indoor plants many of the most attractive shopping centers would be no more than bare, sterile environments with only building materials and people. You can use indoor plants in your home to achieve the same effect of restfulness and comfort, creating your own oasis in today's desert of concrete and steel.

Cuttings and small potted plants can be shared with friends and relatives who can take them wherever they go. In a mobile society indoor plants can be moved to new homes and provide a link with the past. In our own home three plants represent a living legacy passed on by our grandmothers. Nine years ago my wife's grandmother gave us a birdsnest sansevieria and a grape leaf ivy. The third plant was my own grandmother's Christmas cactus. These plants have made four moves with us and are a meaningful part of our plant collection.

## Plants Are Living Organisms

Indoor plants are alive and demand a certain amount of care in order to survive in our homes. If we kept plants in our homes just for the shape and color, plastic plants would be all we would find inside homes. A plant responds to the treatment it receives and the location where it is placed. A plant that does not receive enough light soon shows that it is struggling to survive. If it is not getting enough water, it will wilt or lose its leaves. If it needs fertilizer, it will show deficiency symptoms. Given proper care, it will thrive and you will be rewarded by seeing your plant put on new growth or seeing the first blossoms open. The truly satisfying thing is that the plant is responding to your care, and you are responsible for the plant. Actually plants are "easy-to-care-for pets" requiring only light, water, fertilizer, and an occasional grooming.

In the last few years much has been said about the benefits of talking to your plants. Although a long conversation with your favorite philodendron may make you feel better, horticulturally it will not do a great deal for your plant. It may temporarily increase the carbon dioxide level and increase air circulation but not enough to make an appreciable difference. However, people who talk to plants are probably more conscientious about the cultural needs of their plants. Plants need people to remove the dust from their leaves, to feel the soil and water when dry, and to notice pest infestations before they become problems.

Our perception and awareness of our surroundings is increased through our efforts to grow plants. They function as biological indicators of conditions in our homes. Their response indicates rooms that are too hot or too cold, where the humidity is low, or where drafts exist.

As exploration of formerly impenetrable jungles, mountains, deserts, and rain forests continues, the number of plants which can be grown indoors increases. Even now the phenomenal variety of shape, size, and color in plants currently available allows us to select the right plant for any interior landscaping location.

There is no sharp dividing line between outdoor plants and indoor plants. However, for a plant to grow successfully inside, it must be able to adapt to the conditions which exist within our homes. Of the over 250,000 herbs, shrubs, and trees, less than 2% can be used as house plants without drastically changing conditions in our homes. But that leaves about 5,000 plants that could be grown or used in your home. By understanding how plants grow and the cultural demands of plants, you can create microclimates in your home that will allow you to grow a far greater assortment of plants than you ever thought possible.

# RIGHT PLANT/PROPER PLACEMENT

## Photosynthesis and Plant Growth

Did you know that when you buy a plant, you are really buying an energy converter? Although it sounds a bit bizarre, like something out of *Flash Gordon* or *Star Trek*, plants have the unique ability to capture light energy and convert it to chemical energy. This energy conversion occurs in the biochemical process called photosynthesis. Most people have heard of photosynthesis but somehow too few understand the significance of it all. Photosynthesis is one of the greatest natural wonders of the universe. In order for a plant to survive and grow in your home, you have to provide conditions which allow photosynthesis to occur.

Photosynthesis depends on many factors and may be easiest to understand by examining a growing house plant as shown on the next page.

The chemical solution (water and dissolved chemicals) available in the soil enters the root hairs and is transported into the root and up the stem through the vascular strands. The leaf of the plant takes in carbon dioxide through tiny pores called stomata. The carbon dioxide dissolves in the moisture in the leaf. Light striking the leaf provides the energy to combine the carbon dioxide with water from the soil and produces simple sugars and oxygen. The simple sugars are chemically combined into more complex food products and moved to other parts of the plant. The oxygen produced during photosynthesis exits via the leaf's stomata and increases the atmospheric oxygen content. Photosynthesis takes place mainly in the leaves, but may occur in any cell containing chlorophyll. As light intensity increases, photosynthesis increases until an optimum light level is reached. Each

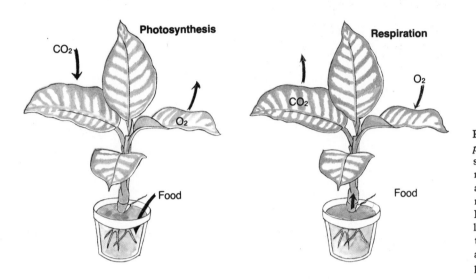

Plants use the process of *photosynthesis* (in which sunlight splits water molecules into hydrogen and oxygen atoms) to manufacture their "food." Excess food is stored and later released for energy through *cellular respiration*, a process opposite of photosynthesis.

plant type has a different optimum light intensity level. Increasing the light intensity beyond this point will not increase photosynthesis and may be detrimental to the plant.

Although higher plants consume energy just as animals do, they differ from animals because they manufacture their own food. All living cells in a plant (and there can be millions) require food in order to stay alive (just as your cells do). Part of the plant's manufactured food is used or consumed by the plant to stay alive; a certain portion of the food may be stored in the roots, the stem, or the leaves. Plants can grow almost forever and consequently excess food is utilized for new growth. Therefore, plants have solved the problem that many humans wish they could solve; they never get fat from stored excess food.

That leaf on your house plant which seems so quiet and inactive is really an intensely active living part of the plant with molecules forming, electrons flowing, gases exchanging, and water flowing—all working together to make food. All these chemical and physical activities are occurring *without* pollution, with the end result being an increased amount of both plant material and oxygen in your home or apartment.

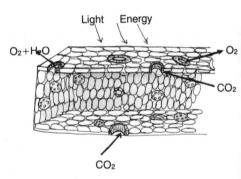

Cross section of leaf showing the *stomata* through which plants cells absorb carbon dioxide from the atmosphere and in turn release free oxygen and excess water.

# Light Intensity

In your home it is easy to provide water and supplemental fertilizer to a potted plant, but providing adequate light for photosynthesis to occur is frequently a problem. Too often people locate plants where light levels are too low and occasionally where light levels are too high.

If plants are located in areas where light levels are too low, there will not be enough energy available to power the photosynthetic process and your plants will be unable to manufacture as much food as they need to stay alive. The plants will continue to consume stored food until the entire organism is so weakened that it no longer can fend off illness, and the plant usually succumbs to a disease or dies of starvation. However, since many of our indoor plants are found naturally growing in heavy shade, they have never developed the ability to withstand full sunlight and the foliage will actually burn if placed in full sun. It is important to know the light intensity levels in our homes so plants can be located where they will grow best.

Similar to other energy or power sources, light energy can be measured so we know how much is available. Traditionally, light energy is measured by a unit called the footcandle, which is the amount of light cast by a candle on a white surface one foot away in a completely dark room. Measuring light energy in footcandles tells us the light intensity or the brightness of the light. Outdoors, the light intensity on a clear, sunny day may range from 10,000 footcandles in an open sunny area to 250 footcandles or less in the shade of a large tree. Inside our homes, light levels may vary from 15 footcandles to over 2,000 footcandles near a south window.

Remember that light intensity indoors is determined by light intensity outdoors. Shade from other buildings, trees, and roof overhangs will all affect the amount of light inside each home. Light intensities will vary during the spring, summer, fall, and winter because the sun's angle with the horizon changes. During cloudy winter weather, outside light levels in the north are as low as 500 footcandles. Consequently, interior light levels are extremely low during these periods.

The only accurate way to determine light levels in your home is to use either a direct reading footcandle meter, a photographic light meter, or a camera equipped with a built-in meter. Table 1 (page 18) converts f-stops at various ASA's to approximate footcandles. Using this method, your home can be divided into four areas which have the following light levels for 8 hours a day.

(1) Low light areas: 25 to 75 footcandles
(2) Medium light areas: 75 to 200 footcandles
(3) High light areas: Over 200 footcandles but not direct sun
(4) Sunny light areas: At least 4 hours of direct sun

Measuring light intensities is necessary to determine how far from windows (normally your brightest areas) you can place your plants. Commercially, all plants discussed in this book are grown under a minimum of 2,000 footcandles. In most homes that figure is exceeded only on window sills of east, south, or west windows,

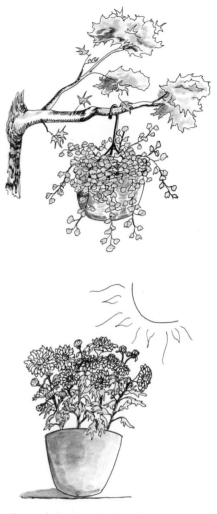

Some plants grow best in shade, others grow best in full sun, while still others grow well in both.

● Memo

Light intensity indoors is often highest during spring and fall when the sun's angle with the horizon is lower and most trees are leafless.

# F-STOP / FOOTCANDLE CONVERSION
## TABLE 1

Converting light meter readings to footcandles:
Built-in light meter. ASA setting of 25.
Shutter speed 1/60.

| f-Stop | Footcandles |
|--------|-------------|
| 2 | 40 |
| 2.8 | 75 |
| 4 | 150 |
| 5.6 | 300 |
| 8 | 600 |
| 11 | 1,200 |
| 16 | 2,400 |

Photographic light meter. ASA setting of 200.
Shutter speed 1/500. Aim camera at a piece
of white paper placed where the plant will
be located.

| f-Stop | Footcandles |
|--------|-------------|
| 4.5 | 150 |
| 6.3 | 300 |
| 8 | 550 |
| 11 | 1,200 |
| 16 | 2,500 |
| 22 | 5,000 |

● Memo

Some indoor foliage plants are native to tropical rain forests where they never receive any sunlight.

or in front of large east, south, or west windows. Without measuring light intensities, the best policy to follow is to place your plants in the best light possible, while avoiding full sun locations for most foliage plants. Low interior light levels can be approximated by knowing that most people find 20 to 30 footcandles necessary for reading.

The growth a plant makes after it is placed in a new location serves as the best indication of whether the light intensity is suitable for the plant. If the light intensity is too low, the internodes (spaces between the leaves) will be much longer than the internodes on the older portion of the plant, new leaves will be much smaller than older leaves, leaf color will be a lighter green on the newer foliage than on the older foliage, and the lower leaves may die.

After evaluating your home in terms of light intensities, you'll probably realize that many locations where you feel a plant is

If you place your plants in inadequate low light areas their new growth will often result in long irregular *internodes* (space between the leaves).

needed don't receive much light. The following list is a selection of some of the best plants available for low light areas.

## PLANTS FOR LOW LIGHT AREAS

Plants listed will tolerate low light levels (25 to 50 footcandles), but will grow better in higher light. A low light area receives no direct light and usually is more than 7 feet from windows.

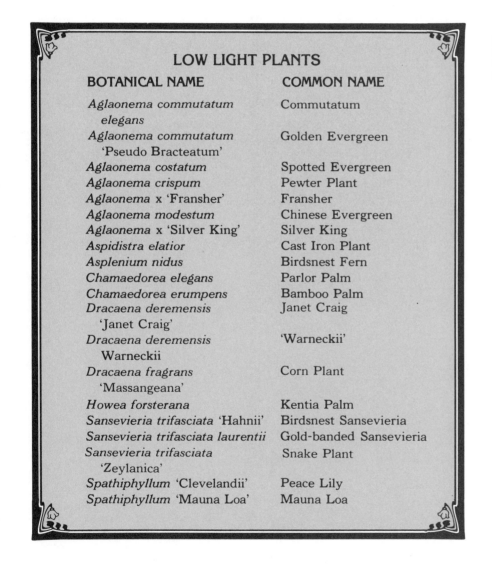

Most indoor plants should not be placed in full sun as sun scorch or leaf burn will make them unattractive.

### LOW LIGHT PLANTS

| BOTANICAL NAME | COMMON NAME |
| --- | --- |
| *Aglaonema commutatum elegans* | Commutatum |
| *Aglaonema commutatum* 'Pseudo Bracteatum' | Golden Evergreen |
| *Aglaonema costatum* | Spotted Evergreen |
| *Aglaonema crispum* | Pewter Plant |
| *Aglaonema* x 'Fransher' | Fransher |
| *Aglaonema modestum* | Chinese Evergreen |
| *Aglaonema* x 'Silver King' | Silver King |
| *Aspidistra elatior* | Cast Iron Plant |
| *Asplenium nidus* | Birdsnest Fern |
| *Chamaedorea elegans* | Parlor Palm |
| *Chamaedorea erumpens* | Bamboo Palm |
| *Dracaena deremensis* 'Janet Craig' | Janet Craig |
| *Dracaena deremensis* Warneckii | 'Warneckii' |
| *Dracaena fragrans* 'Massangeana' | Corn Plant |
| *Howea forsterana* | Kentia Palm |
| *Sansevieria trifasciata* 'Hahnii' | Birdsnest Sansevieria |
| *Sansevieria trifasciata laurentii* | Gold-banded Sansevieria |
| *Sansevieria trifasciata* 'Zeylanica' | Snake Plant |
| *Spathiphyllum* 'Clevelandii' | Peace Lily |
| *Spathiphyllum* 'Mauna Loa' | Mauna Loa |

## PLANTS FOR SUNNY AREAS

As with many things in life, too much light is just as detrimental as too little and the majority of indoor plants should not be placed in full sun. Sun scorch or leaf burn will soon make them very unattractive. The following is a list of plants that can be placed in sunny south, east, or west windows if air circulation keeps temperatures below a maximum of 85°F.

Plants listed will grow on a sunny window sill or floor locations in front of large east, south, or west windows.

### SUN LOVING PLANTS

| BOTANICAL NAME | COMMON NAME |
| --- | --- |
| **FLOWERING PLANTS** | |
| *Abutilon hybridium* | Flowering Maple |
| *Begonia semperflorens* | Wax Begonia |
| *Bougainvillea spp.* | Bougainvillea |
| *Carissa grandiflora* 'Bonsai' | Natal Palm |
| *Chrysanthemum morifolium* | Chrysanthemum |
| *Euphorbia pulcherrima* | Poinsettia |
| *Euphorbia milii splendens* | Dwarf Crown-of-Thorns |
| *Hibiscus rosa-sinensis* | Chinese Hibiscus |
| *Hoya carnosa* | Wax Plant |
| *Justicia brandegeana* | Shrimp Plant |
| *Kalanchoe blossfeldiana* | Christmas Kalanchoe |
| *Pelargonium* hybrids | Geraniums |
| *Punica granatum nana* | Dwarf Pomegranate |
| **CACTI AND SUCCULENTS** | |
| *Aloe barbadensis* | Medicine Plant |
| *Astrophytum myriostigma* | Bishop's Cap Cactus |
| *Beaucarnea recurvata* | Ponytail |
| *Crassula argentea* | Jade Plant |
| *Dyckia brevifolia* | Miniature Agave |
| *Haworthia subfasciata* | Little Zebra Plant |
| *Pedilanthus tithymaloides* | Devil's Backbone or Ribbon Cactus |
| *Sansevieria spp.* | Sansevierias |

● Memo

Most indoor flowering plants require 2 to 4 hours of sun a day to produce flowers. High intensity artificial light can be substituted for natural sunlight.

Not only light intensity but also light duration or the length of time the plant is exposed to light is important. You can compensate for low light levels by increasing the time interval during which the plant can photosynthesize. Twelve hours at 50 footcandles will produce approximately the same results as 8 hours at 75 footcandles. By strategically locating your plants close to supplemental light sources, you can improve both their appearance and the appearance of the room.

# ARTIFICIAL LIGHT

Sunlight is the best and cheapest source of light for growing plants but artificial light is often used to enhance a plant or to prolong the length of time a plant can be kept in a low light area. Supplemental light may be provided by either incandescent or fluorescent light.

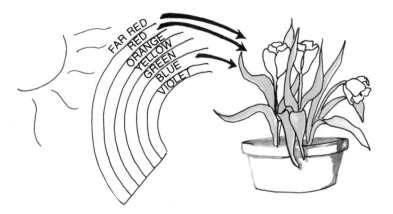

Sunlight consists of the colors we see in a rainbow, and for healthy growth plants utilize the light energy they receive at the blue, red and far red portions of the spectrum.

If you are using artificial light as your only light source, light quality or the color of light the plant receives becomes important. When plants are growing outside, they are exposed to the entire spectrum of the sun's radiation. This radiation includes the colors we see in a rainbow which is called "the visible spectrum." Just as some automobiles run best with premium gas, plants grow best when the light is strong in the blue, red, and far red portions of the spectrum.

Incandescent light is a poor sole source of light energy because it is low in blue wavelengths. Most of its light output is in the red and far red portions of the spectrum. Because incandescent lights convert 75 to 85% of electrical energy into heat energy rather than light energy, they are more expensive to operate. The heat generated by incandescent light bulbs will usually burn the plant's foliage if they are used as the only light source for growing plants. Although fluorescent lights are a better light source for plant growth, standard fluorescent tube light is particularly low in the red and far red portions of the light spectrum. If you want to grow an extensive number of plants in your home, you should investigate the possibilities of using artificial light. In the past

Because light in most building interiors is one-directional, plants should be turned approximately 90° each day. Otherwise, the plants will grow with curved stems.

several years, a number of specialty fluorescent tubes have been developed to more closely approximate the light quality requirements of growing plants. Both these specialty lights and attractive plant growing carts are available from a number of suppliers. (See source of supply, Appendix.) Depending on your skills as a carpenter and electrician, you can choose prefabricated units or order the bare essentials and construct plant growing areas yourself. If your primary interest is in growing plants that produce attractive flowers, we recommend joining a local indoor light society chapter. (See Appendix.)

# DAY LENGTH

Have you ever wondered why the Christmas cactus you purchased last Christmas didn't bloom this Christmas even though you've kept it growing with lots of tender loving care? Your Christmas cactus, poinsettia, and a number of other plants require a successive number of night periods uninterrupted by any light source which shines much brighter than the full moon. In many urban and suburban areas street lights emit enough light to interfere with the flowering process. Commercial growers of poinsettias, chrysanthemums, and Christmas cactus cover their plants with black shade cloth at 5:00 P.M. and uncover them at 8:00 A.M. so the plants will be in flower during any season they desire. Plant response to relative lengths of light and dark periods in a 24 hour period is known as *photoperiodism*. After the discovery in 1920 that some plants would flower only in short days, other plants were found which would flower only in long days. Continued research led to four general day-length classifications:

(1) *Short day plants*: Plants which flower when exposed to light periods of 12 hours or less.
(2) *Long day plants*: Plants which flower when exposed to light periods of 12 hours or more.
(3) *Indeterminate or day neutral plants*: Plants which have no apparent flowering response to day length.
(4) *Intermediate plants*: Plants that flower when days and nights are about 12 hours each.

Since developing this easy-to-understand classification of flowering response to photoperiod, scientists have found that high or low temperatures may modify response to photoperiod. By knowing if your plant has a specific photoperiod or temperature requirement, you will be able to succeed in having your plants flower while other people fail. (See individual plant descriptions.)

● Memo

The further north you live the shorter days are in the winter and the longer they are in the summer; the further south you live the less variation there is between summer and winter day length.

Some plants will flower only when exposed to light periods of less than 12 hours (short days and long nights), while others will flower only when exposed to light periods of 12 hours or more (long days and short nights).

For example, to keep your wax begonia (*Begonia semperflorens*) blooming in the wintertime during natural short days make sure it receives supplemental artificial light or is kept in a cool room since wax begonias won't bloom in short days if temperatures are over 70°F.

# Temperature

Before the energy crisis most of us adjusted the temperatures in our homes for our own comfort. This temperature averaged from 68 to 72°F at night and 76 to 78°F during the day. This temperature range was satisfactory for most house plants, particularly if night temperatures were lower than day temperatures. However, with rising heating and cooling costs, most people are keeping their houses cooler in the winter and warmer in the summer than they did previously. Will these higher or lower temperatures affect your plants? The answer depends on both the plant and its location.

The cooler temperatures in your home during the winter will probably benefit most of your house plants. Most house plants are "cold-blooded" or their temperatures are the same as the surrounding air temperature. The lower night temperatures will slow down the plant's rate of using the food it manufactured

Plants manufacture and store food only during the day, although they need food both day and night. When temperatures increase, plants use more of their stored food for homeostasis and growth.

23

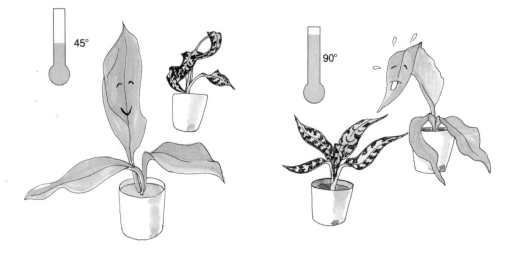

Many foliage plants are cold sensitive and cannot tolerate temperatures below 45°F. However, other plants can tolerate 45°F, but do poorly when temperatures are above 75° to 80°F.

during the day. So, during the winter, when interior light intensities tend to be low, the lower temperatures will keep your plants healthier. Many house plants which are old favorites such as aspidistras or ferns actually grow better with the cooler temperatures. However, many tropical foliage house plants are cold-sensitive and cannot tolerate temperatures much below 55°F. Aglaonemas, crotons, dieffenbachias, and peperomias are among the more cold-sensitive house plants, and they should be located in the warm areas of your home.

With a thermostat of 68°F in homes during the winter, several locations in the house may get colder than 55°F. More cold damage occurs on window sills than any other place in the house. When it is below 0°F outside, window sill temperatures can be up to 30° cooler than the room temperature. This pronounced temperature difference is aggravated when the shades or drapes are drawn, preventing warm air from circulating next to the window. If you have shades, always place the shade between the plants and the window. Many house plant growers tape newspapers on their windows to protect their plants on cold evenings. If newspaper coverings do not aesthetically appeal to you or you do not want to bother putting up papers on many winter evenings, tape a sheet of clear plastic film on the window and leave it up all winter.

Cold air is heavier than warm air and flows much like water. Consequently, floor areas directly under window sills can be cool-

During the winter, window sill temperatures may be much cooler than room temperatures. When shades are drawn always place the shade between the plant and the window.

er than adjacent floor areas. The lower level of split level homes will also be much cooler. Take advantage of the cooler winter temperatures and cooler locations in your home and grow some of the cool temperature loving house plants.

## COOL LOVING PLANTS

Some of the better plants for locations that drop down to the low 50's at night and 60's during the daytime are:

### COOL AREA PLANTS

| BOTANICAL NAME | COMMON NAME |
|---|---|
| Calceolaria crenatiflora | Slipperwort |
| Campanula isophylla | Campanula |
| Crocus spp. | Crocus |
| Cyclamen persicum giganteuna | Cyclamen |
| Fatshedera lizei | Botanical Wonder Plant |
| Fatsia japonica | Japanese Aralia |
| Hedera helix | English Ivy |
| Hyacinthus orientalis | Hyacinth |
| Narcissus hybrids | Daffodils |
| Tulipa hybrids | Tulips |

The higher indoor summer temperatures actually present more problems than the cooler winter temperatures for many house plants. Many of the flowering plants do poorly if kept inside during the warm summer months. The critical temperature is the night temperature. Temperatures should go down to at least the low 60's for the flowers to last more than a few days. In many parts of the United States, these temperatures are impossible to achieve indoors economically and the plants should be moved outside.

Certain areas in your home have a tendency to be warmer than other areas. Areas which can have excessively high temperatures detrimental to your plants include south and west windows and enclosed sun porches. Many house plants will tolerate occasional temperature periods in the high 80's but cool loving plants should

● Memo

Plants that grow best when temperatures are cool will often wilt when temperatures go above 85°.

be moved either outside or to the coolest location in your home. A number of indoor plants will remain healthy and even thrive in the warmer rooms in your home if they cool down in the evenings and have sufficient light.

The easiest way to determine maximum and minimum temperatures in various locations in your home is to use a maximum-minimum thermometer. They average about $15.00, but are worth the investment. Readings can be taken whenever you want as the thermometer will record the maximum and the minimum temperature since the last time you reset the thermometer. You may discover as I did that a south window sill can vary from a high of 95°F in the summer to a low of 40°F in the winter.

Within an average home, temperatures vary from room to room. This temperature variance allows you to use a wide diversity of plant materials in your home. If you evaluate your home to determine the differences which do exist, you'll be able to select the best plants for a location.

● Memo

Most plants that tolerate high temperatures are native to deserts or tropical jungles.

## Air Circulation

Air circulation is more important than most people realize. If you carefully watch a leaf on a plant outside, you'll notice the leaf flutters and moves ever so slightly almost all the time. The natural air currents are continuously replacing the air around each leaf with fresh air. Indoors there is very little air movement and the air tends to "layer" or stagnate over each leaf. Without a certain amount of air movement, the leaf rapidly depletes the air surrounding it of carbon dioxide which the plant uses in the photosynthetic process. As carbon dioxide is less than 1% of normal air, continual air movement is necessary to keep photosynthesis occurring.

Slow air circulation (about 1 or 2 miles per hour) aids plant health by keeping temperatures more uniform and providing air exchange for the photosynthesizing leaf. Homes with central air and forced hot air heating systems provide ample air circulation in most locations during the hot and cold periods when all the doors and windows are shut. In homes with other heating and cooling systems it may be advisable to locate the plant to take advantage of traffic patterns in the home or to use a fan or to open the windows. Windows may be opened even during the winter on warm days if plants are protected or moved away from the cold air stream.

Outdoors, the air around each leaf is constantly being replaced. Indoors, the air tends to form a layer around each leaf.

## PLANTS FOR WARM AREAS

The plants listed will do well in areas occasionally having a daytime maximum of 90 to 95°F.

### WARM AREA PLANTS

| BOTANICAL NAME | COMMON NAME |
| --- | --- |
| *Aechmea fasciata* | Silver Vase |
| *Aechmea* 'Royal Wine' | Royal Wine |
| *Aeschynanthus pulcher* | Lipstick Vine |
| *Aglaonema spp.* | Aglaonemas |
| *Ananas comosus* | Pineapple |
| *Ascocentrum miniatum* | Ascocentrum Miniatum |
| *Beaucarnea recurvata* | Ponytail |
| *Billbergia nutans* | Queen's Tears |
| *Billbergia zebrina* | Zebra Urn |
| *Brassaia actinophylla* | Schefflera |
| *Chamaedorea elegans* | Parlor Palm |
| *Chamaedorea erumpens* | Bamboo Palm |
| *Chrysalidocarpus lutescens* | Areca Palm |
| *Coffea arabica* | Coffee |
| *Cryptanthus spp.* | Cryptanthus |
| *Dieffenbachia spp.* | Dieffenbachia |
| *Dizygotheca elegantissima* | False Aralia |
| *Dracaena spp.* | Dracaena |
| *Epiphyllum* hybrids | Orchid Cactus |
| *Epipremnum spp.* | Pothos |
| *Euphorbia pulcherrima* | Poinsettia |
| *Euphorbia milii splendens* | Crown-of-Thorns |
| *Ficus spp.* | Ficus |
| *Guzmania lingulata* 'Major' | Scarlet Star |
| *Guzmania monostachia* | Striped Torch |
| *Hemigraphis alternata* 'Exotica' | Waffle Plant |
| *Hibiscus rosa-sinensis* | Chinese Hibiscus |
| *Monstera deliciosa* | Pertusum |
| *Neoregelia carolinae* 'Tricolor' | Tricolor Bromeliad |
| *Pedilanthus tithymaloides* 'Variegatus' | Devil's Backbone |
| *Peperomia spp.* | Peperomia |
| *Philodendron spp.* | Philodendron |
| *Pilea spp.* | Pilea |
| *Platycerium spp.* | Staghorn Ferns |
| *Sansevieria spp.* | Sansevierias |
| *Schlumbergera truncata* | Christmas Cactus |
| *Scindapsus spp.* | Scindapsus |
| *Spathiphyllum spp.* | Peace Lily |
| *Syngonium podophyllum* | Nephthytis |

● Memo

Many greenhouses have fans called "turbolators" to keep the air slowly circulating to improve plant growth.

Air circulation may be increased by opening windows from top.

Most house plants cannot tolerate an abrupt and drastic change in temperatures. A sudden change of about 35°F will shock the plant and it will stop growing, lose its leaves, or even die. Plants should not be located close to outside doors where the temperature may plummet abruptly when the door is opened. Other locations to avoid are those in front of heating vents and room air conditioners where temperatures fluctuate drastically.

In homes where it is not feasible to open windows, a hassock fan will gently move air within a room.

During winter months when doors and windows are closed, plants will benefit by being located near traffic patterns in the house and the circulated air they generate.

## Humidity

Although slow air movement aids plant growth indoors, it does increase the amount of transpiration (water loss from the leaves and other parts of the plant). The lower the humidity, the higher the transpiration rate is. The transpiration rate increases as the relative humidity decreases because relative humidity is the ratio of the amount of water vapor in the air to the amount that could be in the air at a specific temperature. The higher the temperature the more water vapor the air can hold and the more water the air removes from the plant. Thus, during the winter when cold outside air is warmed to heat our homes, the relative humidity becomes very low and usually averages somewhere around 10 to 15%. Low humidity is desirable to neither plants nor humans. We feel best when the relative humidity is 40 to 50% at 72°F and plants do best with a minimum of 30 to 35% if cacti and succulents are excluded. Cacti and succulents can tolerate relative humidities down to 10% for years. Many plants cannot be grown successfully indoors without increasing humidity above 25%. Water loss from the leaves occurs so rapidly that the plant cannot supply enough water to keep the leaf from drying out. The leaf margins turn brown, and eventually the entire leaf dies. This type of environmental injury is called desiccation. New leaves are more susceptible to desiccation than old leaves; and if periods of low humidity persist for any length of time, the plant is soon leafless and dies. Fortunately, for both us and our house plants, periods of extremely low relative humidity last only two to four months, and normally there are intervening periods of higher humidities during those months.

During those low humidity periods there are a number of things that can be done to offset the stress caused by low humidity. One commonly used and very natural solution is to group plants in the same general area. When plants are grouped, each plant aids the others by increasing the amount of moisture in the air. The best areas to group your plants are ones with good light intensity and a day temperature between 68 and 72°F.

● Memo

Most of the world's deserts seldom have less than 20% relative humidity.

Avoid placing plants in front of heating vents . . . underneath air conditioners . . . or close to outside doors.

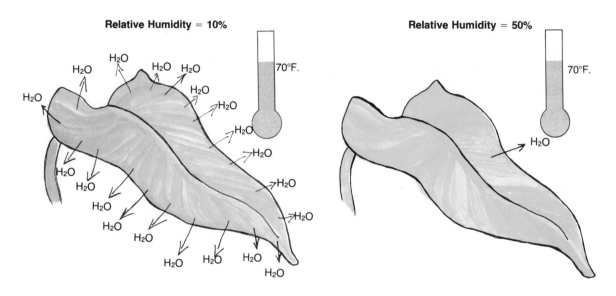

**Relative Humidity = 10%**    70°F.

$H_2O$ $H_2O$ $H_2O$ $H_2O$ $H_2O$ $H_2O$ $H_2O$ $H_2O$ $H_2O$ $H_2O$ $H_2O$ $H_2O$ $H_2O$ $H_2O$ $H_2O$ $H_2O$ $H_2O$ $H_2O$ $H_2O$

**Relative Humidity = 50%**    70°F.

$H_2O$

The lower the humidity, the more water dry air absorbs from each leaf. To counteract periods of low humidity you can use an atomizer to spray the air around the leaves of your plants.

The humidity can be increased even more if we group plants on a shallow tray about 2 inches deep which is filled with pebbles, sand, perlite, or any other inorganic material that the containers can be placed on. Water should be added to the tray as it evaporates but the water level in the tray should be kept below the level of the containers. Trays made of aluminum, plastic, or tin are used by most indoor gardeners. Remember, water will rust trays made of ferrous material.

Another solution is to move your plants to rooms with the highest humidities. In most homes, the bathroom or the kitchen usually has the highest humidity. However, in most homes the bathroom is too small to hold many plants, and if you like plants, your kitchen will probably have all it can hold.

A frequently overlooked location is the laundry room, particularly if clothes are hung to dry in this area. If the light intensity is high enough to maintain growth and the temperature is not too low, the plants placed there will thrive.

For plants that are prone to desiccation, a daily misting with an atomizer will keep them looking much greener and healthier during low humidity periods. The best times to mist are mid-morning and mid-afternoon since foliage will dry before evening. Use water at room temperature since cold water in the atomizer can cause chilling injury to plants with sensitive leaves like the African violet. The secret to using an atomizer correctly is to spray the air around the plant and not the plant itself. Hold the atomizer far enough away so the foliage does not get wet, although a few drops will not hurt anything.

A misting in mid-morning or mid-afternoon keeps plants that dessicate easily looking attractive.

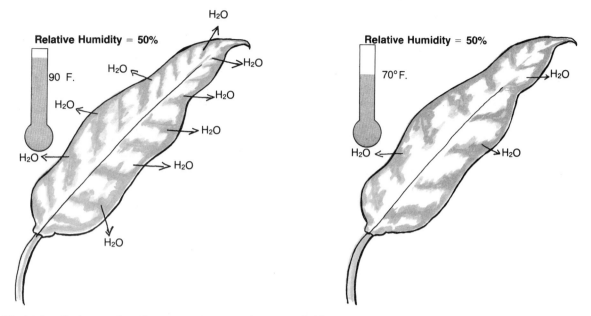

The higher the temperature the more water vapor the air can hold, and the more water will be lost from the plant.

The cheapest atomizers are those that household cleaners come in. Be sure to clean the bottles thoroughly before using as some household cleaners will burn the foliage.

If you have an older hot air furnace without a humidifier, place cans of water in the heating ducts. By keeping them full you can raise humidity in the home by approximately 10%.

Although all of these suggestions aid in raising the relative humidity, the ideal solution would be to have a humidifier running to keep the humidity up.

Serious indoor gardeners should consider the purchase of a small desk top *hygrometer* at their local hardware store. Absolute precision is not necessary and an inexpensive hygrometer can be used to determine which areas in your home have the highest and lowest relative humidities. You can evaluate several locations in one day as most hygrometers will give an accurate reading in an hour. Place the instrument in a south window early on a sunny day and watch the relative humidity drop as the temperature increases.

● Memo

Locate recently propagated plants in the most humid room in your home (often the kitchen or bathroom). This will prevent their newly formed leaves from drying out.

To help your plants cope with periods of low humidity, group plants together.

Humidity can be increased by grouping plants in a shallow tray filled with wet pebbles.

A plant should be appropriately sized to its location. A small plant in a corner looks out of place, and large plants on a coffee table create a visual imbalance in the room.

# Evaluating Your Home

The wisest thing to do prior to purchasing a house plant is to evaluate your home in terms of the previous sections on light, temperature, air circulation, and humidity. This will allow you to select a plant that matches the climatic conditions of the location in your house or apartment. If you have carefully evaluated your home, you will avoid selecting a croton for a low light area, an aglaonema for a full sun location, or a maidenhair fern for a low humidity area.

A plant should be appropriately sized to its location. Jot down the approximate width and height of the area. Actually, when you buy a plant you are not only purchasing an "easy-to-care-for pet" but also a decorative accent to complement your interior decor. Although certain exceptions exist, most plant forms can be used with different furniture styles, either harmonizing or providing contrast. Plant size, however, is a diffferent consideration. A large container of *Asparagus Densiflorus* 'Sprengeri' on a small coffee table creates a visual imbalance in the room. Conversely, a small schefflera in the corner will only bring attention to the bareness of the corner.

You must also consider your own personality. Many plants succumb each year to an inevitable death because the cultural demands of the plant did not mesh well with the owner's personality. Some people want to water their plants twice a day and fertilize them every other day so they can see them grow. The other extreme is the person who buys a plant and puts it in a

● Memo

Plants grow slowly indoors so buy them close to the size you desire.

corner and expects it to live when it is watered once a month and fertilized every two years. Although these are probably exaggerated extremes, it is much easier to be a successful indoor gardener if your plants have been selected with your daily and weekly routine in mind. Success is assured if you select a plant to suit your home and your personality.

# Novice List

If you've grown plants since childhood, you probably will be able to successfully grow the majority of plants listed in this book, but if you've had limited experience with only one or two plants, perhaps none at all, choose one from the novice list.

The following plants are relatively tolerant of varying conditions and will often survive errors made by beginning indoor gardeners.

● **Memo**
A cast iron plant will survive for almost any indoor gardener, but the rest of the plants in the novice list require more care.

## EASY TO GROW PLANTS

| BOTANICAL NAME | COMMON NAME |
|---|---|
| *Aechmea fasciata* | Silver Vase |
| *Aglaonema spp.* | Aglaonema |
| *Aspidistra elatior* | Cast Iron Plant |
| *Brassaia actinophylla* | Schefflera |
| *Chamaedorea elegans* | Parlor Palm |
| *Chamaedorea erumpens* | Bamboo Palm |
| *Cissus rhombifolia* | Grape Leaf Ivy |
| *Crassula argentea* | Jade Plant |
| *Cryptanthus bivittatus* 'Minor' | Dwarf Rose Stripe Star |
| *Dracaena spp.* | Dracaena |
| *Epipremnum aureum* | Golden Pothos |
| *Ficus spp.* | Ficus |
| *Haworthia subfasciata* | Little Zebra Plant |
| *Hedera helix* | English Ivy |
| *Pelargonium spp.* | Geraniums |
| *Philodendron spp.* | Philodendrons |
| *Sansevieria spp.* | Sansevierias |
| *Schlumbergera truncata* | Christmas Cactus |
| *Soleirolia soleirolii* | Baby Tears |

By selecting plants tolerant of widely varying conditions, you can gain both experience and confidence and join the evergrowing ranks of successful indoor gardeners.

# Choosing a Plant Store

A few years ago it was almost impossible to find a good selection of indoor plants except in large urban areas. Today most communities have one or more stores specializing in indoor plants. The increase in plant shops allows for comparison shopping in plants, accessories, and the general horticultural knowledge of the people operating the stores.

What should you look for in a store before buying? The most important area to consider is how well the conditions in the shop match the maintenance requirements of the plants.

As in your home, the most important factor to consider is the light intensity in the store. Is it well lighted and are plants requiring high light intensity located close to the window or in brightly lit areas? The light intensity in the plant holding areas should be a minimum of 50 to 75 footcandles and preferably about 150 to 200 footcandles. If plants are grouped into those requiring high light and those requiring low light, the store owners know their plants and anticipate repeat sales.

The watering practices in the store have a significant bearing on how well the plant will survive after you take it home. Without shopping in the store several times a week, it is difficult to evaluate the degree of watering frequency, but the area where the plants are located should have provisions for drainage and the containers should never be standing in water. Overwatering in the retail store will predispose plants to root-rotting organisms. If the plants have not been watered often enough, a number of plants will show brown edges on leaves, and yellowing and dropping of older leaves. If the soil has been allowed to dry out in the store, the roots may be severely damaged and the plant may die after you purchase it.

What about other places that sell plants such as hardware stores, dime stores, and supermarkets? These sources rely on high volume and quick turnover of usually lower-priced plants. If you purchase a plant shortly after its arrival from commercial producers in Florida, California, or Texas, you may have an excellent buy. However, the management in supermarkets and dime stores usually doesn't have the time to properly supervise watering practices or plant location in relation to light. Consequently, the longer the plants are in the store, the less attractive a buy they are.

● Memo

Check prices and plant quality at several stores to make sure you are getting the best buy.

# How to Buy a Plant

Be selective and critical when buying indoor plants. If all goes well you may have the plant or its progeny for the next quarter century. Purchase the plant close to the size you desire; don't plan on having the plant grow to fill your needs. Most plants selected for interior decorative purposes will be located in areas where they will grow slowly.

Compare plants of the same type and select the most attractive plant both in shape and leaf color. Although plant leaves have an endless variety of greens, generally the darker green the foliage, the better the plant will adjust to your home. If the plant has variegated leaves, select the one with the best color development. Leaf tip and margins should not be brown or yellowed. The foliage should be free from necrotic (dead) spots or holes. Most indoor plants should appear "full" with foliage retained down to the soil line with straight stems. Notable exceptions to this include corn plant and marginata, which are appreciated for their distinctive stems as well as their foliage.

Examine the plant carefully for insects, especially scale, mealy bugs, and mites. Carefully turn the leaves over and examine the underside of each leaf. Do not forget to look in the leaf axils (where the leaf joins the stem) where insect pests frequently hide.

Occasionally the leaves will have spray residue on them. The residue is material left from the grower's weekly spray program. It will hurt neither you nor the plant. Although the residue may be difficult to remove completely, usually enough can be removed to make it unnoticeable at a distance.

When purchasing a flowering plant, the most common mistake people make is to buy one with most of the flowers open. The attraction of the flower color automatically draws us to the plant, but the plant to buy is the one with buds just beginning to open. By purchasing the plant with the flower buds just opening your home will be brightened for a much longer time period.

After you have made your purchase, remember your newly acquired plant should be protected from cold, heat, or windburn. When the temperature is below 40°F, most plants should be wrapped in newspaper or other protective material and taken to your home as quickly as possible to prevent chill damage. In the summer, most plants need protection from full sunlight and should be placed in a shaded location if transported in a car. Plants should never be left in a car with the windows rolled up as temperatures can easily reach 110 to 130°F. Most plants will die if subjected to those temperatures for any length of time.

When purchasing a plant, examine it carefully. Turn the leaves over and examine leaf axils where plant pests frequently hide.

● Memo

Never buy wilted plants as this indicates root damage from soluble salts or root rot.

# Acclimatization of Plants to Your Home

Horticulturists have defined treatments or procedures used either by a wholesale grower or a retail store operator that condition a plant to adapt to your house as "acclimatization." Acclimatization is done to minimize leaf drop and shock that plants undergo when transferred from their "pampered" greenhouse surroundings to the low light, low humidity, and reduced watering rate that most plants experience when brought into the home. Until shortly before it was put on sale in the retail store, the plant you purchased may have received between 250 to 300 inches of water a year, all the fertilizer it could use, weekly spraying for diseases and insects, a constant high humidity, optimum night and day temperatures, and the correct light intensity for maximum photosynthesis. It is up to you to help the plant make the transition from ideal greenhouse conditions to the ones prevailing in your home. Many commercial plant growers are now acclimatizing their plants before they are shipped to retail stores. Unfortunately, it is not easy to determine if your plant has been acclimatized by the grower.

When you bring your plant home, the first thing to do is to water it thoroughly. Since commercial growers want their plants to grow as rapidly as possible, the soil ball usually has a high level of fertilizer in it; and if you let the soil dry out (more than the top ¼ to ½ inch), the roots can be burned by the high concentrations of fertilizer. After watering the plant, place it in isolation if you have other indoor plants. By placing the new plant in isolation, you avoid the possibility of an insect infestation spreading from the new plant to other plants you may have. If the plant does develop pests, check later chapter for control measure. Choose a location with high interior light intensity but do not place the plant in direct sun. The plant will need special treatment for approximately two weeks, and then if it has no apparent problems, it can be moved from isolation to take its place with your other plants. During the adjustment cycle, keep the soil moist but do not keep it continuously saturated. As the plant has undergone a drastic change in growing conditions, one or two of the lower leaves may fall off. Loss of a few leaves is nothing to be concerned about as the plant is just adjusting to interior conditions. Whenever environmental conditions are changed, plants adjust by shedding leaves that can no longer function under the new conditions. Most foliage house plants have been grown under reduced light intensities and if they start dropping many of their

● Memo

During the summer a new plant can be isolated from your other indoor plants by placing it outside in a shady area.

leaves and the remaining are wilting, it usually means that a root-rotting organism has destroyed their root system. There is little hope of saving a plant that has reached this stage of decline. (See disease recommendations, page 56.)

Flowering plants, especially azaleas and gardenias, with buds just beginning to open require special care in the home to prevent bud drop. Budded plants should be placed in an area that is moderately cool (65 to 70°F) and where there will be no sudden temperature fluctuations. Large plants in small containers with a lot of foliage may need to be watered twice a day. Increase the humidity by using an atomizer or by placing the pot on a tray of wet pebbles. These practices will help the plant retain its blossoms and keep your home more colorful longer.

Occasionally the plant brought home has been mistreated before you bought it and the plant will look steadily worse from day to day. If you bought your plant at a reputable retail plant store, they normally will exchange the plant for you if you return it within two weeks after purchase.

● Memo

Flowering plants will often drop their buds if the humidity is kept too low.

# HOW TO KEEP PLANTS GROWING

## Watering Techniques

A clue to correct watering practices for indoor plants is found in the old horticultural adage, "To maintain proper growth, plants require adequate amounts of water." The secret word in the statement is *adequate*. Improper watering procedures kill more indoor plants than any other single factor.

Knowing what constitutes adequate watering for your plants is something that is gained with experience. Most beginning indoor gardeners want to be told to water at specific intervals as if water were a medicine or food that a plant needed every so many hours. Not only do most plant types have different water needs, but each location may require different watering practices. It is perfectly possible to have two rubber plants, both in the same size container, with the same soil mix, and about the same height with the same number of leaves, with one located in the kitchen and the other in the living room, and one plant will require twice the amount of water as the other. Your plant's water requirements will change from week to week and from season to season as the environment changes. During the summer when temperatures are high, and the windows are open or the air conditioner is running, your plant's transpiration rate will increase drastically. However, during periods of rainy weather and high humidity, your plants may not need watering for a week or longer. Understanding the basic principle of indoor watering combined with experience will allow you to provide the proverbial *adequate* amount of water for each of your plants.

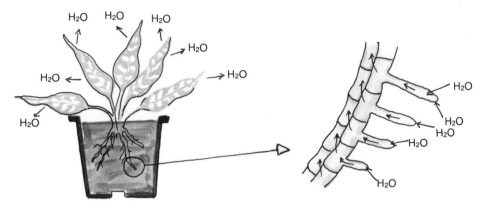

A plant absorbs water from the soil, transports it up the stem and into the leaves. Most of this water evaporates through small openings in the leaves called stomata.

To understand when to water, it is necessary to understand how plants absorb water and use water. Most water enters a plant through the root hairs. In order for the roots and root hairs to function properly, they need air (oxygen). The water absorbed by the roots is transported from the roots, up the stem, and into the leaves. Plants are continuously losing water, primarily through their leaves, as they must keep the small pores called stomata open to absorb carbon dioxide from the air. Most of the water a plant takes up from the soil is lost to the atmosphere through the leaves on the plant. In essence, a plant is really functioning as a natural humidifier, taking water from the soil and dispersing it into the air. Therefore, plants in warm, windy locations will require more water than plants in cool locations with slow air circulation.

Most indoor plants will remain healthier for the indoor gardener if they are grown a little on the dry side. (Exceptions are discussed in the plant identification section.) Water when the top portion of the soil has dried out. How much the soil should dry out depends on container size, but it should approximate $1/6$ of the soil height or about 1 inch in a 6 inch container. When you water, apply enough water to wet the soil ball thoroughly and to drain through the bottom of the container. Wait before watering again until the top portion of the soil has dried out. Following these procedures for plants growing in single containers will minimize the possibilities of losing your plants because of overwatering.

Usually people water plants where they are growing and have a saucer or similar shallow container to catch the excess water that drains through the soil ball. Your plants should not sit in this excess water for more than 15 to 20 minutes. If the containers sit in this water for any extended length of time, the soil will become saturated with water, displacing the soil air, and the roots will stop functioning. Low oxygen levels in the soil also favor the

When using a container without natural drainage to display a potted plant, elevate the pot with blocks of wood, bricks or stones. This allows space for drainage water.

Use a layer of stones in containers without drainage holes to provide space for drainage water.

growth of root-rotting organisms which can destroy part of the plant's roots. If the plant is transpiring water rapidly and the supply of water from the roots slows down, the plant will wilt. The normal reaction of most people is to water it again. Obviously, more water will make the soil wetter, displacing even more soil air, and more of the plant's root system will stop functioning from both oxygen deprivation and infestation by the root-rotting organisms. This vicious cycle normally ends with a dead plant and a discouraged ex-plant owner.

The majority of plants sold in retail stores are in light-weight plastic pots. Although these are not unattractive, many indoor gardeners prefer to slip them inside more decorative containers made of fiberglass, brass, or ceramic materials. Usually the more attractive containers are watertight and the containers slipped inside need to be elevated with blocks of wood, stones, or other materials to provide space for the drainage water.

Plants potted in containers or jardinieres without natural drainage present special problems to provide conditions for growing plants for an extended time. Without provisions for drainage, water will accumulate in the bottom of the container and the roots will die of either oxygen starvation or root-rot. A layer of stones in the bottom of the container will allow space for excess water. However, it is so easy to overapply water to containers without drainage that I recommend this only for experienced indoor gardeners, or plantings of succulents which can tolerate extended intervals between waterings. Larger containers and planters without drainage are actually easier to maintain because it is possible to install a hollow plastic tube or pipe through the soil and into the stone layer. Then you can use a dipstick to check water levels. When the level approaches the bottom of the soil, it is easy to siphon the water out of the container using a gasoline siphoner. Small containers as dishgardens without drainage should be watered in the sink, and the excess water drained from the container by tilting it while holding the soil in place with your hands. If the container is small enough, you can hold it upside down until the excess water stops dripping. Sometimes when I felt we needed a plant in a decorative container, I used a hand drill with a masonry bit. If the glaze is not too thick, a number of holes can be made to aid drainage. Naturally, the drilling must be handled carefully or you will end up with a shattered pot.

Most references on indoor plants will suggest watering your plants early in the morning. Although this is good advice, it is not always feasible to find the necessary time. You should water your plants as early as possible each day to allow the top layer of soil and the crown (plant part closest to soil line) to dry before tem-

A masonry drill can be used to drill holes in decorative containers without preformed drainge holes.

When the water level in a container without drainage approaches the soil line, it can be drained out with a gasoline siphon.

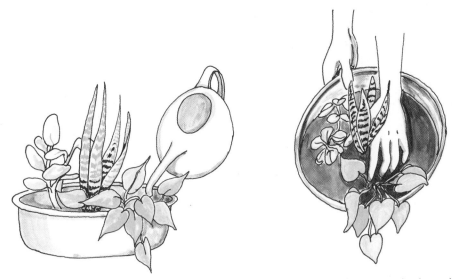

Water dish gardens and other small containers near a sink, so excess water can be drained from the container by tilting. Use your hands to hold the soil in place.

peratures drop in the evening. You can alleviate some of the problems associated with watering late in the day by using water at room temperatures. Cold water from the tap can temporarily stop the roots from growing and may suppress flowering on some indoor plants.

In many parts of the United States, tap water temperatures are as low as 45°F. If you have a number of indoor plants, having enough water at room temperature poses problems. One easy solution is to add hot water to the tap water. Unfortunately that solution does not allow for the aeration needed with some water supplies. Most municipal water is treated with chlorine gas to destroy harmful bacteria in the water. Allowing the water to warm up to room temperatures will lower chlorine levels and minimize any potenitial damage to your plants. By saving plastic gallon milk containers or distilled water containers, you can draw a reserve of water which can be left open for aeration. Many municipalities are adding fluorides to the water supply to pevent dental decay. Research now has proven that dracaenas, cordylines, and marantas will suffer foliar tip burn (browning or burning of the leaf tips) if fluoride is added to the water supply. To prevent fluoride-induced tip burn you can adjust the soil pH to 6.5. (See sections on soils and repotting.) Other alternatives include using distilled water, water from a dehumidifier, or rain water, or of course not growing plants susceptible to fluoride damage. Rain water is free, but not always pure. If you live in an area of the United States with high pollution level, it is advisable to wait until it has rained 30 minutes before collecting rain water, because by then the majority of the pollutants will have been washed from the air.

● Memo

Plants grow best when watered with room temperature water. This prevents "shocking" the root system.

## TOP WATERING

Watering practices vary among indoor gardeners but the most common method is to flood the soil surface and allow the water to drain through the soil ball. Horticulturally, this is known as top watering. Top watering requires a half inch to one inch of space from the top of the soil to the top of the container to act as a reservoir for the applied water. The entire surface of the soil should be flooded or the pot rotated so the water percolates uniformly and wets the entire soil ball. If water is applied too slowly to a porous mix, only a portion of the soil ball will be wetted. An extremely porous soil such as recommended for orchids and bromeliads requires that you turn the pot as you water so the entire soil ball is wetted evenly.

Top watering means wetting the soil surface at the top and allowing the water to drain through the soil ball.

## BOTTOM WATERING

A number of indoor plants have a rosette growth habit which makes top watering difficult. (African violets are good examples of plants with rosette growth habit.) Many indoor gardeners prefer bottom watering for those plants or others that are subject to crown rot (diseases occurring at the soil line). Bottom watering consists of filling a shallow container with water and allowing the water to be absorbed into the soil. Applying water from the bottom eliminates white spots on the foliage caused by high calcium levels in the water. To work properly the soil should be well packed because the water has to be drawn up by capillary water movement. Continual use of bottom watering will result in an accumulation of fertilizer salts in the top of the soil and the top ring of a clay container. If the soil and the pot are not leached (flushed with water), the continual build-up of salts will result in "salt burn" to the crown and any petioles which touch the rim of the clay pot will burn also. Burned petioles will rot, and you will lose the entire leaf. Top watering once every two weeks will leach the salts from the soil ball and the clay container. If you water to leach salts, fill the reservoir completely to carry away any salts in the clay container. Leaching should be done early in the morning so both the crown and soil surface will dry rapidly. A weekend morning fits well with many plant enthusiasts' schedules.

Bottom watering allows the water to be absorbed into the soil. Water moves up the soil until the soil ball is wet.

## IMMERSION WATERING

Another method that is favored by some indoor gardeners is total immersion of the plant and its container in a pail of water. The water should be somewhat higher than the soil line. After air

Immersion watering consists of lowering a potted plant into a partially filled pail of water. The water should be just above the soil line.

bubbles stop emerging from the soil surface, the plant can be removed from the pail. Although an excellent method for throughly wetting the soil ball and leaching excess fertilizer from the container, it presents two disadvantages as a routine watering practice for an indoor plant collection. One is the extra work involved in moving the plants to an area where the plants can "drip dry" after being soaked in water. The other is the possibility of spreading diseases and insect pests from container to container unless the water in the pail is changed every time another plant is immersed. Immersion watering is more appropriate for special watering situations when a good soaking or leaching is necessary.

One of those occasions is when the indoor gardener finds a severely wilted plant among his/her well-watered plants. Commercially produced flowering plants, especially chrysanthemums, are prone to use more water than your other house plants because they have not fully adjusted to the conditions in your home and they have a large number of leaves which are continuously losing water. Usually when a plant has wilted severely, the soil ball has pulled away from the side of the container. Top watering will not rewet the soil ball as the applied water will run down the side of the container and out the drainage holes. Total immersion is the fastest way to rewet the entire soil ball and revive the plant.

Immersion watering is also the best way to leach accumulated fertilizer salts from the soil media and clay containers. If you fertilize often, your plants will remain healthier longer if you use immersion watering twice a year. Plants that are bottom watered frequently have an accumulation of salt crystals on the soil surface and may require treatment more often.

Occasionally you may purchase a plant which does not have enough space between the soil surface and rim of the container for top watering. These plants will require bottom or immersion watering until you can find time to repot them.

When bromeliads are used as indoor plants, the cup formed by the rosette of leaves should be kept filled with water.

## WICK WATERING

Wick watering is a self-watering system that uses a wick, usually made from fiberglass, to draw water from a water supply located beneath the pot. The wick draws water the same way a paper towel soaks up water. To demonstrate this, just stick a paper towel into a colored liquid solution and watch the liquid climb to the top. You can make a wick watering system for plants you already have by knocking the soil ball out of the container, pulling the wick through the drainage hole and unraveling the wick in the bottom of the pot. Replace the soil ball, ensuring that

Wick watering is really a modification of bottom watering. The fiberglass wick keeps the bottom soil moist and the water is absorbed into the soil.

firm contact is made between the soil ball and the wick fibers. Any drainage material should be removed from the bottom of the soil ball or container. All you need is a support to keep the bottom of the pot above the reservoir water level and a 2 to 3 inch deep container to function as the water reservoir. The free end of the wick should be unraveled and inserted in the water. Never allow the reservoir water level to touch the bottom of the pot. Top water the plant to establish water contact between the wick and the soil ball. The moisture level of the soil will be determined by the reservoir water level. If the soil becomes too wet, lower the water level; if the soil becomes too dry, raise it.

Small attractive wick pots with a matching water reservoir section are available commercially in a variety of colors. The next time you see these in a store buy a couple. Even if you decide not to use wick watering, the color-coordinated water reservoir makes an attractive catch basin for drainage water when you top water.

Wick watering seems to work best with plants that do well in a continually moist soil, such as African violets or ferns.

Although almost all indoor plants can be watered using a variety of methods, bromeliads or vase plants need special consideration. The cups formed by the rosette of leaves should be filled with water at all times when grown indoors. The soil may be watered with any of the other methods that work well for you.

You can purchase ready-made containers for wick watering. Make your own containers for wick watering using a margarine tub container.

Use a larger container with a support to keep the potted plant above the water level.

# Fertilizers

Knowing how to use fertilizers correctly can make the difference between having healthy vigorous plants or plants that are struggling to maintain their existence. Improper use of fertilizers is exceeded only by improper use of water when plants are grown indoors. I believe much of the confusion surrounding fertilizer usage results from the long established practice of calling fertilizers "plant foods." A plant makes its own food but needs elements supplied by fertilizers to keep its food manufacturing cells and other cells healthy. Most indoor gardeners wonder when to fertilize and when not to fertilize until they understand how fertilizers relate to plant growth. Determining the best time to fertilize house plants requires understanding what a fertilizer is and knowing how plants differ in their fertilizer needs. Once you understand and apply these two ideas, you will be able to fertilize your plants with confidence.

"What is a fertilizer?" is a question asked at one time or another by most people who grow plants. A fertilizer is any substance which supplies one or more of the elements required by plants that they do not obtain from either water or air. Plants require sixteen elements for normal growth and development. They are carbon, hydrogen, oxygen, boron, calcium, chlorine, copper, iron, magnesium, manganese, molybdenum, nitrogen, phosphorus, potassium, sulfur, and zinc. The plant obtains carbon, hydrogen, and oxygen from water and air. The thirteen remaining elements must be available in the soil in water solution so that the root hairs can absorb them. Plants use more nitrogen, phosphorus, and potassium than the remaining elements. The plant's need for the other elements depends on the plant and the soil mixture. Because nitrogen, phosphorus, and potassium are used in larger quantities than the other elements, you are more apt to notice deficiencies in these three elements.

Nitrogen is part of every protein molecule in plants and forms part of many other important compounds within plant cells. Typical nitrogen deficiency symptoms in plants are a slower growth rate, a yellowing of the older, more mature leaves, and light green new leaves. Too much nitrogen promotes an excess of weak vegetative growth. On some flowering plants, it induces bud drop.

Phosphorus is necessary for growth of new roots, shoots, and flowers. Phosphorus accumulates in seeds and fruits of mature plants. Typical phosphorus deficiency symptoms are dwarfed growth and dull dark green or purple cast to the foliage. Too much phosphorus can interfere with iron uptake and alter the nitrogen balance of the plant.

Potassium is necessary for the plant to build protein, and it regulates the manufacture of starches and sugar. Potassium-

● Memo
Plants use fertilizers the same way we use mineral supplements of iron and zinc.

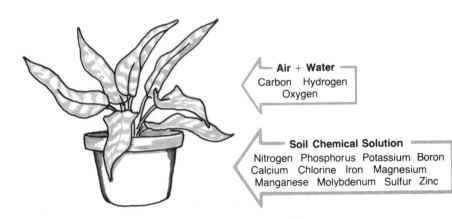

**Air + Water**
Carbon   Hydrogen
Oxygen

**Soil Chemical Solution**
Nitrogen  Phosphorus  Potassium  Boron
Calcium  Chlorine  Iron  Magnesium
Manganese  Molybdenum  Sulfur  Zinc

Plants require 16 elements for normal growth and development. These are supplied from either the air or the soil-water solution.

deficient plants have leaves that look burnt on the tips and margins. Extremely potassium-deficient plants may drop their leaves. High potassium levels in the soil may inhibit root growth and cause foliage to turn yellow.

● Memo
Many types of fertilizers are available, but the most important selection criteria is the fertilizer analysis.

## WHAT THE NUMBERS MEAN

Long before most consumer protection laws were passed, all states had passed laws and regulations stating that the chemical content of a fertilizer must be clearly labeled on the bag or bottle in which it was packaged. If you know how to interpret the statement on the container you'll know exactly what you are buying. Unless you are an avid plant specialty grower, the best buy is a balanced fertilizer containing nitrogen, phosphorus, and potassium. By law these fertilizers are defined as complete, even though many essential elements are missing. The content of each can be determined from the three numbers found on the label. Nitrogen is listed as the element N, phosphorus is listed as phosphoric acid ($P_2O_5$), and potassium is listed as potash ($K_2O$). A sack of 12-4-8 contains 12% nitrogen, 4% phosphoric acid, and 8% potash. If one of the three elements is missing, a zero is included in the series of three numbers; e.g., 20-0-20 would be the analysis of a fertilizer with no phosphorus. Unless otherwise stated on the label, the remainder consists of materials which have little nutrient value to the plants. If other essential elements are available, they usually will be listed on the label as secondary elements or micronutrients. Each time you water, a small fraction of fertilizer solution leaves the soil ball and runs out with the drainage water. Not all elements dissolve or leach at the same rate. Of the three elements that plants require in the largest amounts, nitrogen is the most water soluble. Phosphorus is the least water soluble, whereas potassium is intermediate between nitrogen and phosphorus. Because of the difference in leaching rates, many successful indoor plant growers apply a fertilizer with a higher percentage of nitrogen than the other elements. Other growers insist a fertilizer with a high phosphorus ratio, as a 5-10-5, is the best for your plants. Much depends on what is in your soil media (see Soils and Repotting p. 193), the light intensity where your plants are grown, how often you fertilize, and the plant itself. I recommend a 1-1-1 ratio fertilizer, as 6-6-6-,10-10-10, or 20-20-20, for most plants. Specific requirements of individual plants are discussed in the plant information section. Certain plants (azaleas, camellias, and gardenias) require an acid-forming fertilizer to maintain the proper soil acidity.

Major garden centers or plant stores usually have a large display area filled with a wide selection of fertilizers. Each type has

Each time you water, more nitrogen leaches from the soil ball than potassium or phosphorus.

certain advantages and disadvantages and purchase depends on intended use and individual preference. Fertilizers for indoor plants can be divided into two categories, one for mixing with the potting soil and the other for supplemental fertilization. Potting soil fertilizers will be discussed on page 196. Fertilizers suitable for supplemental fertilization include water soluble powders, concentrated liquid fertilizers, and special formulations of slow-release fertilizer in pill or tablet form.

Concentrated liquid fertilizers are easy to use; amounts per gallon or quart can be determined easily with standard measuring spoons. Do not buy more than you will use in six months, as many of the liquids form precipitates which settle to the bottom. Water soluble powders are almost as easy to use as concentrated liquids. To avoid accidentally increasing the recommended rate, level your measurements. Powders are probably the cheapest indoor plant fertilizers.

Slow-release fertilizers may be plastic coated and look like BBs or large tablets which slowly dissolve in the soil. Both products function better if incorporated in the soil rather than broadcasted on the surface.

Cost of fertilizer does not necessarily reflect quality. Comparison shopping will permit you to save money on your fertilizer purchases. If you remember the essentials of a good fertilizer, you can pick up the best composition at the lowest price. An attractive package will not make your plants grow better.

## APPLICATION

Unfortunately many indoor gardeners have the same problem with fertilizer that they have with water. They want to give their plants too much. They remind me of a mother who constantly urges her children to eat because food is good for them and will make them strong. But we all know too much food will make them fat and prone to various diseases. Too much fertilizer also has disastrous results—a dead plant.

The danger from overfertilization occurs because any fertilizer used (whether liquid, powder, or tablet) will dissolve in the water of the soil and form "salts" in the water. If you continue to add more fertilizer when the plants have not yet used the fertilizer already present, the water in the soil becomes so "salty" that it "burns" the plant's roots by removing water from them. The term horitculturists use to describe the amount of fertilizer "salts" in the soil is "soluble salts." The higher the soluble salt level in the soil, the greater the possibility of salt damage to the plant's root system.

If you have just bought a plant from a plant store or garden

● Memo
Never overapply any fertilizer as this can kill plant roots.

center, do not rush to fertilize it. In most cases the amount of fertilizer applied by the commercial producer while growing the plant will supply enough nutrients for two to three months in your home. This rule is flexible and if you notice deficiency symptoms, you should fertilize.

The secret to fertilizing plants indoors is to apply small amounts of fertilizer as the plant grows. Without new growth, the plant has only a limited need for more fertilizer. During the winter months when light intensities are reduced, a plant's need for fertilizer is reduced. When light intensities increase in the spring and the plant starts to grow at a faster rate, more fertilizer is needed. Plants that completely stop growing and become dormant (e.g., amaryllis and gloxinias) should not be fertilized until new growth appears.

How often should you fertilize your plants? The best answer may be "less is better than more." Even when your plants are growing actively, once a month fertilization at suggested rates may be too much. Label rates have been determined for plants growing under optimum conditions where light, humidity, and temperatures are perfect. These conditions seldom occur for most house plants. As a starting point, you could use about ¼ the label rate for monthly applications. If the overall plant color becomes lighter green, fertilize every two weeks. If the new growth is dark green but leaves are small and distances between leaves seem longer than on older growth, decrease the fertilizer rate. House plants will last longer and look better with less care if they grow slowly. Unless you are growing plants in a greenhouse or other areas where conditions are optimum for plant growth, too much fertilizer will cause far more problems than too little. If you do over fertilize a plant occasionally, use immersion watering to stop fertilizer burn.

If you repot your plants about once a year, minor element fertilizer can be incorporated in the soil. However, if your plants remain in the same container for more than a year and a half, they should be fertilized with a minor element fertilizer. Several companies formulate minor element fertilizers in different strengths, so use the suggested rate or less for indoor plants. Some house plant fertilizers contain a small amount of minor elements with the nitrogen, phosphorus, and potassium. If you use this type when your fertilize, yearly supplemental minor element fertilization will not be necessary.

## Grooming

When you water or inspect your plants, you can maintain their charm by removing unsightly leaves or faded flowers. To remove

Do not fertilize gift plants, newly potted, or dormant plants for 2-3 months.

Cut off flowers before seed and fruit development begin to keep new flowers forming and to maintain plant health.

faded leaves on stemless plants as aspidistra, most ferns, and some aglaonemas, you should cut the petiole just above the soil surface. Many foliage house plants grow slowly and removal of an entire leaf for a brown leaf tip would seriously affect the plant's aesthetic appearance. Professional plant personnel just reshape the leaf with a pair of sharp scissors. It is important to cut off flowers before seed and fruit development begins, to keep new flowers forming and to maintain plant health. Most indoor plants do not have the necessary food reserves to develop seed without seriously weakening them. (See Seed Propagation.)

Just like your coffee table and book ends, indoor plant leaves collect dust and dirt. Outdoors the wind and rain keep plant foliage clean and attractive but indoors your plants have to depend on you. Once every two to four weeks you should gather up your smaller plants and take them to the kitchen or utility room sink to rinse off the foliage. This includes your fuzzy or hairy-leaved plants as African violets or gloxinias. Room temperature water will not cause leaf spot on hairy leaves but cold water will. If you do not have a spray attachment on the sink use a plastic spray bottle adjusted for coarse spray and filled with tepid water. Tilt the plant or spray at an angle to avoid washing the soil from the container. Larger plants can be moved to your shower for a cleansing, or take advantage of a gentle, warm summer rain and move them outside. Be sure to bring them inside before the sun starts shining again. Always give your plants a shower early in the day so the foliage can dry quickly. Occasionally it may be necessary to use a mild soap solution (¼ teaspoon per one quart of tepid water) and cotton balls or a moist soft cloth to clean plants

● Memo
A few minutes of time once a week to groom your plants will not only make them look better, but also prevent diseases.

Your plants should have a shower once every 2-3 weeks to keep the foliage clean and remove insect pests.

with hard, firm foliage. Avoid placing wet plants in full sun or the foliage may burn.

I prefer the natural sheen of clean foliage on my plants but some indoor gardeners prefer a little added luster on plants with hard, firm foliage as schefflera, ficus, and philodendrons. Most plant stores carry small aerosol cans of leaf polish which can be used without damaging the foliage. Read the label and ensure that you can use the product on the desired plant. Clean the foliage and water the plant well before using any leaf polish to reduce the chances of damaging the foliage. Spray only the top surface of the leaf. This will leave the stomata on the lower leaf surface functioning since leaf polish can clog the plant's stomata openings and interfere with photosynthesis and respiration. Leaf polishing is not a new idea, and before aerosol sprays were available, many commercial florists used skim milk to increase leaf sheen. Skim milk is still recommended and used to impart luster to leaves without creating an artificial appearance.

When using leaf polish, spray only the top leaf surface. This prevents clogging the stomata (small openings) on the lower leaf surface.

## Pruning

You can control the growth and ultimate shape of your house plants by pinching and pruning at the appropriate time. Many indoor plants will look more attractive if the soft growing tip or *meristem* is pinched back at the proper time. Pinching will increase branching on the stem and the result will be a stockier, fuller plant. Remove the growing tip before the plant becomes too large so the new growth will be proportional to the older

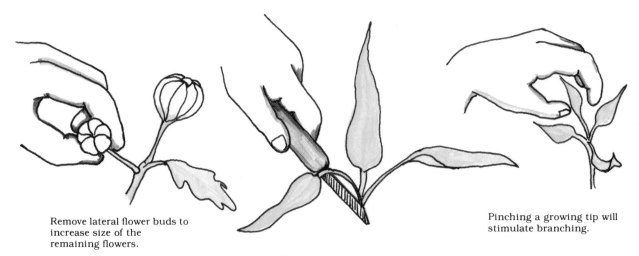

Remove lateral flower buds to increase size of the remaining flowers.

To remove faded leaves on stemless plants, cut the petiole just above the soil surface.

Pinching a growing tip will stimulate branching.

growth. Begonias, coleus, geraniums, gynuras, ficus, and ivies are just a few examples of plants whose beauty can be enhanced by selective pinching. Of course, pinching will work only with plants that branch or can form additional growing tips. Read the specific cultural information on your plant to prune it properly.

The objective is to remove the meristem with as little damage to the plant as possible. Make the cut or pinch just above a node, where the leaf joins the stem, and the new growth will look more natural. On very succulent plants you can remove the meristem by exerting pressure on your index finger with your thumbnail. I find that a single-edge razor blade or sharp knife works best and causes the least amount of damage.

Prune plants by cutting back to bud so the new growth will cover the pruning scar.

Occasionally older plants require more drastic treatment to keep them attractive and in correct size for their location. Because light in most homes comes from one direction only, indoor plants occasionally become misshapen. Often removal of one or more branches is necessary. Cut close to the main stem or major branches. This will avoid dead stubs on your plant. Even though they grow slowly, schefflera and other indoor trees will require some pruning to keep them in balance with the room. Prune indoor trees at regular intervals to keep them at the correct size rather than waiting until they have completely overgrown their location.

Flowering plants such as azaleas, hydrangeas, and geraniums are best pruned back just before they start active growth in the spring. Remember, proceed with caution as you can always prune more, but it is difficult, if not impossible, for most indoor gardeners to put branches back on! If you would like additional plants, make preparations to use the cuttings for propagation before you prune your plants. (See Plant Propagation.)

## Vacation Care

● Memo
Many communities now have professional "plant sitters" that will take care of your plants while you are gone on vacation.

Although some large urban areas have plant clinics that will take your plants while you are on vacation, most plant enthusiasts do not have that option. If you have just a few plants, the simplest procedure is to move the plants over to a friend's house. However, moving a large collection takes time and could pose a space problem in your friend's home. To solve this problem I have grouped my smaller plants on the kitchen table and the larger plants on the floor and had a friend come in and water them on a regular basis of every four or five days. When you do this, provide very shallow trays for drainage water. This reduces the possibility of your friend's overwatering your plants. The first time I did this I was not so cautious and had several plants that required treatment for root-rot when I returned home from vacation. By grouping all your plants in a cool, low light area you reduce the possibility of one plant being overlooked and collectively the plants increase the relative humidity. I usually have another group of plants that I keep outside in the summer. Before leaving on vacation, I group these together in a shaded area and set up a lawn sprinkler. Plants grouped outside usually need more water, and if it does not rain every two or three days, the sprinkler should be turned on. Another solution is to plunge all your plants in a trench similar to the one suggested for plants in summer plant care. Laying a soaker hose along the trench will minimize watering effort by the person caring for your plants.

If it is not possible to have someone water your plants, you should water your plants thoroughly, wrap the pots in polyethylene plastic, and fasten the plastic to the soil close to the base of the plant. The plastic will reduce water loss from the soil and through the container. Small plastic bags work well, and if you have clay pots, pack the bags with moist peat moss. Don't pack the peat moss around the plant's stem as it may induce stem rot. If you are going to be gone longer than two weeks and you are going to leave your plants alone, it may be worthwhile to purchase automatic watering wicks. (See discussion on watering.)

If you can't arrange for a 'plant sitter' during vacation, water your plants thoroughly and wrap the pots in polyethylene plastic, fastening the plastic to the soil close to the base of the plant.

## Summer Care

If your house plants could read, they would undoubtedly agree with James Russell Lowell when he said, "And what is so rare as a day in June? Then if ever, come perfect days." During the long gray winter days in your home many of the high light requiring

Protect indoor plants from strong winds, cold temperatures, and direct sun when you place them outside.

Summer plant care can be minimized by digging a trench outside about a foot wide, 8 inches deep, and as long as necessary to accommodate your plants.

plants produce only weak, spindly growth, if any. The more favorable growing conditions outdoors in summer with higher light intensities, higher humidity, and cool night and warm day temperatures are just what many of your plants need to restore depleted food reserves and to produce strong, vigorous new growth.

Not all plants should be put outdoors, nor should you place your plants in direct sun. Choose a shaded location; remember, your plants have adjusted to the much lower indoor light intensities. Unless your have been growing your plants in a sunny south window, the foliage will sun scorch if placed in direct sun. Even sun loving plants have to be acclimatized to the higher light intensities prevailing outside. Gradually move them from deep shade into higher light areas until they are located in an optimum area.

Keep most of your tropical foliage plants inside if night temperatures in your region go down to the low 50's. Even where night temperatures stay in the 60's, African violets, gloxinias, and some orchids are easier to care for if moved no further outdoors than a north porch.

Avoid wind burn, caused by excess water loss from the leaves, by locating your plants where they receive protection from strong winds. The stronger air circulation outdoors will increase the amount of water your plants need, especially if they are in clay pots. Choosing a protected location also prevents the pots from being knocked over. Many indoor gardeners plunge their pots in the ground to avoid these problems. Plunged pots need far less water as the soil does not dry as rapidly. A solution that works well for many people is to have a special area on the north side of

● Memo

The fastest way to rejuvenate a "sick-looking" plant is to move it outdoors during the summer.

their house where their indoor plants can be plunged during the summer. Dig a trench about a foot wide and approximately 8 inches deep and as long as necessary to accommodate your plants. Fill the bottom of the trench with gravel to ensure good drainage. Coarse bark mulch is a good material to use between the pots as weed growth will be kept to a minimum and any "volunteers" in the mulch can be easily pulled. Locating the holding area on the north side of your home provides a variety of light intensity locations to match your plants needs: the northwest corner for sun loving plants, the northeast corner for high light plants, and the center for plants that should not be placed in full sun. Without special precautions your plants will root through the drainage holes, making removal and adjustment to your home difficult in the fall. Prevent this problem by lifting or twisting the pot once a month. Remember that the increased growth rate outside will increase the amount of fertilizer needed for your plants. Water and fertilize when placing them outside and repeat fertilizer application once every two weeks at about ½ the label rate. Reduce rates if your plants seem to be getting too much fertilizer.

When temperatures are expected to go down to the middle 40's, it is time to prepare your plants to come back indoors. Before your bring them in, prune and groom them, hose or spray them, clean the pots, and then put them in your plant isolation area for two weeks to ensure that they are essentially pest free. This is also a good time to take care of repotting for those plants that have outgrown their containers.

## When You Move

In our mobile society, people move an average of every 3 to 5 years. For many plant enthusiasts moving day is particularly traumatic as moving companies will wrap and move just about all your household possessions except your plants. Abruptly you are faced with deciding what to do with your plants. Too often, your neighbors are bequeathed a number of plants that they may not really want and a few select plants are placed in the car. Sound familiar? It does to me, because that is what happened the first time I moved.

Since then I have learned that there are a number of ways to move plants. Plants may be mailed, sent by commercial bus carrier, parcel delivery, or railway express companies. If not shipped commercially, they can be carried in a rented enclosed trailer or transported in your car. All that is required is proper wrapping and packaging.

● Memo

To avoid moving several plants of the same kind choose the healthiest and take cuttings to propagate new plants after you move.

However, before preparing plants for transportation across state lines, check with that state's Department of Agriculture. Several states have plant quarantine laws to prevent diseases and/or insect pests from entering the state.

Plants can be ready to travel in your car with a minimum of preparation. The plants should be well watered, but not soggy, before packing. Each plant can be slipped inside a sleeve made of brown wrapping paper. A cardboard box can be easily prepared by lining the bottom and ¼ of the sides with wax paper or aluminum foil. If most of the plants are in clay pots, reinforce the

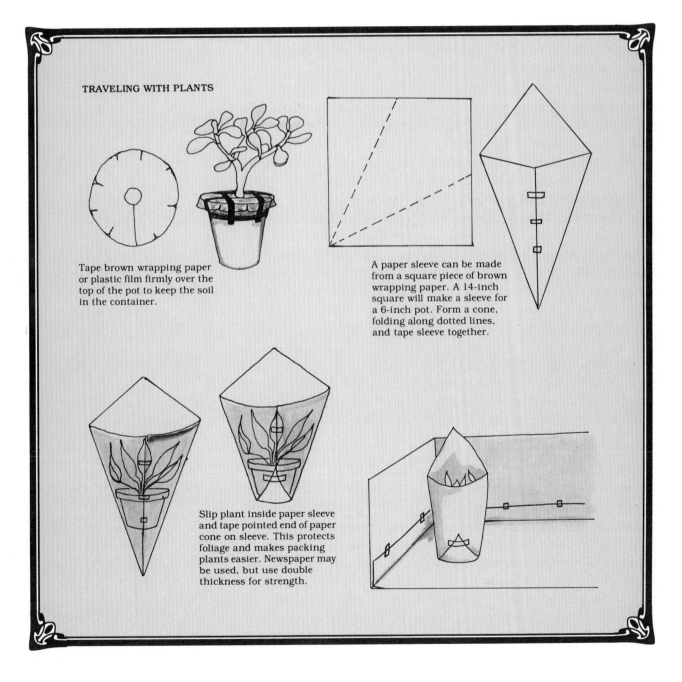

**TRAVELING WITH PLANTS**

Tape brown wrapping paper or plastic film firmly over the top of the pot to keep the soil in the container.

A paper sleeve can be made from a square piece of brown wrapping paper. A 14-inch square will make a sleeve for a 6-inch pot. Form a cone, folding along dotted lines, and tape sleeve together.

Slip plant inside paper sleeve and tape pointed end of paper cone on sleeve. This protects foliage and makes packing plants easier. Newspaper may be used, but use double thickness for strength.

bottom with additional cardboard. If possible, choose a box slightly taller than your tallest plant which will prevent any possibility of sun scorch or chill damage in your car. Having all your plants in an easy-to-handle box will make it easier if you have to take them out of the car when stopping in the evening. Remember to protect your plants from temperature extremes, below 45°F or above 90°F.

When using an enclosed trailer to move a larger plant collection, prepare your boxes similarly to car transporting but fix each box so the top can be closed and smaller boxes can be stacked upon each other. During the summer, park the trailer in the shade or open the doors when you stop to keep the plants from getting too hot. Small air holes should be cut in each box to allow air exchange except during cold weather. Cover your boxes with insulated paper during cold weather.

Additional preparations have to be made to ship plants commercially or by mail. All plants in clay pots should be repotted in plastic pots or the soil ball should be packed in peat inside a plastic bag to reduce shipping weight. Group your plants by pot size and approximate height. Insert a bamboo stake as long as the box is tall into each container. The stake will prevent the soil ball from crushing the foliage if the box is accidentally upended. Tape brown wrapping paper or plastic film firmly over the top of the pot to keep the soil in the container. Cut in the shape indicated in the drawing. Sleeve the plants. Place each plant on the bottom of the carton and make sure the plants cannot shift. To prevent shifting use crumpled newspaper or excelsior between plants. The carton should be sealed, the top clearly labeled, and the contents identified as living plants. In the summer air holes should be placed on top of two opposite sides for ventilation. In the winter line the carton with insulated paper and do not make air holes. Do not mail or ship plants when temperatures are below 30°F, as most indoor plants freeze or suffer cold damage when temperatures are below 30°F.

# Disease and Insect Control

Although conditions in your home may not be ideal for growing plants, they permit rapid insect and mite reproduction. Even isolating newly purchased plants for two to four weeks will not prevent plant pests from becoming established on your plants. Mites and aphids can spread from a bouquet of cut flowers to your potted plants or enter through open windows or doors. In order to keep plants completely pest free, it would be necessary for you and your family to go through a re-entry decontamination chamber every time anyone came indoors, as insects and mites frequently are brought in on clothing.

Initial infestations are difficult to detect and constant surveillance is necessary to spot insect damage before pest populations cause extensive damage and make control difficult. Insect infestations can reduce or prevent flowering, stunt the plant's development, distort new growth, cause browning or yellowing of the older foliage, and in extreme cases, bring about the death of the entire plant.

The most convenient time to inspect your plants is when you are watering or grooming them. House plant pests usually escape detection because they inhabit parts of the plant that are seldom examined carefully. Although insects feed on both leaf surfaces, infestations usually start on the lower leaf surface. Do not overlook the leaf axil as mealybugs can be detected there before spreading to other plant parts. Look carefully at the stem and growing points and be sure no unwanted guests are enjoying a free meal at your plant's expense.

The area that most home growers overlook is the soil surface. Move the soil media with your finger or a stick and see if anything hops, jumps, or crawls. Water and watch to see if small white worms float to the surface.

You can determine what insect or other pest is plaguing your plants by being familiar with the type of damage they cause and the description of the pest. A small hand lens makes identification much easier.

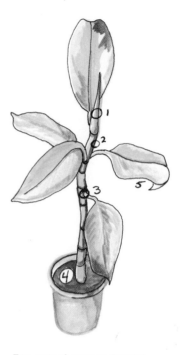

Five critical areas to inspect carefully for insect pests: (1) new growth; (2) stem surface; (3) leaf axil; (4) soil surface; (5) underside of leaf.

## COMMON PESTS

MEALYBUGS. Mealybugs are among the common pests on houseplants. Mealybugs are soft-bodied insects covered with a white powdery material. These tiny insects look like small pieces of cotton that have attached themselves in the leaf axils and on the main veins on the undersides of leaves. When mature, they are about ⅛ inch in length and live under white, cottonlike protective masses. African violets and other plants may become infested with the ground mealybug which feeds on plant roots. Mealybugs damage plants by sucking plant juices and severe infestations can kill plants. Most pesticides will require a repeat application in 2 weeks or less to control mealybugs. Inspect plants with previous mealybug infestations at weekly intervals for 3 or 4 weeks to be sure pests are eradicated.

SPIDER MITES. Spider mites are about 1/50 inch long when mature. They may be greenish, yellowish, reddish, or virtually colorless. They reproduce fastest in hot dry environments so the conditions that prevail in our homes during the winter are

Mealbybug

Spider Mite

ideal. They are commonly found on the underside of leaves, but spread to other parts of the plant as populations increase. When plants are heavily infested, fine webbing will be noticed on the plant. White or yellow speckled areas on the upper leaf surface indicate an established infestation. As mite populations build up, the leaves become bronzed or yellowed and may drop from the plant. If left untreated, mites can kill plants. Most pesticides require repeat applications every 3 to 7 days until all mites, including those hatching from eggs are eliminated. Inspect plants with previous mite infestations at weekly intervals for 3 or 4 weeks to be sure pests are eradicated.

Aphid

APHIDS. Aphids may be green, pink, black, brown, yellow, or blue in color. They are usually less than ⅛ inch long and may or may not have wings. Their bodies are pear-shaped and they have long antennae and two short tubes extending from the rear of the body. They usually cluster on the underside of leaves or on young succulent growth. If left untreated, young leaves and new growth will become curled and distorted. While feeding, aphids excrete honeydew, a sticky, sweetish liquid. Aphids are easy to control with pesticides, but susceptible plants should be inspected frequently to be sure they have not been reinfected.

Scale

SCALES. Scales can be almost any color, but brown is the most common. They are ⅛ to ⅓ inch long when mature and surrounded by a waxy covering that may be circular, oval, oblong, or pear-shaped. Scales are found on upper and lower leaf surfaces, stems, and branches and in leaf axils. Scales suck plant juices and excrete droplets of honeydew. Infestation usually results in growth reduction. Most pesticides will require a repeat application in 2 or 3 weeks to control scales.

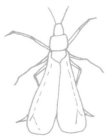

Whitefly

WHITEFLY. Whitefly adults are about 1/16 inch long, white in color, and resemble tiny moths. When an infested plant is disturbed, the agitated adult flies remind me of flying dandruff. Immature whiteflies are pale green and scalelike in appearance. They feed on lower leaf surfaces and excrete a lot of honeydew. Their favorite hosts seem to be soft and hairy-leafed plants. Plants infested with whitefly have mottled leaves which turn yellow and die or drop off. If the flies are not controlled, an infested plant may die. Most pesticides will require a repeat application in 5 to 10 days to control whitefly. Adults and young congregate on the underside of the leaf. Spray both leaf surfaces.

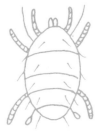

Cyclamen Mite

CYCLAMEN MITES. Cyclamen mites are extremely small mites which require a hand lens to be seen. Adults are oval, semitransparent, and light tan in color. They are found on young leaves before they have fully expanded, and on flower buds of African violets, gloxinias, begonias, cyclamens, and geraniums.

Their feeding causes growth deformities; leaves of infested plants are curled, hairy, and brittle. Buds may not open and the flower will be deformed and streaked with darker color. Most pesticides require repeat applications every 3 to 7 days until all mites, including those hatching from eggs are eliminated. Inspect plants with previous mite infestations at weekly intervals for 3 or 4 weeks to be sure pests are eradicated.

**FUNGUS GNAT MAGGOTS.** Fungus gnat maggots are white, wormlike in shape, and ¼ inch long when mature. The adult flies cause no damage but can be a nuisance. The maggots feed on decaying organic matter and plant roots. They will burrow into the crowns of plants. Infestations will usually retard plant growth and affect foliage color. Fungus gnats are usually controlled with a pesticide soil drench. Check and be sure the pesticide can be used indoors; if not, treat plants outdoors.

Fungus Gnat Maggot

**PSOCIDS.** Psocids are soft-bodied, oval insects about 1/16 inch or smaller. Some types may have wings, whereas others are wingless. Psocids are not known to damage plants but sometimes will be present in such large numbers they become a nuisance. Psocids are usually controlled with a pesticide soil drench. Check to be sure the pesticide can be used indoors; if not, treat plants outdoors.

Psocid

**SPRINGTALES.** Springtails are the small jumping insects you may have noticed in the soil around your plants. They are never more than 1/5 of an inch long and vary in color from white to black. Usually they feed on decaying organic matter but if present in large numbers, they sometimes injure seedlings or new shoots emerging from the soil surface. Springtails are usually controlled with a pesticide soil drench. Check to be sure the pesticide can be used indoors; if not, treat plants outdoors.

Springtale

**SYMPHYLIDS.** Symphylids or garden centipedes are less than ½ inch long. They feed on young roots and root hairs. Without functioning roots, plants wilt and growth is greatly reduced. Garden centipedes are usually controlled with a pesticide soil drench. Check to be sure the pesticide can be used indoors; if not, treat plants outdoors.

**EARTHWORMS.** Earthworms are fine outdoors but they can clog drainage holes in potted plants. Earthworms are usually controlled by removing them from soil mix by hand.

**NEMATODES.** These small unsegmented worms are too small to be seen with the naked eye but the damage they can cause is all too visible. Most nematodes live in the soil, feeding on or in plant roots. Plants growing in nematode infested soils grow slower, wilt easier, and develop light green leaves. These symptoms can be caused by poor cultural practices or other pests

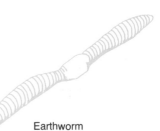

Earthworm

and diseases, too. If you suspect nematode infestation, the best way to check is to examine the roots of the plant. Although many nematodes are serious plant pests, the one with the worst reputation is the root-knot nematode. This nematode lives within the roots causing enlargements called galls. Plants susceptible to root-knot nematode include African violets, begonias, chrysanthemums, gardenias, and marantas. The damage caused by other nematodes is not as easy for the indoor gardener to detect but all involve damage to the plant's root system. No chemical control measures are available to home owners. The best procedure to follow if you suspect a nematode infestation is to take cuttings and propagate new plants. Discard the soil and sterilize the pot before using it again. (See section on Repotting.)

## HAND CONTROL MEASURES

The best controls are measures to prevent infestations. Always use sterilized or pasteurized soil for potting to help prevent infestations of soil pests such as nematodes, springtails, psocids, and fungus gnats. If you have been working with outdoor plants, wash your hands before handling your house plants. Aphids and mites are easily transmitted by your hands.

SYRINGING. If you spray your plants with a stream of room temperature water every two weeks, many insect pests will not have a chance to become established. Rotate the plant to ensure that the lower leaf surface where most plant pests are found is well sprayed. Hold the pot at an angle to wash the pests down the drain or on the ground. Syringing is best done outdoors or in a laundry sink. Spraying also keeps the foliage free from dust and the plants looking more attractive.

WASHING. Washing with soapy water and a soft cloth may be all that is needed to remove aphids, mealybugs, and scale insects from broad-leaved plants. Use 2 teaspoons of a mild detergent to a gallon of water. Large plants that are difficult to move can be cleaned in place. Recent studies have shown that many insects are repelled by soapy water. Washing and syringing help keep mite infestations to a minimum.

● Memo

Most insects avoid plants that have been washed with soapy water.

HANDPICKING. If only one or two plants are infested, you may be able to control aphids and mealybugs by removing them with a toothpick or tweezers. Scales that cannot be washed off can be squashed in place and the residue picked off with a tweezers. Caterpillars may be picked off plants by hand and destroyed. Cutworms, slugs, and snails may be found in their hiding places during the daytime and destroyed.

ALCOHOL. An easy way to control a light infestation of mealybugs or aphids is to wet or remove the insects with a swab that has been dipped in rubbing alcohol. Swabs recommended for babies are excellent. Be careful not to overapply as alcohol may damage the foliage.

## CHEMICAL CONTROL

If your regular grooming and hand control measures fail to keep a particular plant pest under control, you can fall back on chemical control. Different manufacturers produce the same pesticide in different concentrations and you should always read the label carefully before mixing and applying any insecticide.

Certain plants, begonias, ferns, and kangaroo vine, will be damaged by some insecticides. This damage is called phytotoxicity and usually shows up as marginal burn, chlorosis, or spotting. Distortion or abnormal growth is also a common symptom of plants injured by pesticides. Although any portion of the plant may be affected, the new growth is most likely to show damage. In order to minimize chances of plant damage, spray your plants early in the morning so foliage will dry before it warms up. Pesticides are manufactured in two forms; wettable powders marked WP on the label and emulsifiable concentrate sprays marked EC on the label. Wettable powders are less likely to cause phytotoxicity but will leave a residue on the foliage. Wettable powders must be agitated while mixing and spraying.

A variety of pesticides may be purchased at plant stores and garden centers in concentrated forms and mixed with water prior to spraying. Read the label carefully for dosage rates and precautions. Use ⅛ teaspoon of liquid household detergent per quart of spray to increase wetting efficiency. Application to house plants is probably best made with a hand atomizer or sprayer. The type which holds ½ pint to one quart spray is suitable for most homes and small greenhouses.

Ready-to-use spray preparations for plants in pressurized cans are available wherever house plant products are sold. When buying an aerosol spray, read the label on the container to be sure the spray contains the recommended pesticide for the pest to be controlled and that it can be used safely on house plants. Some aerosol sprays contain oils or other materials that will burn foliage or kill plants. Most commercial preparations contain pesticides which provide control against a broad spectrum of common plant pests including spider mites, scales, aphids, whiteflies, and mealybugs. Always read the label and follow the directions on the container. All insecticides are poisons and should be used only in areas with good ventilation. Never spray plants in rooms where fish aquariums, birds, or other pets are located. When you are through spraying, dispose of leftover spray materials and empty containers.

● Memo

To receive the latest information on chemical controls for plant pests, contact your local agricultural extension office.

61

The following is a list of common pesticides and the plants that have been damaged by them when used at recommended rates. The amount of damage depends on many factors. Before treating the whole plant, you may want to spray just a few leaves to see how severe the damage will be.

## PLANT / PESTICIDE CAUTION LIST

| BOTANICAL NAME | COMMON NAME |
| --- | --- |

### Pesticide-Diazinon:

| *Anthurium* spp. | Anthurium |
| --- | --- |
| *Asparagus setacus* | |
| *Asparagus densiflorus* 'Sprengeri' | Asparagus Fern |
| *Begonia* spp. | Begonia |
| *Cissus antarctica* | Kangaroo Vine |
| *Epipremnum* sp. | Pothos |
| *Hoya* spp. | Wax Plant |
| *Nephrolepsis* sp. | Fern |
| *Peperomia* spp. | Peperomia |
| *Pilea* spp. | Pilea |

### Pesticide-Kelthane:

| *Anthurium* spp. | Anthurium |
| --- | --- |
| *Asparagus setacus* | |
| *Begonia* spp. | Begonia |
| *Brassaia actinophylla* | Schefflera |
| *Cissus antarctica* | Kangaroo Vine |
| *Codiaeum variegatum* | Croton |
| *Cordyline terminalis* | Ti Plant |
| *Chamaedorea elegans* | Parlor Palm |
| *Epipremnum* sp. | Pothos |
| *Peperomia* spp. | Peperomia |

### Pesticide-Malathion:

| *Anthurium* spp. | *Anthurium, Aralia* |
| --- | --- |
| *Asparagus setacus* | |
| *Asparagus densiflorus* 'Sprengeri' | Asparagus Fern |
| *Begonia* spp. | Begonia |
| *Brassaia actinophylla* | Schefflera |
| *Cissus antarctica* | Kangaroo Vine |
| *Crassula argentea* | Jade Plant |
| *Dieffenbachia* spp. | Dumb Cane |
| *Epipremnum* sp. | Pothos |
| *Ficus* spp. | Ficus |
| *Nephrolepis exaltata* 'Fluffy Ruffles' | Fluffy Ruffles |
| *Peperomia* spp. | Peperomia |
| *Pilea* spp. | Pilea |
| *Syngonium podophyllum* | Nephthytis |

# COMMON DISEASES

Commercial growers of indoor plants maintain regular spray schedules to control plant diseases. Fortunately, the low relative humidity in your home and dry foliage are not favorable for development of most diseases. Good cultural care and use of pasteurized soil mix will minimize disease problems in your plants. The following problems commonly occur on indoor plants.

ROOT ROT. Root rot is one of the most common diseases of indoor plants. Usually it occurs because the plant has been over-watered, or grown in a container with poor drainage, or the soil mix has not been porous enough. Plants with root rot will wilt even when the soil is moist. The roots will be soft and pull apart easily. When you pull on the root, the outer portion will slip off, leaving a central threadlike portion attached to the remainder of the root. Whether or not a plant that has root rot can be saved depends on the severity of the disease and the specific plant. The easiest solution is to take one or more cuttings and propagate new plants. Sometimes providing better drainage and allowing surface of the soil mix to dry between waterings will save the plant. Remember the plant has to regrow part or all of its root system. Anything you can do to reduce transpiration while the plant is regenerating a root system will help. Some plant growers tape a plastic bag to the top of the pot and attach it to stakes placed inside the container. Leave the bag open for air circulation. If you have many plants with root rot, review your cultural practices.

CROWN ROT. Crown rot occurs on plants that are essentially stemless and have a rosette growth habit. The plant part closest to the soil line becomes soft and slimy and plants react as they do when they have root rot. Treat as described for root rot. Another method is to knock the plant out of the pot, cut off all decayed tissues, and repot in a pasteurized soil mix. If crown rot is a chronic problem, you are keeping the soil next to the crown wet for too long a period of time.

VIRUSES. African violets, dieffenbachias, chrysanthemums, and geraniums are some of the house plants that may have a virus disease. Leaves are usually characteristically mottled or the foliage is distorted. Virus infected plants grow slowly and lack vigor. As with the common cold, little can be done when plants have a virus and infected plants should be discarded. Do not take cuttings to start new plants as the disease is systemic or contained within the plant.

DAMPING OFF. This disease affects germinating seeds and seedlings after they have emerged from the soil media. Some times it can destroy an entire flat of young seedlings as they rot at the soil line and fall over. Check with your local retail nursery to see what fungicides can be used.

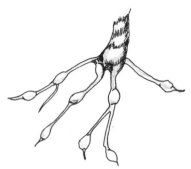

Plants with root-knot nematode have small swollen areas on roots.

Plants with root rot will have soft roots which pull apart easily, leaving a central threadlike portion attached to the remainder of the root.

Irregular color patterns and distorted leaves are characteristic of virus diseases.

# PLANT GENEALOGY

Have you ever tried to trace your family tree? Some family trees can be traced back several hundred years, others just a few generations. How far back your heritage can be verified depends on what kinds of documents and records are available.

The complexities and problems encountered in finding out who your ancestors were and who your relatives are is similar in some ways to determining what plants are related and to which family they belong. Only when tracing plants, there are no written documents. During the past two centuries or so, botanists and horticulturists have studied plants intensively to group them into meaningful categories. Their efforts have been quite successful, and most of the complex interrelationships between the half million or so living plants are well understood. Various classification categories have been established, and a detailed record of how a plant growing in your home relates to all other plants can now be constructed.

Before revealing how all the relatives of your favorite philodendron can be determined, you may wonder what facts and methods scientists use to construct a genealogical record. Although there are no graveyards with nicely-inscribed tombstones or church records of marriages and births, the past history of some plants is written in stone. Fossil records of plants shed a great deal of light on the ancestors of modern plants and suggest how plants have evolved through the eons. Not only do these fossils document how plants have changed, but they also indicate in what ways plants have not changed or have changed very little. Some plant families, like the cactus family, have undergone extensive evolutionary changes as they have adapted to a particular environment. Fossils document how some cacti have evolved into drought-tolerant plants that can survive for six months or longer without rain. These same fossils show that cacti flowers have changed very little during the milleniums. Over a given time period, other plant families also show the least amount of change in flowers as compared to leaves, stems, or roots. Consequently, scientists studying plant classification (taxonomists) examine flowers, particularly the male and female reproductive organs. So even though fossil records are sometimes incomplete, they have shown us what to look for to determine how closely or distinctly related today's plants are.

In summary, the genealogical record of each plant is based on fossil records, detailed chemical and microscopic examination of flowers or reproductive structures, fruits, seeds, and other internal and external parts.

The easiest way to show how plants are organized into different groupings of related plants is to select a common indoor plant and follow it through the various categories to which it belongs. First we have to know what it is called—not its common name, but its scientific name. Each scientific name consists of two words, usually given in Latin. Using just two words to identify a plant is known as the binomial system of nomenclature and was introduced in 1753. It was quickly adopted because it is easy to use and simplified naming new plants. Before adoption of the binomial system, each plant was identified by a list of Latin words so its name would be a brief description of the plant. This sometimes took ten or more complex names for the same plant. The first word in a binomial is the genus to which the plant belongs, and the second word designates the species. The genus of a plant is always capitalized whereas the species is not. Scientific names may seem difficult to pronounce and hard to remember, but they correctly identify the plant whereas common names are often confusing, in that they are used for more than one plant and the same plant may have several common names. For example, *Saxifraga stolonifera* is called strawberry geranium, strawberry begonia, creeping sailor, and mother of thousands. When a plant is referred to by its species, the species really designates a certain type of plant, but there can be minor differences within a species. If you have grown a number of plants of the same kind, you know that there are often small but noticeable differences between plants of the same species. A commercial grower who cultivates a more desirable plant among thousands of the same species may want to distinguish it in some way from other plants of the same species. This is done by using a cultivar name. Cultivar names are always capitalized. There is a selection of *Saxifraga stolonifera* with dark green and ivory leaves with pinkish young leaves. This is the cultivar Tricolor, and is identified by writing *Saxifraga stolonifera* 'Tricolor.' Differences sometimes occur in plants growing in their natural habitat, and these are given a botanical variety name to distinguish them from other members of the species. Thus, if a red-flowered *S. stolonifera* were found it could be called *Saxifraga stolonifera rubra*. (The genus name is often abbreviated by using one capital letter and a period—in this case *S.)*

Scientific names also identify a specific plant's closest relatives. The name *Saxifraga stolonifera* means that the species *S. stolonifera* is closely related to the other 300 plants in the genus, *Saxifraga,* and sometime in the past they all had a common ancestor. A genus may contain only one or hundreds of species, but all the species in a genus have similar flowers and fruits and often similar leaves, roots, and stems. Usually species within a genus can be bred to produce hybrid plants.

The next grouping of plants related to *Saxifraga stolonifera* are in the family Saxifragaceae. However, all of the other plants in the Saxifragaceae family are not as closely related to *Saxifraga stolonifera* as plants in the genus *Saxifraga*. Members of a plant family have more characteristics in common with each other than with members of other plant families. And plants are grouped in the same family because the evidence shows that they all had a common ancestor. This plant, the common ancestor of the Saxifragaceae, gave rise to those plants which produced the 80 genera in the Saxifragaceae.

Plant families sharing certain characteristics such as similarities in flowers, fruits, and seeds are grouped into categories called orders. The Saxifragaceae are placed in the order Rosales which includes the rose family and the pea family along with 13 other plant families. All the plants in an order are assumed to also have a common ancestor, but much further back in time than the plant family ancestor. Similar orders are grouped into categories called classes. *Saxifraga stolonifera* is placed in the plant class called Angiospermae. The Angiospermae include those plants we call flowering plants. The flowering plants are grouped with classes of plants as the conifers and ferns into a category called a division. In the case of *Saxifraga stolonifera,* the division (or phylum) is Tracheophyta. Thus the "family tree" of *Saxifraga stolonifera* looks like this:

Division: Tracheophyta
Class: Angiospermae
Order: Rosales
Family: Saxifragaceae
Genus: Saxifraga
Species: stolonifera

This then is the genealogical history of *Saxifraga stolonifera* and shows both what its close and distant relatives are.

This book discusses 150 species or cultivars of plants that are commonly grown indoors. These plants are arranged alphabetically by genus because many members of the same genus have similar cultural needs. Forty-four plant families are represented by the 150 plants. To give the reader more information about the plants covered in the book, a short discussion of each plant family precedes the cultural care instructions. A list of plants in each family is included and selected members of each family are illustrated.

## Acanthaceae

### Acanthus Family

This family is named after a plant genera found in southern Europe and West Africa, but you could expect to find its relatives in other temperate or tropical countries. The family contains about 180 genera and around 2,000 species and includes nonwoody (herbaceous) plants, shrubs, vines, and even a few trees. Most members of the family grown indoors are either herbaceous plants or shrubs found in shady woods or jungles in tropical or subtropical parts of the world. Although leaf color and growth patterns of plants in this family differ, they all share certain similarities. The leaves grow directly opposite each other and are simple. Each new set of leaves grows at right angles to the leaves beneath it, so when you look down from the top you see just four leaves. The flowers are borne on long, erect spikes and each flower has a relatively large, often colorful bract directly beneath it. Each flower is short lived, usually lasting only a day, but the bracts may remain on the flower spike for a month or more. If seeds are formed they will be found in a fruit known as a capsule. Most of the 2,000 plants in this family are grown for their attractive flowers or foliage, but a few are grown for medicinal or food value. Whether they are grown indoors or out, members of the acanthus family can be grown successfully in rich, well-drained soils if protected from full sun.

Acanthus Family Members:
*Aphelandra squarrosa*
*Crossandra infundibuliformis*
*Fittonia verschaffeltii*
*Fittonia verschaffeltii argyroneura*
*Hemigraphis alternata* 'Exotica'
*Justicia brandegeana*

Many plants in acanthus family might in shady woods

Family is named for a plant resembling a thistle.

## Agavaceae
### Agave Family

Some of our best and more durable indoor plants are found among the 20 genera and 500 species in the agave family. Most of these plants are native to tropical and subtropical regions where rainfall is often limited during part of the year. Their ability to survive a certain amount of neglect makes them ideal plants for the novice. Plants of the agave family have long narrow leaves which have fiber strands to prevent them from wilting and collapsing when water is unavailable. Although plants vary from the stemless sansevierias to the palmlike 25 foot dracaenas, the leaves are usually arranged in a rosette.

Members of the agave family are grown to produce fiber for ropes, twine, and weaving material, or as ornamentals. Indoors, many members of this family have become cherished plants because of their interesting stems and attractive foliage. Flowers are seldom seen on indoor plants, but when conditions are just right they produce panicles of small flowers which clearly resemble those found on some plants in the closely related lily family. In fact, some horticulturists and botanists refuse to admit this family exists and put all of its members in the lily or amaryllis family. Whether you believe this family exists or not, the plants in it do and can be grown with a minimal effort if protected from cold temperatures and burning sun.

Agave Family Members:
*Beaucarnea recurvata*
*Cordyline terminalis*
*Dracaena angustifolia honoriae*
*Dracaena deremensis* 'Janet Craig'
*Dracaena deremensis* 'Warneckii'
*Dracaena fragrans* 'Massangeana'
*Dracaena marginata*
*Dracaena sanderana*
*Dracaena surculosa*
*Sansevieria trifasciata* 'Hahnii'
*Sansevieria trifasciata* 'Laurentii'
*Sansevieria trifasciata* 'Zeylanica'

Fiber products are produced from many plants in this family.

## Amaryllidaceae
### Amaryllis Family

This is an important horticultural plant family with many of its 90 genera and 1,200 species native to the dryer parts of South America, South Africa, and the Mediterranean. Most members of this large family form underground bulbs which store food and water for those periods when no water is available and the above ground leaves shrivel and dry up. Al-

Amaryllis Family Members:
*Clivia miniata* 'Grandiflora'
*Hippeastrum* hybrids
*Narcissus* hybrids

68

though many plants in this family, like the daffodil, contain poisonous alkaloids, several plants in the family are used for food, the best known being the common onion. However most members of the amaryllis family are grown for their attractive, colorful flowers. Usually the flowers are carried well above the green, strap-shaped leaves on relatively long stems called scapes. Each scape may have from one to fifty flowers depending on the plant species.

Most members of this family grow best in full sun locations; several can be grown indoors if a sunny spot can be found. Some, like daffodils, require special cold treatment to flower; most require a dormant period to flower, and only Kafir lily (*Clivia miniata*) will remain green all year.

Many plants in this family produce bulbs.

## Apocynaceae
### Dogbane Family

Containing some 180 genera and 1,500 species of plants, members of the dogbane family are found around the world, but most grow in warm tropical regions. Within this family we find nonwoody plants, shrubs, vines, and even trees. Many of these are grown as ornamentals, usually for their showy flowers. However, as pretty as some of the plants are, some members of this family, like oleander, are very poisonous. But some poisonous plants also have medicinal value. *Rauwolfia* or Indian snakeroot provides the original source material of tranquilizers so widely used today. Several family members, including *Carissa*, have edible fruit.

Although many of the plants have a milky sap, this large family is not neatly tied together by one single characteristic but rather by several technical characteristics of the flower.

Dogbane Family Member: *Carissa grandiflora*

Milky sap and opposite leaves are characteristic of plants in this family.

## Araceae
### Aroid Family

Most of the 15 genera and 2,000 species in the aroid family are found in tropical countries, with just a few hardy varieties able to withstand the cold winters in the temperate zones. Aroids are a diverse group of plants that includes herbaceous plants, vines, epiphytes, and even a few plants that spend their entire lives in the water. Some members develop woody tissue with age and resemble shrubs and trees, although technically they are neither. In contrast to these treelike plants, some aroids have no above ground stems and the leaves grow from underground corms or rhizomes.

The leaves of the aroids vary from small and heart shaped to large and egg shaped. Some are over three feet in length with a great number of indentations and sometimes perforations. Whatever the size or shape of the leaf, it is usually held aloft by a long petiole that wraps around the stem. In the case of a vining aroid, this stem will also have roots just opposite the leaf which will adhere to tree bark or other available support.

Perhaps because aroids usually have such attractive foliage, many family members contain small needlelike crystals in the leaves and tubers which make tiny cuts in the mouth or throat. The cuts themselves cause little pain, but the leaves contain an enzyme which when penetrating a cut can cause extreme swelling and pain. Many aroids are used as food crops in tropical countries but the tubers or leaves, also poisonous, are boiled to destroy the enzyme thus making them edible.

As diverse as plants in this family are, the one common trait that ties them together is the flower cluster or inflorescence they produce. The flower cluster is composed of two parts: a round, sticklike structure called a *spadix* which is covered with tiny male and female flowers and a protective covering called a *spathe*. On some aroids like anthuriums and spathiphyllums it is very colorful and showy, whereas on others, like dieffenbachia, it only opens partially to expose the spadix.

As important as aroids are in the tropics for their food value, they are even more important as indoor plants. About ten of the fifteen genera in the aroid family are grown indoors for their attractive foliage or showy inflorescence. Provide moist, but well-drained soil mixes, shade, and warm temperatures.

Aroid Family Members:
*Aglaonema commutatum elegans*
*Aglaonema commutatum* 'Pseudo-Bracteatum'
*Aglaonema costatum*
*Aglaonema crispum*
*Aglaonema* 'Fransher'
*Aglaonema modestum*
*Aglaonema* 'Silver-King'
*Anthurium scherzeranum*
*Caladium* spp.
*Dieffenbachia amoena*
*Dieffenbachia* 'Exotica Perfection'
*Dieffenbachia maculata* 'Rudolph Roehrs'
*Epipremnum aureum*
*Monstera deliciosa*
*Philodendron bipennifolium*
*Philodendron* hybrids:
   'Burgundy'
   'Emerald Queen'
   'Florida'
   'Prince Dubonnet'
   'Red Emerald'
*Philodendron scandens oxycardium*
*Philodendron selloum*
*Scindapsus pictus*
*Spathiphyllum* 'Clevelandii'
*Spathiphyllum* 'Mauna Loa'
*Syngonium podophyllum*

The spathe and spadix are two unifying characteristics of the aroids.

## Araliaceae
### Aralia Family

Most of the 84 genera and 700 species in the aralia family are found growing in shaded areas around the world, primarily in the tropics. The family encompasses small trees, shrubs, nonwoody plants, and some vines. Among this diversity of plant material, we find a number used as ornamentals, some for medicinal purposes, and one for paper production. Ginseng is probably the most publicized member of the family, but English ivy may be the most popular member.

A taxonomist might call this the chameleon family, as the leaves change shape as the plant matures, and some plants have three different types of leaves representing juvenile, intermediate, and mature stages. When grown indoors, these plants seldom achieve maturity, and people often fail to recognize mature specimens in botanical conservatories even though they may have grown the plant for years. When members of the aralia family achieve maturity they do flower, producing flowers clustered on long stems or grouped together in a clump.

As a general rule, aralias succumb to root rot if overwatered.

Aralia Family Members:
*Brassaia actinophylla*
*Brassaia arboricola*
*Dizygotheca elegantissima*
*Fatshedera lizei*
*Fatsia japonica*
*Hedera helix*
*Polyscias fruticosa*

Plants in this family often change leaf shape as they mature.

## Araucariaceae
### Araucaria Family

In prehistoric times, the araucaria family was widespread and found throughout the world. Today most of the 2 genera and 30 species are found growing on islands in the South Seas. All araucarias are tall trees growing to over sixty feet with straight, majestic trunks. Few conifer families contain plants suitable for growing indoors, but araucarias do well indoors because they grow naturally where temperatures are above freezing and young trees thrive in the dense shade of their parents.

In the tropics, most species are grown for lumber, but the symmetrical growth form and attractive needles have made Norfolk Island Pine an indoor favorite.

Araucaria Family Member:
*Araucaria heterophylla*

This family is an important source of lumber in the tropics.

# Asclepiadaceae
## Milkweed Family

Although named for a plant that grows in temperate zones, the majority of the 130 genera and 2,000 species of the milkweed family are found in the tropics. Most of its members are nonwoody plants or vines, with just a few woody shrubs and treelike plants. The family members have several common characteristics: for example, they have simple, opposite leaves and usually produce a milky sap.

Some family members yield fiber for ropes and cloth, whereas others have a milky sap that can yield rubber; however most are grown for their attractive flowers or interesting foliage. Many of the plants in this family grown indoors are succulents and some resemble members of the cacti family, but they have no thorns. However, their flowers bear little similarity to cacti. In fact, the flowers may look like wax or even rotting meat.

When grown indoors, all the members of the milkweed family require good light, porous soil, and protection from cold.

Milkweed Family Member:
*Hoya carnosa* 'Variegata'

Many members of this family have unusual star-shaped flowers.

# Balsaminaceae
## Balsam Family

Although there are only 2 genera, the family contains 500 species of herbaceous plants and small shrubs. A few hardy members grow in temperate zones, but most are found in the warmer regions of Asia and Africa. A majority of these plants are found growing in moist, shaded areas and have juicy stems swollen at the nodes.

Some family members are used for medicinal purposes, whereas others yield dyes that are used to produce green, yellow, or black cloth. Of course, the best known are those grown for their attractive, colorful flowers which highlight shaded areas in the garden or the home. This ability to produce flowers continuously has led florists and nurserymen to evaluate (for cultivation) several new species in the family for commercial production. This is a plant family that will probably become more important horticulturally.

Balsam Family Member:
*Impatiens wallerana* 'Variegata'

Seeds of plants are forcibly expelled.

## Begoniaceae
### Begonia Family

The begonia family contains only 3 genera but over 1,000 species and all but just a few are in the important *Begonia* genus. Most of these plants are herbaceous or small shrubs native to moist shaded areas in the tropical and subtropical areas of the world.

The 1,000 species share a number of family chraracteristics. The most noticeable characteristic has to do with the leaves. Begonia plants have an alternate leaf arrangement; one side of the leaf is larger than the other side, and the leaves are borne on a slanting leaf base. Stems and leaves are usually hairy. The showy red, pink, white, or yellow flowers are borne on flower stalks which grow from the leaf axil. After flowering, plants in the begonia family produce seeds somewhat like orchids. The flowers are capable of producing thousands of tiny seeds which contain little or no stored food. Thus, growing conditions have to be just right or seedlings die.

Although roots and leaves of begonias are used medicinally in the tropics, most members of this family are grown as ornamentals, both indoors and out. More than 10,000 hybrids have been developed in the begonia family, but most have similar cultural requirements: moist, acid soils and protection from burning sun and freezing temperatures.

Begonia Family Members:
*Begonia semperflorens cultorum*
*Begonia x rex cultorum*

Plants in this family have a leaf with one side larger than the other.

## Bromeliaceae
### Bromeliad Family

All of the 45 genera and 2,000 species with but one exception are native to the American tropics. Like orchids, they are both epiphytes, growing on trees, or terrestrial, growing in the ground. They vary in height from 1 inch to plants that are 35 feet tall. Usually they grow as single plants, but some epiphytes like Spanish moss grow in tangled strands. Within the 2,000 species we find plants like the pineapple that are used for food and plants that have fibers used for mats or rope, but most cultivated plants are grown as ornamentals.

Bromeliad Family Members:
*Aechmea fasciata*
*Aechmea* 'Royal Wine'
*Ananas comosus*
*Billbergia nutans*
*Billbergia zebrina*
*Cryptanthus bivittatus* 'Minor'
*Dyckia brevifolia*
*Guzmania lingulata* 'Major'
*Guzmania monostachia*
*Neoregelia carolinae* 'Tricolor'
*Nidularium innocentii nana*
*Vriesea x mariae*
*Vriesea splendens*

The majority of these ornamentals are stemless, and have long, often stiff leaves arranged in rosettes. In many bromeliads, the leaves form a water holding cup or vase. Usually the leaves have spines or thorns along the margins, perhaps to discourage hungry plant eaters.

Although we think of bromeliads as jungle inhabitants, some of them grow in areas where it is relatively dry during most of the year. You can frequently tell whether a bromeliad is native to arid desertlike areas or to the moist jungle areas by the number of silvery scales on the leaves that give many bromeliads their silver stripes. Usually the more scales on the leaves, the drier the region from which they come.

Bromeliads are grown as ornamentals as much for their attractive leaves as for their colorful bracts, which may last for months. Many bromeliads produce exotic, showy flowers, some of which are hidden in the middle of the cup formed by the upright leaves; however most bromeliad flowers are short lived. After this show of color, bromeliads die. As a survival mechanism, new plants grow from the base.

All bromeliads require a soil mix that provides good drainage and aeration but other cultural requirements may vary.

The pineapple is probably the best-known member of the bromeliad family.

## Cactaceae
### Cactus Family

The cactus family is another plant family with members native to the Americas, with but one exception. Even though this family has been extensively studied by many taxonomists, or perhaps, because it has, there is some dispute over how many genera and species it contains. Most authorities will agree that it contains between 100 and 200 genera, and 1000 to 2,000 species.

Cactus Family Members:
*Astrophytum myriostigma*
*Epiphyllum* hybrids
*Schlumbergera truncata*

Many of the plants in the cactus family really do not fit our mental conception of what a cactus should look like, as family members include herbaceous plants, shrubs, trees, even a few vines and an occasional epiphyte. Stems show as much variation, and they may be the familiar round form, flattened, or even triangular. Most cacti native to arid deserts have numerous thorns scattered up and down the stem, but the epiphytic cacti that grow in tropical rain forests are thornless. Most cacti either have no leaves or quickly lose them; however, a few primitive

Cacti inhabit both deserts and jungles.

vinelike cacti have simple, alternate leaves. This varied group of plants is tied together in a family by certain technical characteristics of the flowers, which are often quite spectacular. Several epiphytic cacti are grown and sold as flowering plants because they can be flowered by providing seven weeks of short days.

This diverse family has some members which produce edible fruit, and some spiny forms may even be used for living fences in arid regions. But the smaller, more manageable cacti have captured the interest of plant enthusiasts. Literally hundreds of species are grown as ornamentals both indoors and out. The indoor gardener's interest in cacti is increasing and more plants are becoming easier to find.

## Campanulaceae
### Bell Flower Family

The bell flower family contains about 40 genera and 700 or more species which are widely distributed in the temperate and tropical regions. Within this family we find herbaceous plants, a few shrubs and small trees, and an occasional vine.

Plants in the bell flower family are grown as ornamentals almost exclusively for their showy white, bluish, or purple flowers. Some are sown as annuals, others are sold as flowering pot plants, and some are grown as garden perennials.

Bell Flower Family Member: *Campanula isophylla*

Note the bell shaped flowers common to many family members.

## Commelinaceae
### Spiderwort Family

Almost all of the 40 genera and 400 species are native to tropical areas where many of them have become weedy. Unlike other large plant families, members of the spiderworts are almost exclusively nonwoody plants or herbaceous vines. Characteristics common to the spiderwort family include: alternate, simple leaves, stem-clasping leaf bases, parallel

Spiderwort Family Member: *Zebrina pendula*

veins in the leaves, and certain similarities of the flowers. Some spiderworts are stemless but if plants have stems, they are usually jointed. Many cultivated spiderworts have purple leaves, flowers, or purplish markings on the foliage.

Spiderworts commonly grown indoors have attractive, often variegated, or otherwise colored leaves. If provided with bright light, water, and fertilizer, it is soon clear how these attractive plants could become weeds.

## Compositae
### Composite Family

Often called the sunflower, daisy, or dandelion family, the composite family is regarded as the largest plant family. Among the 950 genera and 20,000 species are nonwoody plants, vines, a few shrubs, and in the tropics, an occasional tree. With so many in the composite family, there is no single leaf or stem characteristic that unites them. However, what does group these diverse plants together is the floral structure and the fruit. Throughout this family, flowers are arranged in an inflorescence called a head. What is commonly called the flower in the composites is really a collection of flowers. Each "petal" on a daisy, marigold, or dandelion is really a ray flower. The "eye" of a black-eyed Susan or the center of a sunflower is a grouping of disk flowers. Thus, composites often produce hundreds of flowers, and from each flower within the composite we get one seed. This partially accounts for their worldwide distribution.

Members of the composite family are grown for many reasons. We find them used for food, medicinal purposes, dyes, ornamentals, and some yield a milky sap that can be used for rubber production.

The strangest thing about this large family is the relatively few plants that can be grown indoors or that are suitable for flowering-pot plant production.

Composite Family Members:
*Chrysanthemum morifolium*
*Gynura aurantiaca* 'Purple Passion'

Flowers in this family are tightly clustered together in an inflorescence called a head.

# Crassulaceae
## Stonecrop Family

The stonecrop or orpine family has about 30 genera and 1,500 species distributed around the world; many of them are found in the temperate zone. The plants in this family are nonwoody plants or shrubs; there are no trees or vines. Some are stemless with their leaves arranged in rosettes. Stonecrops with stems usually have opposite leaves. With or without stems, many stonecrops have thick, fleshy leaves that are capable of storing water, and they are sometimes confused with cacti although their stems carry no thorns. Leaves of some stonecrops have the unusual characteristic of producing small plants on the edges of their leaves either while the leaves are still attached to the parent plant, or after the leaf is cut off.

Their use as medicinal plants dates back to ancient times but most are grown as ornamentals, often for the attractive red, yellow, or white clustered flowers. A number of these plants can be flowered if given several weeks of short days.

Although some stonecrops are grown indoors, many require higher light than other indoor plants.

Stonecrop Family Members:
*Crassula argentea*
*Kalanchoe blossfeldiana*

Plants in this family form small plantlets on their leaves.

# Ericaceae
## Heath Family

The heath family contains some 70 genera and 1,900 species of shrubs and small trees. Most members of the heath family grow on acid soils in the temperate zone, either as food plants (blueberries) or ornamentals.

The majority of ornamental heaths are grown outdoors for their showy flowers. Only the florist's azaleas seem to have met with enough popularity to be available in any quantity.

The family characteristic of cultural importance is that most heaths have small, fine, delicate roots which die if the soil mix gets too dry or too wet.

Heath Family Member:
*Rhododendron* hybrids

Showy flowers are characteristic of many cultivated members of this family.

## Euphorbiaceae
### Spurge Family

The 280 genera and 7,300 species in the spurge family are found worldwide but it is believed they originated in the tropics and spread into temperate areas. A large family, it contains nonwoody plants, shrubs, trees, and a few vines.

Within the spurge family are plants used for food, fiber, oil, medicinal purposes, dyes, rubber, lumber; and many are grown as ornamentals.

Leaves and other vegetative characteristics show a great deal of variability. Some plants in the spurge family have undergone parallel evolution with the cactus family and have thick, water-storing, leafless stems with sharp spines. However, careful examination will show that spines on plants in the spurge family grow directly out of the stem whereas spines on cacti grow from a round structure known as an areole.

Flowers are usually very small, but the inflorescence may be very showy with colorful bracts which resemble flower petals.

Most plants commonly grown indoors in the spurge family are native to dry tropical climates and tolerate low humidity.

Spurge Family Members:
*Acalypha hispida*
*Codiaeum variegatum*
*Euphorbia milii splendens*
*Euphorbia pulcherrima*
*Pedilanthus tithymaloides* 'Variegatus'

Many plants in this family have evolved traits similar to cacti.

## Geraniaceae
### Geranium Family

The geranium family contains 11 genera and about 600 species of herbaceous plants and shrubs, most of which are native to the temperate zones. Most cultivated members of the geranium family are grown as ornamentals or for their oil which is used in the manufacture of perfume. The oil is extracted from leaves of the scented-leaf geraniums.

The showy pink, white, or red flowers usually have their flower parts arranged in fives. The old favorites in the geranium family have been greatly improved in the last few years by releases of better and more floriferous plants developed in breeding programs. As the programs have just recently begun, we can expect to see more improvements in the cultivated members of the geranium family.

Geranium Family Member:
*Pelargonium* hybrids

Many cultivated plants have fragrant leaves whose extracts are used in the perfume industry.

## Gesneriaceae
### Gesneria Family

The gesneria or African violet family includes about 120 genera and 1,200 species. The greatest number of these plants are native to Mexico, the West Indies, and Central and South America, but they are found in other tropical and subtropical regions. In warm, moist areas, the gesneriads grow both as terrestrials and as epiphytes. Most gesneriads are nonwoody with just a few shrubs or trees.

Although the plants show considerable variations (stemless gesneriads have their leaves in whorled rosettes whereas plants with stems have opposite leaves), usually the leaves are covered with thick, soft hairs.

Flowers are often showy and clustered on ends of flower stalks or appear singularly in leaf axils.

During the seedling stage, many gesneriads develop underground storage stems. These gesneriads alternate between periods of growth when they leaf out and flower and periods when the leaves die back and they go dormant.

More and more gesneriads are being grown as indoor plants because they combine attractive foliage and flowers. However, they require more care than other plants, as light intensities must be high, but the foliage is easily sunburned; and many require higher humidities than are usually found indoors. Even with these minor problems, they are highly recommended plants because of their beauty.

Gesneria Family Members:
*Achimenes* hybrids
*Aeschynanthus pulcher*
*Saintpaulia* hybrids
*Sinningia speciosa*

A number of plants in this family have short stems and leaves arranged in rosettes.

## Iridaceae
### Iris Family

Plants in the iris family are found throughout the world but a large number of the 60 genera and almost 1,000 species are native to South Africa and South America. All of the plants in this family have an underground stem, which may be a bulb, corm, or a rhizome. There are no trees or shrubs in this family. The sword- or strap-shaped leaves either grow directly from the

Iris Family Member:
*Crocus* spp.

The underground stem called a rhizome.

underground stem in a fan-shaped cluster or the leaves are alternate along a cylindrical stem and appear to be folded almost around the stem.

Plants in this family have been used for medicinal purposes, perfumes, dyes, and food. However, most members of the iris family are grown for their colorful flowers, which resemble flowers in the closely related amaryllis and lily families. The flowers, like the leaves, may grow directly from the underground stem or be scattered along a flower stalk. In addition to these common traits, many members of the iris family are bearded! This is a term botanists use to describe the coarse velvetlike growth found on the petallike parts of the flower.

Few members of the iris family are grown indoors, as they require high light levels and special temperature treatments.

A number of plants in this family have bearded flowers.

## Labiatae

### Mint Family

Other names used for this family are Lamiaceae or Menthaceae. Almost all of the 160 genera and 3,500 species in the mint family are herbaceous plants, shrubs, or vines. Although you might find mint family members in almost any country in the world, many are native to the Mediterranean region. Plants in this family and man have had a long association, with a number of species cultivated for centuries. Many plants in the mint family are grown as ornamentals, but perhaps the largest group is grown as kitchen herbs. Members of this family have also been grown for medicinal purposes or for oils used in the perfume industry, and even as natural insect repellents.

Mint Family Member:
*Coleus blumei*

There are a number of characteristics common to this large group of plants which help tie them together as a plant family: if one were to view the stems of these plants in cross section, one would see that new stem growth is square whereas older stem growth is round. The plants have simple opposite leaves and each pair of leaves grows at right angles to the pair below and above it. If leaves are torn or crushed, they usually have a noticeable fragrance. The flowers of the mint family plants are usually small, but are densely arranged on flower stalks which grow from the leaf axils and the growing tips.

Cultural requirements of plants in this family are relatively diverse: some plants require moist soils and shade, whereas

Square stems and opposite leaves make the mint family easy to recognize.

others grow best in full sun and drier soils. With over 3,000 members, it would seem that more plants in this family would be grown indoors, but only a few make good foliage plants and only a dozen or so are grown on sunny window sills as kitchen herbs.

## Liliaceae
### Lily Family

The 240 genera and 3,000 species in the lily family are widely distributed around the world but the greatest number are found in temperate and subtropical regions. Most plants are herbaceous (nonwoody plants) and grow from bulbs, corms, rhizomes, or tubers; a few are vines and some are shrubs. If all the species in this family are considered, there are no leaf or stem characteristics common to all family members; and membership in the family is based predominately on floral characteristics.

Some species in the lily family are used for food, others for medicinal purposes, but most cultivated species are grown as ornamentals. Contrary to popular belief, only some members of the lily family have showy colorful flowers; the greatest number have attractive foliage with small inconspicuous flowers. The lily family includes a number of small succulents that grow well in or close to a sunny window. The succulent members of the family often have an extremely long inflorescence with small bell like flowers. Due to an increased interest in small succulents, an even wider plant selection will soon be available.

Lily Family Members:
*Aloe barbadensis*
*Asparagus densiflorous* 'Sprengeri'
*Aspidistra elatior*
*Chlorophytum comosum*
*Haworthia subfasciata*
*Hyacinthus orientalis*
*Lilium longiflorum*
*Tulipa* spp.

Bulbs are common throughout the lily family.

## Malvaceae
### Mallow Family

The mallow family is widely distributed and contains about 95 genera and 1,000 species of herbaceous (nonwoody) plants, shrubs, and trees. Several common traits help identify members of this family. Leaves are always alternate, often lobed, usually hairy, and the veins are palmate. The flowers are all variations of those found on the best-known member, the hol-

Mallow Family Members:
*Abutilon hybridium* cultivars
*Hibiscus rosa-sinensis*

lyhock, which could be described as resembling a hoopskirt.

Although a large family, no members are known to be poisonous, and many are used to provide food (okra), fiber (cotton), medicine, oil, or ornamentation. Whether grown indoors or out, mallow family members are cultivated more for their colorful flowers than their foliage. Those grown indoors require a sunny spot to continue producing flowers, and reasonable humidity levels to keep the foliage attractive. Currently our selection of plants from this family for indoor use is limited, but the increasing interest in flowering pot plants may result in future plant breeding and selection programs to increase availability of colorful plants for our interiors.

Large showy flowers and rough hairy leaves are typical of family members.

## Marantaceae
### Arrowroot Family

A predominantly tropical plant family, the arrowroots contain about 25 genera and 400 species of herbaceous (non-woody) plants. Family members are characterized by underground storage stems, either tubers or rhizomes. These often produce new plants, thus it is not unusual to find members forming large colonies in swampy areas or damp jungles. A rather distinctive feature in this family is the ability of many of its members to fold their leaves at night. This is possible because the petiole and the leaf blade are connected by a swollen joint that functions as a hinge.

Some plants have starchy tubers that are used for food and some plants are used for fiber products, but most cultivated members are grown as ornamentals. A few arrowroots are grown outdoors for their flowers, but the majority are grown for their highly colored or distinctly marked foliage both outdoors in the tropics and indoors in the temperate zone. Cultural problems with members of the arrowroot family can be minimized if the soils are kept moist and relative humidity is kept above 25%.

Arrowroot Family Members:
*Maranta leuconeura erythroneura*
*Maranta leuconeura kerchoviana*

Many family members have the ability to hold their leaves.

## Moraceae
### Fig Family

This is a diverse family containing up to 75 genera and perhaps 1,800 species of shrubs, trees, vines, and herbaceous (nonwoody) plants. Although family members are found in temperate areas, most are native to tropical and subtropical regions. Plants differ a great deal and have a variety of leaf shapes and arrangements on the stem. Flowers also vary in shape and size, but family members are identified by technical characteristics of the flower and fruit. Many members have a milky sap when stems are cut or broken.

Plants of the fig family are grown for their fruit (breadfruit, fig, mulberry), fiber (hemp), wood, medicinal value (marijuana), and as ornamentals. With almost 2,000 species, it is unusual that there are no plants with showy or colorful flowers. Many of the larger members of the fig family are grown as shade trees in tropical and subtropical areas. A number of these trees are able to adapt to the indoor conditions of homes and most tolerate and survive the varied cultural practices of indoor gardeners.

Fig Family Members:
*Ficus benjamina*
*Ficus elastica* 'Decora'
*Ficus lyrata*
*Ficus pumila* 'Minima'

The fig is a flower turned inside out.

## Myrsinaceae
### Myrsine Family

This family contains 32 genera and 1,000 species that are confined to tropical and subtropical countries. With but one exception, all the plants in the myrsine family are trees or shrubs. Usually family members have simple, alternate, and leathery leaves, and small starlike white or pink flowers arranged in clusters.

In tropical countries a number of plants in the family are grown for lumber, dyes, food, or as ornamentals. Considering the size of the myrsine family, it is surprising that more members are not grown indoors.

Myrsine Family Member:
*Ardisia crenata*

A good many plants in the myrsine family are tropical tress.

# Nyctaginaceae

## Four-O'Clock Family

Many of the 32 genera and 300 species of herbaceous (non-woody) plants, shrubs, and trees in the four-o'clock family are native to tropical America. The leaves of family members are always simple, but may be opposite each other or alternate on the stem. However, the flower offers the biggest asset in identifying members of this family. They have no petals, and other flower parts are often showy, colorful, and petallike.

Although a few are grown for food or wood, most four-o'clock members are cultivated for their showy inflorescence. Most of these are colorful landscape plants; only two or three species in the family are commonly grown indoors. Even these require a sunny spot and good cultural care to thrive.

Four-O'Clock Family Member: *Bougainvillea spp.*

Plants in this family have colorful sepals and small flowers.

# Onagraceae

## Evening Primrose Family

Most of the 21 genera and 700 species of herbaceous (non-woody) plants, shrubs, and trees in the evening primrose family are native to temperate regions in America. Leaf and flower arrangements vary throughout the family but flower parts are arranged in fours or multiples of four.

Some plants in the evening primrose family are used for food, others for medicinal reasons, and a few for dyes, but most are grown as ornamentals. Their colorful flowers are used to enliven landscapes wherever the climate is cool and somewhat moist. Out of the 700 species in the family, only fuchsia has become widely used as an indoor or patio plant.

Evening Primrose Family Member: *Fuchsia hybrida*

Flower parts are usually arranged in fours.

## Orchidaceae
### Orchid Family

The exact number of genera and species in the orchid family is a much-debated point among specialists. Depending on what expert is consulted the number of genera can vary from 600 to 800 and the number of species from 17,000 to 30,000. Enthusiastic orchid breeders have added another 20,000 or so cultivars, making for a grand total of almost 50,000 plants. This makes the orchid family either the largest or second largest plant family, depending on how you classify plants. Whether the orchid family is the world's largest plant family or not, these plants are found in all parts of the world except deserts and polar regions. The majority of species however are native to tropical parts of the world. Where native, they may be found growing on tree trunks and branches (epiphytes), in the ground (terrestrials), or on rocks (lithophytes). Most of the 50,000 plants of the orchid family are usually categorized as herbaceous (nonwoody) plants but a number are nonwoody vines. Based on their growth habit, orchids are divided into two major categories, those that are sympodial and those that are monopodial. Sympodial orchids have a horizontal underground or surface stem which produces a set of upright leaves, goes through a dormant period, then a new stem grows sending up another set of leaves. The growth cycles are about a year apart. Monpodial orchids usually have an upright stem and growth may be continual or alternate between dormant and growing periods. Frequently, leaves on monpodial orchids are alternate, with a row of leaves on each side of the stem, and the stem is unbranching. Another special feature found in orchids is a structure called a pseudobulb, which is a thickened bulblike stem which may vary in shape from being almost round to an elongated stick form.

With the exception of vanilla which is grown for food flavoring, orchids are cultivated for their colorful, unusual flowers. Many orchids have small flowers usually found in clusters of ten or more. After flowering , orchids produce seed pods which can contain four million tiny seeds. If you are wondering why the world is not overrun with orchids, it is because the seeds contain no stored food, and after germination seeds have to form a symbiotic relationship with a mycorrhizal fungus in order to grow. Orchids were

Orchid Family Members:
*Ascocentrum miniatum*
*Epidendrum atropurpureum*
*Oncidium sphacelatum*
*Paphiopedilum* hybrids
*Vanilla planifolia*

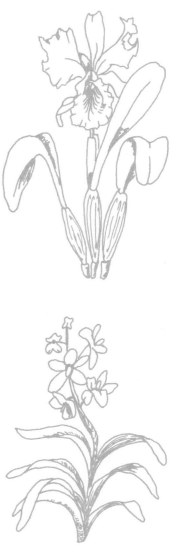

Orchids may grow along the surface (sympodial) or upright (monopodial).

very expensive at one time; now hundreds of plants can be produced in a short time by a new technique. An ever-increasing number of small orchids are being grown indoors, and many species are more adaptable than previously thought.

## Oxalidaceae
### Oxalis Family

Most of the 7 genera and 1,000 species in the oxalis (wood sorrel) family are found in the tropics, but a few hardy species are native to temperate regions. They are usually herbaceous (nonwoody) plants which grow from bulbs, tubers, or rhizomes, with some shrubs and a few trees. Most family members have compound leaves (with an appearance similar to shamrocks) which are alternate along the stem. The leaves may be palmate or pinnate. Flower parts are arranged in fives or multiples of five. Many family members grow from small bulbs which produce a set of leaves and flowers, then go dormant for several months before growing again. Another family characteristic is the interesting "sleep" movement of the leaves. The individual leaflets fold up as soon as night falls to reopen with the morning light.

Some of the treelike members have edible fruit, and a number of smaller plants in the oxalis genera have edible bulbs, tubers, or rhizomes. Bulbous oxalis are becoming more popular as small flowering pot plants, and a number of them make interesting and colorful indoor plants if their dormancy requirements are met.

Oxalis Family Member:
*Oxalis deppei*

Most plants in this family fold their leaves at night.

## Palmae
### Palm Family

The palm family is restricted in distribution to areas where temperatures seldom go below freezing. Most of the 210 genera and 2,780 species are native to tropical and subtropical regions; just a few are found in warmer temperate regions. Although many of the 3,000 species of palms have a single trunk with a cluster of leaves on top, there are some atypical plants in the

Palm Family Members:
*Chamaedorea elegans*
*Chamaedorea erumpens*
*Chrysalidocarpus lutescens*
*Howea forsterana*
*Phoenix roebelenii*

family that are vines, have creeping stems, and even a few that form branches.

Palms are usually divided into two major groups based on their leaf characteristics. These two categories are pinnate and palmate. Pinnate palms have compound leaves with leaflets attached to both sides of the main axis of the leaf. These palms are often called feather palms because their leaf resembles a feather. Palmate, or fan-leaved, palms have a large circular or triangular leaf that is not divided or only slightly so at the margins. Individual flowers on palms are usually small but often grouped together in an unusually large and noticeable inflorescence.

Palms are extremely important in many tropical countries, providing fruit (dates), sugar, starches, fermented beverages, fiber products, timber, and oils used in industry. In addition, many are grown as landscape plants. Many palms, particularly young palms, make excellent indoor plants because they tolerate a reduced light intensity and grow slowly. Formerly a much wider variety of palms were grown indoors than presently. However, interest in palms for interior use is now increasing and a wide selection should soon be available.

Palm leaves are divided into two categories—pinnate and palmate.

## Piperaceae
### Pepper Family

The 9 genera and 1,200 species in the pepper family are only found in subtropical or tropical regions. Within the 1,200 species we have herbaceous (nonwoody) plants, shrubs, vines, and small trees. Throughout the pepper family, leaves are usually simple with smooth margins, and arranged alternately along the stem. The flowers have no petals or other showy parts and frequently appear tightly arranged on a catkin-like spike which often grows straight up from the group of leaves.

Pepper Family Members:
*Peperomia caperata*
*Peperomia obtusifolia*
*Peperomia obtusifolia* 'Variegata'

Pepper family plants have flowers with no petals.

Plants in this family are grown for food flavoring (pepper), beverages, and ornamentals. Most ornamentals are small plants used as ground covers outdoors; a number of these adapt to indoor use, making attractive foliage plants. Many plants of the pepper family have succulent properties and store limited amounts of water in their fleshy leaves. These plants have become increasingly popular with indoor gardeners and more members of the pepper family are now available for purchase.

# Pittosporaceae
## Pittosporum Family

The pittosporum family is found in the warm temperate and tropical regions of the world. Many of the 9 genera and 200 species are native to islands in the South Pacific but are also found in Africa and warmer parts of Eurasia. The 200 species are all woody, and include trees, shrubs, and vines. Leaves are simple, alternate or whorled, and leathery in texture. Flower parts are usually grouped in fives, arranged in clusters, and often fragrant.

A few members of the pittosporum family are grown for their wood, but most cultivated species are grown as ornamentals for their attractive foliage. Many members of the family can tolerate short periods of drought and can grow both in full sun locations or in shade. These characteristics make some family members adaptable to indoor use.

Pittosporum Family Member:
*Pittosporum tobira*

Some plants in this family are used for lumber.

# Podocarpaceae
## Podocarpus Family

This is another family of woody plants native to tropical and subtropical regions of Africa, Asia, and the South Pacific. The 7 genera and 100 species in the podocarpus family are mostly trees and include only a few shrubs. A coniferous plant family, the leaves are usually needlelike with a few members having flat, broad leaves. The genera in the podocarpus family either have separate male and female plants, or separate male and female flowers on the same plant. The female flowers are in a conelike structure but differ from many cone-bearing plants in that only one seed develops, usually at the end of a fleshy stalk.

Cultivated species in the family are grown either for lumber or as ornamentals. Most of these ornamentals are used as landscape plants but several species tolerate low light as seedlings and

Podocarpus Family Member:
*Podocarpus macrophyllus* 'Maki'

Female plants in this conifer family have a single seed often attached to an aril.

young plants. These members of the podocarpus family and members of the araucaria family are among the few conifer plants that can be grown indoors.

# Polypodiaceae
## Common Fern Family

The common fern family is one of the eleven families of true ferns and contains 180 genera and about 7,000 species. True ferns differ from seed plants such as asparagus fern and fern begonia because true ferns never form flowers or seeds but reproduce from microscopic one-celled structures called spores. The spores are produced in cases called sporangia. Ferns are grouped into different families based on technical characteristics of the sporangia. The common fern family is the largest family of ferns and includes most of the commonly encountered ferns without treelike trunks. Common fern family members are distributed around the world, even in some desert regions. However, most species are native to moist, shaded, cool areas.

Many of the ferns in this family grow from underground or surface stems called rhizomes. Fronds (leaves) vary within the family and may be simple or compound. The sporangia are produced on the lower surface of the leaves, and may be scattered or grouped in patches or neat rows along the leaf margins. Some ferns produce two types of fronds, fertile fronds which produce spores and sterile fronds which never produce spores.

Most of the plants in the common fern family are rather small, seldom attaining heights over four feet. Like orchids, members of the common fern family may be terrestrials (growing in the ground), epiphytes (growing on tree branches and trunks), or lithophytes (growing on rocks). Ferns are often thought to require a rich, organic soil but many have the ability to grow in or on areas that offer a limited supply of plant nutrients.

Members of the common fern family have been grown for medicinal purposes, food, ornamentation, and even as ingredients for witches brew. Although many of the common ferns can be grown outdoors, only a limited number will tolerate the low humidity levels in our interiors. A wide variety of ferns can be grown successfully indoors if humidity can be kept at 50% or higher, but there are several varieties that will grow well in most homes.

Common Fern Family Members:
*Asplenium nidus*
*Cyrtomium falcatum* 'Rochfordianum'
*Davallia fejeensis*
*Nephrolepis exaltata* 'Bostoniensis'
*Nephrolepis exaltata* 'Fluffy Ruffles'
*Platycerium bifurcatum*
*Pteris ensiformis* 'Victoriae'

Ferns are ancient plants and were growing during the age of the dinosaur.

# Punicaceae
## Pomegranate Family

One of the smaller plant families, there is only one genus and two species in the pomegranate family. Native to southern Europe and Asia, pomegranates are now grown in many countries with similar climates. Both species grow either as small trees or shrubs. Young twig growth has square stems and opposite, simple leaves. As the stems mature they lose this square shape and become circular when viewed in cross section.

Pomegranates are grown for their edible fruit and as medicinal plants and ornamentals. During the centuries in which they have been cultivated, many forms have been developed, and several cultivars adapt to growing indoors on sunny window sills.

Pomegranate Family Member:
*Punica granatum nana*

Fruits in this family are large and showy.

# Rubiaceae
## Coffee Family

Most of the 400 genera and 5,000 species in the coffee family are native to tropical and subtropical regions in the world. Members of the coffee family include herbaceous (nonwoody) plants, shrubs, trees, and even vines. Although the plants in this family differ in the way they grow, they all have simple leaves which may be opposite or whorled on the branches. The flowers vary in size but the total inflorescence is usually quite showy as they often appear in dense clusters. Whether large or small, the individual flowers are funnellike with flaring petals, and flower parts are often found in fives.

Many plants in the coffee family have considerable economic importance (coffee being the best-known product to most Americans) but the family also includes cinchona, the source of quinine used for the treatment of malaria. Several other members have medicinal value and some are grown for dyes, wood, and of course, as ornamentals.

Coffee Family Member:
*Coffea arabica*

This family contains the important coffee plant.

Most members of the coffee family grown as ornamentals have showy flowers but indoors they require high light intensities to produce their inflorescence. A few species are grown indoors for their attractive foliage and do not require a high light intensity.

## Rutaceae
### Rue Family

Although members of the rue family are distributed in tropical and temperate regions, few of the 150 genera and 1,600 species are native to Europe. Most of the plants are either trees or shrubs, with only a few nonwoody plants in the family. Even though the family is smaller and contains fewer plant types than many other plant families, considerable variation exists within the rue family. Leaves may be simple or compound and are alternate or opposite on the stem, but they are usually smooth and contain oil glands and are frequently fragrant when crushed or torn. Flowers may also be fragrant, and they are often clustered.

Members of the rue family are grown for medicinal purposes, oils for perfumes, foods (citrus), and as ornamentals. Many citrus are grown outdoors for their attractive foliage as well as for their fruit. Several citrus plants make interesting indoor trees if they are given enough light.

Rue Family Member:
*Citrofortunella mitis*

This family contains the citrus group of plants.

## Saxifragaceae
### Saxifrage Family

The saxifrage family has about 80 genera and 1,200 species of herbaceous (non-woody) plants, shrubs, and some small trees. In contrast to other plant families in this book, most of these plants are native to temperate and artic regions of the world. The family name means "rock breaker" and it was given to this family because several species are native to moun-

Saxifrage Family Member:
*Hydrangea macrophylla*

Some plants in this family form plantlets on the end of long runners.

91

tainous areas of the world where their roots have actually broken through rocks. Many of the herbaceous plants in this family have leaves growing in rosettes. Family members with stems may have simple or compound leaves that are alternate or opposite on the stem. Usually many clustered flowers in shades of white or pink make up the inflorescence.

With the exception of currants and gooseberries, cultivated plants in this family are used as ornamentals both indoors and out of doors. Some woody species are grown as flowering pot plants, and several small herbaceous plants are grown for their attractive foliage or unusual characteristics. Saxifrage family members grow best in cooler rooms indoors.

Many plants in this family grow in rosettes and send up flowers on a slender stalk.

# Scrophulariaceae
## Snapdragon Family

This is a widely distributed plant family with 210 genera and 3,000 species. Most family members are herbaceous (non-woody) plants or shrubs, but a few are trees and vines. There is considerable variation within the 3,000 species, and leaves may be alternate, opposite, or whorled; and although leaves are simple, they are often lobed. Family membership is determined predominantly on several technical characteristics of the flower.

Snapdragon Family Member:
*Calceolaria crenatiflora*

Although a few plants are used for medicinal purposes, most cultivated species are grown as ornamentals. Most of these are grown outdoors for their showy, colorful inflorescences, but several members of the family make attractive flowering pot plants. Due to their cultural requirements snapdragon family members are usually temporary visitors indoors, and new plants are purchased when desired.

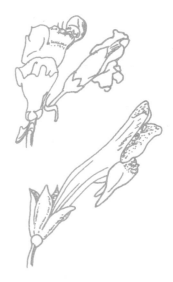

Flowers with a tubular structure are common to this family.

# Theaceae

### Tea Family

Most of the 25 genera and 380 species in the tea family are native to cool tropical and subtropical regions of Asia. Members of this family are either trees or shrubs, and they share a number of common characteristics. The simple leaves are usually leathery, smooth, and arranged alternately on the stem. The flowers show more variation, as they may be single or arranged in clusters; and in some species, flowers are found in leaf axils, whereas in others they are on stem tips. The showy flower parts are usually found in fives or multiples of five.

Members of this family are grown for oils, tea, and as ornamentals. Many of the ornamentals are grown outdoors both for their attractive foliage and colorful flowers. Indoors, most of the plants in this family require high light intensities and cool temperatures for best growth.

Tea Family Member:
*Camellia japonica*

This family contains the source of tea.

# Urticaceae

### Nettle Family

The nettle family has 40 genera and 500 species of herbaceous (nonwoody) plants, shrubs, trees, and vines which are found in the temperate and tropical regions of the world. This is a rather diverse group of plants that are united by technical characteristics of the inflorescence. However, they do have several similarities. The leaves may be alternate or opposite but they are always simple. A number of plants in this family have evolved stinging hairs on the stems and leaves which can cause

Nettle Family Members:
*Pilea cadierei*
*Pilea microphylla*
*Soleirolia soleirolii*

minor to severe discomfort and pain. Most family members have small, often greenish flowers which are grouped together in clusters.

Some plants of the nettle family are grown for food, fiber, and medicine, and a few are grown as ornamentals. Most of the ornamentals in the family are small plants used as ground covers in shaded, moist areas in the tropics and subtropics. Several of these grow well indoors if soils are kept moist and the humidity is not too low. They usually make good hanging-basket subjects and are more popular now than previously.

Several members of this family have stinging hairs.

# Vitaceae
## Grape Family

The grape family contains 12 genera and about 500 species of vines, shrubs, and a few small trees. Family members are found in the tropics and subtropics; only a few hardy members may be found where winter temperatures are often below freezing.

Several common characteristics help identify family members. Leaves of mature plants are alternate, and vining members have tendrils. The small, often greenish flowers are formed opposite the leaves and are borne in clusters. If pollination occurs, members of the grape family have fruits that are classified as berries.

The cultivated plants in this family are grown for their fruits or as ornamentals. Almost all of the ornamentals in the grape family are grown for their attractive foliage and interesting stem characteristics rather than their flowers. A number of vining grape family members are used indoors as hanging baskets, totem poles, or cascading plants on pedestals. Most of these make excellent indoor plants if soils are not kept too wet.

Grape Family Members:
*Cissus antarctica*
*Cissus rhombifolia*

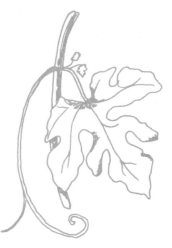

The vines in the grape family may support the stems by coiling tendrils.

# History and Cultural Care

Contrary to the old wives' tale, a "green thumb" is no mystical appendage bestowed at random on those lucky souls able to make plants and flowers grow and grow and be beautiful. Rather, it is the simple combination of common sense, knowledge applied and time spent. Any successful houseplant "family," species by species, has been carefully chosen to fit the owner's interests and requirements—and the results are lush and beautiful—as if by magic.

To that end, this collection of popular houseplants offers specific in-depth information to enable you to choose and grow the right plants. About a third of the plants are traditionally grown for their flowers, and the remaining ones grown for their attractive foliage. All of the plants are readily available in florist's shops throughout the country. Under the proper conditions they are durable and will grow and thrive indoors for many years.

Some plants are easy growers, while others are more challenging and require more indoor gardening experience. Before selecting a particular plant for your home, be sure and carefully read its cultural care requirements indicating proper light, temperature, humidity, water and fertilizers. This will enable you to choose those plants best suited to your degree of indoor gardening expertise, home conditions, and—of special importance—time limitations.

As most of these plants should be expected to remain in your home for years to come, a short discussion of soils, repotting, pruning and grooming information is also included along with the most common propagative techniques for each plant. In addition, the most frequently occurring pests are listed so you can protect your plants.

Extensive cultural care charts for over 300 plants, starting on page 245, augment this information and offer answers to most any plant care query that may arise.

One word of advice—sound horticulture is somewhat akin to good cooking. The cultural care prescriptions for each plant are merely guidelines. Since few homes approximate the ideal conditions of plant stores and greenhouses, they will most likely require slight or at times even radical "recipe" changes to suit your particular climate or spot in the house.

# ABUTILON
## (Malvaceae)

**Abutilon hybridium** cultivars—Flowering Maple, Parlor Maple

Flowering maples are woody shrubs from Central and South America whose leaves resemble maple leaves. Although there are numerous species in the tropics and subtropics, most abutilons grown as houseplants are *A. hybridium* cultivars. Abutilons produce attractive, hanging bell-like flowers which resemble small hollyhocks. Depending upon the cultivar, the 2-inch flowers may be various shades of white, yellow, salmon, or red, with conspicuous yellow stamens and pistil. Foliage size and color also vary from cultivar to cultivar, and may be 2 to 8 inches long and vary from soft green to attractive variegated patterns.

CULTURE—*Light:* Place in full sun locations indoors. Outdoors locate in partial shade or morning sun. *Temperature:* Parlor maple does best with cool night (55 to 60° F) and day (60 to 70° F) temperatures. *Humidity:* New growth may need misting to prevent desiccation. *Water:* Allow soil surface to dry between waterings; adjust watering frequencies to prevent wilting. *Fertilizer:* Use reduced rates every 2 or 3 weeks. *Soil and repotting:* Use soil mix number 1. Repot older plants in the spring; younger plants as needed to balance plant and container. *Pruning and grooming:* Young plants (6 to 12 inches) need pinching to promote branching. Older plants should be pruned back in spring and fall to desired height. Syringe foliage as needed to remove dust. *Propagation:* Terminal cuttings. *Pests:* Aphids and spider mites.

*Abutilon hybridium*

# ACALYPHA
## (Euphorbiaceae)

*Acalypha hispida*—Chenile Plant

Chenile plants may reach 10 feet or more in the tropics but they look best when kept to 2 feet or less as indoor plants. Female plants have small red flowers grouped together to form velvety, crimson-red hanging spikes up to 20 inches long. The long pendulous spikes are very attractive displayed against the 4 to 6 inch deep green leaves. One other color form exists with cream white spikes.

CULTURE—*Light:* Place in full sun locations for best indoor flowering. *Temperature:* Chenile plant tolerates normal house temperatures. Do not put outdoors unless night temperatures remain above 50°F. *Humidity:* Use humidity increasing methods during the winter when relative humidity is low. *Water:* It may require more water than your other plants but allow top surface of soil to dry before watering again. *Fertilizer:* Use reduced rates every 3 to 4 weeks. *Soil and repotting:* Use soil mix number 1. Repot older plants in the spring; younger plants as

needed. *Pruning and grooming:* Prune plants back in the spring and fall. Young, single stemmed plants have the longest flower spikes, but plants that have been pinched and have a number of flower bearing branches are more attractive. Syringe plants as needed to remove dust. *Propagation:* Terminal cuttings. *Pests:* Mites during dry periods.

*Acalypha hispida*

97

# ACHIMENES
## (Gesneriaceae)

**Achimenes hybrids**—Magic Flower, Nut Orchid

Magic flowers grow 6 to 12 inches high and make excellent flowering plants for indoor hanging baskets or outdoor window boxes. The cascading stems with oval hairy leaves bend and grow upright carrying attractive, showy flat-faced flowers that range from ½ to 3 inches across. Flower color depends on the cultivar, and includes yellows, whites, blues, reds, and violets. The plants have a tuber or rhizome which some people feel resembles a pine cone or pineapple. The scaly rhizomes can be planted in late winter or early spring. Some indoor gardeners prefer to start magic flowers in flats and transplant when they are about 2 inches high. Use a mixture of peat moss and perlite or builder's sand in the flat. Use an African violet soil mix when transplanting. Achimenes will grow and flower for about 8 months and then need a 4 month dormant period. The great variety in flower color and size, and their free blooming habit, make magic flowers worth attempting to grow.

*Achimenes hybrid*

CULTURE—*Light:* Magic flowers need high interior light but avoid prolonged full sun locations. Outdoors, place in partial shade. *Temperature:* Normal home temperatures are acceptable. Avoid locations where temperatures drop below 50° F. *Humidity:* Use methods to increase humidity during the winter. *Water:* Keep the soil surface moist, but avoid overwatering. *Fertilizer:* Use reduced fertilizer rates when the plants are 3 to 4 inches high and fertilize every 2 to 3 weeks when growing actively. *Soil and repotting:* Use soil mix number 7. After dormancy has occurred, tubers may be stored at 60°F in peat moss or left in the pots. *Pruning and grooming:* Syringe foliage as needed to remove dust. *Propagation:* Division of tubers. *Pests:* Aphids and mites.

# AECHMEA
## (Bromeliaceae)

**Aechmea fasciata**—Silver Vase

Aechmeas are the most widely grown of the bromeliads and *Aechmea fasciata* is the most popular of the Aechmeas. The large rosette of 8 to 12 inch, silver coated, gray-green leaves deserves the name silver vase. The flowering spike arises from the center of the cup formed by the rosette of stiff leaves. Usually silver vase is sold after the plant has been induced to flower. Although each tiny blue flower lasts only a short time, the pink bracts last 2 months or longer.

Although *A. fasciata* grows as epiphytes on tree branches in tropical rain forests in Central and South America, it is an easy-to-care-for house plant. After flowering, the parent plant dies but the offsets which form naturally can be used to propagate the plant.

All epiphytic bromeliads should be grown in a porous organic mixture. In their native habitat, they obtain much of their nourishment and water through their specialized leaves. The roots function primarily to keep the plant on the tree. It is very important when growing *A. fasciata* and other bromeliads indoors to keep water in the leaf rosette, but it is also necessary to water the soil.

by placing mature specimens (2 year old plants) in a sealed plastic bag with a ripe apple for 5 to 7 days. Before putting the bromeliad in the bag, empty the water from the leaf rosette. Flowering should occur within 30 to 80 days depending on the bromeliad species. *Pruning and grooming:* Very little care is needed other than to syringe your *A. fasciata* once every 2 weeks if possible. *Propagation:* Remove the side shoots or offsets formed after the plant flowers. Pot them in a half and half mix of peat and perlite. *Pests:* Scale sometimes may become a problem.

### Aechmea 'Royal Wine'

'Royal Wine' has softer, more pliable leaves than *A. fasciata*. The leaves are shiny apple green overlaid with maroon coloration which increases in intensity from the base to the tip of the leaf. The inflorescence has orange bracts and blue flowers on a flexible wine colored stalk.

CULTURE—Care is the same as *A. fasciata* except that 'Royal Wine' requires more frequent watering to keep the soil moist.

*Aechmea 'Royal Wine'*

# AESCHYNANTHUS
## (Gesneriaceae)

**Aeschynanthus pulcher**—Lipstick Vine, Scarlet Basket Vine

In its native Java, lipstick vine grows on tree branches where the slightly woody stems

*Aechmea fasciata*

CULTURE—*Light: A. fasciata* will grow best where it receives medium to high interior light but it will tolerate lower light areas for several months. Do not place in direct sun. If placed outside, select shaded locations. *Temperature:* Although *A. fasciatas* are easy to grow, do not allow temperatures to go below 50°F. *Humidity:* Keep the rosette filled with water indoors. The foliage will remain attractive longer if the relative humidity can be kept above 25%. *Water:* If the rosette is kept filled with water, soil moisture is not critical but do not allow the soil to become completely dry. *Fertilizer:* Aechmeas can absorb fertilizer from either their roots or leaves. Use a water soluble fertilizer at dilute concentrations, applied to the soil (⅛ recommended strength) and fertilize every 3 weeks. *Soil and repotting:* Bromeliads seem to look most attractive in containers just large enough to keep the plants from falling over. Use soil mix number 3. *Flowering:* You can induce flowering in home grown bromeliads

*Aeschynanthus pulcher*

hang gracefully for about 2 to 3 feet. The 2 to 4 inch tubular, bright red flowers are clustered at the stem tips, contrasting with the smooth, green, succulent 2 inch leaves.

CULTURE—*Light:* Lipstick vine does best in east or west windows. Direct sun for about 4 hours during the winter is acceptable but direct sun should be avoided during the summer. *Temperature:* Keep day temperatures above 70°F, and night above 65°F during most of the year. Lipstick vine flowers best if kept cool (55 to 60°F) and a little dry from January through February. *Humidity:* When the plant is actively growing, strive for 50% humidity. *Water:* Keep soil moist, except for the rest period when it should be watered sparingly. Use water at room temperature and avoid getting it on the foliage or flowers. *Fertilizer:* Use reduced rates every 3 or 4 weeks. *Soil and repotting:* Use soil mix number 7. Repot, if necessary, just before active growth starts in the spring. *Pruning and grooming:* When plants have completed their flowering cycle, cut back to about 6 inches. *Propagation:* Stem cuttings. *Pests:* Aphids and mites.

# AGLAONEMA
## (Araceae)

People who grow aglaonemas are constantly amazed at the plant's ability to thrive indoors in low light locations. Although aglaonemas are native to tropical rain forests in Indonesia and the Pacific Islands, they are among the best of indoor plants. Hybrid aglaonemas with excellent color have been developed in the past few years. The hybrids seem to grow even better indoors than most of the naturally occurring species. Flowers appear at

spasmodic intervals but as the flower's stems are short, the leaves usually cover them and the flowers go unnoticed. If pollinized, bright red fleshy berries are formed. Aglaonemas spread by

*Aglaonema* 'Silver King'

Aglaonema
commutatum elegans

Aglaonema
costatum

weeks. *Soil and repotting:* Use soil mix number 2. Repot when the plant becomes pot-bound. *Pruning and grooming:* As the stem continues to grow, it usually starts to lean or with time lose its lower leaves. Cut the stems off close to the soil line and when necessary use the cuttings to propagate the plant. New growth will start from the underground rhizomes and the plant will be as attractive as before or more so. *Propagation:* Aglaonemas can be propagated by seeds, division, or cuttings. *Pests:* Mites and sometimes aphids.

### Aglaonema costatum —Spotted Evergreen

Spotted evergreen is essentially a stemless aglaonema spreading by underground rhizomes. Usually no higher than 8 inches, it makes an ideal desktop plant. Its broad, dark green, leathery leaves are spotted with white and have a broad white stripe down the center. It adds color and contrast to low light areas.

CULTURE–Similar to other Aglaonemas but *A. costatum* needs higher humidity. Group with other plants, mist daily, or place on a tray of wet pebbles. Because of its unique foliage, this plant is worth a little extra care.

### Aglaonema crispum —Pewter Plant

Pewter plant is the largest aglaonema commonly grown indoors; it may exceed 3 feet. The stems are about as thick as your thumb and the leaves are grayish-green with

underground stems and fill the container with short stemmed plants with long lasting leaves. Although they grow well with a moderate amount of watering, cuttings can be taken and kept alive for extended periods in just plain water.

### Aglaonema commutatum elegans —Commutatum

Commutatum has long, deep green lanceolate leaves with distinct silver markings The plant reaches an ultimate height of about 2 feet when grown in a large container, but does well in small containers, too. It can be used as a table or desk plant, as a filler plant in a large planter, or as a low floor plant.

CULTURE—*Light:* Place in low to medium interior light locations. *Temperature:* Avoid temperatures below 50 to 55°F as the plant is cold sensitive. Aglaonema grows well with 70 to 80°F day temperatures and 60 to 70°F night temperatures. *Humidity:* Commutatum tolerates low humidity fairly well. *Water:* Allow top soil surface to become dry. *Fertilizer:* Use reduced rates every 4 to 5

Aglaonema
crispum

silver markings over most of the upper surface. It will tolerate low light as well as the other aglaonemas but it makes a better floor plant because of its upright growth habit and broad leaves. Pewter plant is a good substitute for dieffenbachia in low light areas.

CULTURE—The same as other *Aglaonemas*.

### Aglaonema 'Fransher'—Fransher

Fransher is an exciting new hybrid which will brighten up any low light area. The stems are not much larger than your ring finger and the attractive lanceolate leaves are variegated with silver markings. If placed in a favorable light location, it grows rapidly for an aglaonema and spreads by underground rhizomes. It makes an attractive table plant or a low floor plant if planted in a large container. It is an excellent plant choice for beginners.

CULTURE—The same as *A. commutatum elegans*, but it tolerates low humidity and occasional dry soil better.

### Aglaonema modestum—Chinese Evergreen

Indoor plant gardeners are most likely to be familiar with Chinese evergreen. The plant has solid green leaves which may be a foot or more in length on slender canes which may be up to 20 inches long. Although durable and an excellent house plant, it has a tendency to drop its lower leaves sooner than other aglaonemas.

CULTURE—The same as for *A. commutatum*.

### Aglaonema commutatum 'Pseudo-Bracteatum'—Golden Evergreen

Botanically, golden evergreen is classified as *A. commutatum* but it differs in having larger leaves. The leaf blades with white petioles are over a foot long and marbled with silver and cream markings. It can be used as a low floor plant as it obtains a height of about 2½ feet.

*Aglaonema*
'Fransher'

*Aglaonema*
*modestum*

*Aglaonema commutatum*
'Pseudo-Bracteatum'

CULTURE—Golden evergreen requires the same care as *A. commutatum* except it is just a little more cold sensitive, and night temperatures should never go below 55°F. Stems seem to have less rigidity than other aglaonemas and may require stem pruning sooner.

## *Aglaonema* 'Silver King'

'Silver King' is another new hybrid with very attractive silver markings on the foliage. Its leaves are a little broader than Fransher's. It grows to about 2 feet and makes a good floor plant.

CULTURE—The same as other aglaonemas.

# ALOE
## (Liliaceae)

### *Aloe barbadensis*—
Medicine Plant

*Aloe barbadensis* has been grown for over 2,000 years as a medicinal plant for treating burns and cuts, and leaf extracts have been drunk for stomach ulcers. Aloe is the "Medicine Plant" that is widely advertised in magazines and Sunday news supplements. Although sold when small, mature plants have grayish green thickened leaves which are 2 to 3 inches wide at the base but taper gradually to a point. The 15 inch long leaves are arranged in a rosette. Young plants have spotted leaves with spines. The flowering stem is about 3 feet high and the upper portion is covered with yellow flowers about an inch long. Some forms of *A. barbadensis* have 3 red outer petals and 3 yellow inner petals. Medicine plant is an interesting plant to have on a sunny window sill.

CULTURE—*Light:* Place in a full sun location indoors. Outdoors, place in an area receiving morning sun and partial shade the rest of the day. *Temperature:* Normal home temperatures are acceptable. *Humidity: A. barbadensis* does well in low humidity areas.

*Aloe barbadensis*

*Water:* As with most succulents, avoid overwatering. Soil can become moderately dry. *Fertilizer:* Apply reduced rates once a month when actively growing. *Soil and repotting:* Plants should be shifted up into larger containers as needed. Use soil mix number 5. *Pruning and grooming:* Give *A. barbadensis* a good shower when dust and dirt build up on the foliage. *Propagation:* Offshoots. *Pests:* An occasional caterpillar may chew young leaves.

*Ananas comosus*

CULTURE—*Light:* Pineapples do best in sunny south windows but they will survive in bright indirect light. *Temperature:* Normal home temperatures are acceptable. Avoid temperatures lower than 50°F. *Humidity:* Usually no special treatment is necessary. *Water:* Water often enough to keep the soil moist. *Fertilizer:* Use reduced rates every 4 weeks. *Soil and repotting:* Repot when the plant becomes too large for the container. Use soil mix number 3. *Pruning and grooming:* An occasional shower to remove dust will keep your plant attractive. *Propagation:* Offsets on the base of the plant or along the stem. You can also use the rosette of leaves from the fruit you purchase in the grocery store to start a new plant. *Pests:* Scale.

# ANTHURIUM
## (Araceae)

*Anthurium scherzeranum* —Flamingo Flower

Anthuriums present a real challenge to the indoor gardener. These beautiful flowering plants are native to South America where

# ANANAS
## (Bromeliaceae)

*Ananas comosus* —Pineapple

Most people associate the Hawaiian Islands with pineapple but all bromeliads including pineapple are native to tropical and subtropical America. Most bromeliads grow in tree branches or in crotches of large trees, but pineapple and a few other bromeliads grow in the ground. The cultivated pineapple has a short stem with long, stiff, spiny-edged leaves arranged in a rosette that may be 3 feet high. Leaf color varies with light intensity and ranges from silvery-green to a medium green. The edible pineapple is formed by pollination of a mass of violet flowers topped by a cluster of leaves. Usually commercial pineapples are grown indoors as curiousity items, but other pineapple cultivars are also very attractive. *A. Comosus* 'Nanus' is a dwarf form which is more ideally suited for most home locations. Several forms with red or white marginal bands occasionally are available.

*Anthurium scherzeranum*

104

temperatures are relatively constant and humidity is high. *A. scherzeranum* is grown for its glossy 2 inch bract which varies from scarlet through white and surrounds the true flowers which are crowded together on a yellow, twisted, taillike structure called a spadix. Many indoor gardeners consider any difficulties in growing the plant worthwhile as the colorful bracts will last for months on the plant, and for several weeks when used as cut flowers. The deep green foliage is clustered on a short stem. Usually less than 15 inches high, the plant is an attractive decorative plant that can be displayed in various locations in the house when blooming. Other anthuriums are worth trying to grow but are more difficult.

CULTURE—*Light:* Choose a high light location but not direct sun. *Temperature:* Night temperatures should never go below 55°F and day temperatures should stay below 85°F for best growth. *Humidity:* The critical factor in growing anthuriums is humidity. Try to maintain at least a 50% relative humidity. Daily misting will aid the plant's growth. *Water:* Do not allow the soil to dry excessively. Frequent watering using lukewarm water will be necessary in most homes. *Fertilizer:* Use dilute fertilizer rates and apply once a month. *Soil and repotting:* Use soil mix number 6. Repot in the spring. *Pruning and grooming:* Removing old yellowing leaves and cleaning the foliage is all that is required to maintain anthurium's appearance. *Propagation:* Division, cuttings, or fresh seeds. *Pests:* Mealybugs, mites, aphids, and scales.

# APHELANDRA
(Acanthaceae)

*Aphelandra squarrosa* —Zebra Plant

Zebra plants would be worth growing even if they never flowered as their large opposite leaves with ivory stripes against a dark green background are very attractive. Although the yellow flowers are short lived, the persistent yellow bracts arising in a terminal spike

*Aphelandra squarrosa*

provide color in the home for about a month and a half. A number of cultivars are grown but *A. squarrosa* 'Dania' and 'Louisae' are probably the most common. In most homes, zebra plant will remain an attractive foliage plant but it will not rebloom. However, the plant may be brought into flower by locating it in a high light area in your home and maintaining high humidity. Zebra plants make attractive decorative plants when in bloom.

CULTURE—*Light:* Zebra plants do best in a high light area but with no direct sun. *Temperature:* Keep night temperatures above 55°F and day temperatures below 85°F. *Humidity:* Make provisions for increasing humidity. *Water:* Keep soil moist; plants use quite a bit of water but water frequency depends on location. *Fertilizer:* Fertilize once a month or more with reduced rates. *Soil and repotting:* Use soil mix number 2. Repot the plants when they become pot-bound. *Pruning and grooming:* Plants should be cut back when they are through flowering. Zebra plants look best when kept between 12 and 18 inches tall. *Propagation:* Propagate new plants from stem or tip cuttings. *Pests:* Mites, scale, and aphids.

# ARAUCARIA
(Araucariaceae)

### *Araucaria heterophylla* —
Norfolk Island Pine

"Storybook Christmas Tree" is the only description that seems appropriate for Norfolk Island Pine. Large potted specimens look almost artificial because of their perfect shape, with 3 to 5 branches radiating from the stem at each tier. As the tree grows over 200 feet tall in its native habitat, it will eventually become too large for your home. There is no way to preserve the symmetry of the tree by pruning techniques, and eventually (10 to 20 years) a new plant will have to be propagated from the terminal growth. Use Norfolk Island pine as a living Christmas tree. When young,

*Araucaria heterophylla*

the trees do well as east or north window sill plants. As they become larger, shift them into floor plants.

CULTURE —*Light:* Norfolk Island pines need to be placed in at least a medium light intensity area. The terminal portion of the plant will stop growing and the upper branches will continue to elongate if placed in a low light area. *Temperature:* Temperatures should be between 50°F and 80°F. Avoid locations where temperatures fluctuate rapidly. *Humidity:* Usually Norfolk Island pine does not require special care, but avoid strong air currents indoors or out. *Water:* Maintain a consistent amount of water in the soil. The tree may drop some of its needles if it is allowed to become too dry and then soaked. *Fertilizer:* Use reduced rates every 5 to 6 weeks. Apply minor elements once a year. *Soil and repotting:* Use soil mix number 2. Repot every 2 or 3 years, shifting to larger containers as necessary. *Pruning and grooming:* A good shower once a month will keep the plant looking more attractive. The tree cannot be pruned and maintain its symmetry. *Propagation:* Must be propagated from seed or terminal cuttings. Do not remove terminal of plant you have until you are ready to discard it. Branch cuttings will root, but they will not form a tree. *Pests:* Scales and mealybugs.

# ARDISIA
(Myrsinaceae)

### *Ardisia crenata* —Ardisia, Coral Berry, Christmas Berry

Ardisia is widely used in the south as a landscaping plant but it makes an interesting indoor plant. White or pink flowers form in the spring and if pollinated persistent red berries contrast with the dark, thick 3 inch leaves in the fall. The berries in large hanging clusters may stay on the plant for up to 6 months, providing attractive color during the Christmas season. There is also a white berried form. With age the lower leaves fall off and the plant assumes the appearance of a miniature tree. Ardisia is suitable for cool north porch. *Humidity:* It tolerates indoor conditions. *Water:* Uniform soil moisture is best for ardisia. If the soil becomes too dry, the lower leaves will drop off. *Fertilizer:* Use reduced rates every 4 or 5 weeks. *Soil and repotting:* Use soil mix number 2. Repot in the spring. *Pruning and grooming:* Cut the terminal back to induce branching. Older plants may be cut back within a few inches of the soil line if they have become too large for their growing area. *Propagation:* Propagate from cuttings taken when pruning the plant or from seed. *Pests:* Mites and somtimes scale.

# ASCOCENTRUM
## (Orchidaceae)

***Ascocentrum miniatum*** —Miniatum

*Ascocentrum miniatum* is a small upright epiphytic orchid which grows with 3 to 8 inch dark green, fleshy, rigid, ½ inch wide leaves. With age it may reach a height of 12 inches. The inflorescence is usually about 5 inches in length and covered with small ¾ inch orange to red flowers. It is an excellent small orchid

*Ardisia crenata*

*Ascocentrum miniatum*

attempts at creating pseudo-bonsai. Initially it makes a good window or low table plant; with age it becomes a floor plant with character.

CULTURE—*Light:* Maintain coral berry in medium or higher light intensity areas but avoid full sun. If taken outside for the summer, it should be located in a shaded area. *Temperature:* Ardisia will tolerate temperatures down to 30°F, and extremes of 90°F, but avoid locations where temperatures fluctuate drastically. It is an ideal plant for a for the window. If you have not grown orchids before, this is a good one to start with. Miniatum requires no resting period.

CULTURE—*Light:* High interior light, an east, south, or west window. If foliage bleaches, move plant to a lower light intensity area. *Temperature:* Average home temperatures are acceptable. *Humidity:* Maintain humidity about 25%. *Water:* Allow soil surface to dry between watering. *Fertilizer:* Use about ¼ ounce of liquid 10-10-10 per gallon of water and fertilize once every 6 weeks if plants are growing in osmunda fern soil mix. *Soil and repotting:* Use soil mix number 4. Repot once every 2 or 3 years. *Pruning and grooming:* Syringe leaves as needed to remove dust. *Propagation:* Stem cuttings. *Pests:* Usually scales are the only problem.

Asparagus densiflorus 'Sprengeri'

# ASPARAGUS
## (Liliaceae)

***Asparagus densiflorus 'Sprengeri'*** —
Sprengeri Fern, Asparagus Fern

Sprengeri fern is not really a fern at all, but a member of the lily family. In addition, what look like leaves on the plant are really modified branches which botanists call cladodes. The plant has thin woody stems covered with short spines and clusters of cladodes which cascade gracefully over the side of the container. During spring, the plant may be covered with small white flowers and in early fall with bright red berries. It is excellent for hanging baskets and raised

planters. Cuttings can be used as a delicate accent for floral arrangements.

CULTURE—*Light:* Sprengeri fern needs at least medium light indoors but preferably high light. Avoid full sun locations, although east windows are all right. Outdoors it does well in partial shade. *Temperature:* It will tolerate cool temperatures (45°F) during winter; high temperatures (95°F) during summer. *Humidity:* Plant tolerates normal room humidity. Hot dry air blowing on plant will dry out the cladodes and you will find them dropping all over the floor. *Water:* Allow top soil surface to dry between waterings. Avoid overwatering during periods of slow growth. *Fertilizer:* Use reduced rates once a month. *Soil and repotting:* Use soil mix number 2. Repot and divide either in the spring or fall. It does best and looks most attractive if grown in large containers. *Pruning and grooming:* Cut old woody stems off at soil line to induce new growth. The tuberous roots contain enough food to allow rather drastic pruning. Shower foliage once a month. *Propagation:* Seed or division. Extra divisions in the spring can be used for outdoor landscape plantings. *Pests:* Sometimes aphids.

Aspidistra elatior

108

# ASPIDISTRA
(Liliaceae)

*Aspidistra elatior —*
Cast Iron Plant, Saloon Plant

*Asplenium nidus*

The common name, cast iron plant, reflects the abuse the plant will withstand. It is an extremely tough and durable plant that has been used as an indoor plant for over a hundred years. The dark green, leathery foliage arises directly from underground stems. Petioles are about half the length of the 1 to 2 feet leaf blades. Forms with variegated foliage are available but I do not find them attractive. Most people never know that their cast iron plants flower because the purplish ¾ inch flowers form just at the soil line and are usually overlooked. It is one of the easiest plants to grow indoors and looks very attractive used as a low floor plant in an 8 inch container.

CULTURE—*Light:* It tolerates low light but it can be grown in high interior light, too. Full sun locations will burn the foliage. *Temperature:* Aspidistra will withstand temperatures down to 28°F and up to 95°F but it does best in cool locations under 75°F. *Humidity:* No special treatment is necessary. *Water:* Water when necessary to keep the soil from drying out. *Fertilizer:* Use reduced rates every 4 or 5 weeks. *Soil and repotting:* Use soil mix number 2. Repot when crowded in the container. *Pruning and grooming:* Cut old leaves just above the soil line when they become unattractive. Foliage will be more lustrous if washed or cleaned once a month. Cut foliage can be used for floral arrangements. *Propagation:* Division when repotting. *Pests:* None of importance.

# ASPLENIUM
(Polypodiaceae)

*Asplenium nidus* —Birdsnest Fern
If you have ever seen a large birdsnest fern, it is hard to realize that this plant is an epiphyte in its native habitat, the Pacific Islands. The smooth, shiny, leatherlike fronds may attain a length of 4 feet. The leaves have

a prominent blackish midrib which radiates from a short stem covered with black hairlike scales. Although native to tropical rain forests, it is one of the better ferns for indoor use. It grows well in most homes with moderate care and is most attractive as a floor plant or low table plant. Birdsnest fern is an excellent plant for creating a tropical effect if you have room.

CULTURE—*Light:* It can be used in low light areas, but does better in medium light or higher. Avoid full sun. *Temperature:* Protect from drafts and sudden temperature changes. Do not let temperature drop below 50°F; normal room temperatures will cause no problems. *Humidity:* Fronds will look better if measures are taken to keep humidity above 50%. When the humidity is too low, new growth may be deformed. *Water:* Maintain a moist soil but do not saturate. *Fertilizer:* Be sure to use reduced rates and fertilize once a month. *Soil and repotting:* Use soil mix number 6. Repot in spring when necessary, maybe once every 2 or 3 years. *Pruning and grooming:* Trim edges of fronds if they become brown. Do not mistake the spores which form on the underside of the frond at right angles to the midrib for disease or damage. Remove fronds when they become unattractive. Keep the foliage clean by syringing every 2 to 4 weeks. *Propagation:* Spores. *Pests:* Scale and mealybugs.

# ASTROPHYTUM
(Cactaceae)

***Astrophytum myriostigma***—Bishop's Cap, Star Cactus

The bishop's cap is one of the more interesting small cacti that can be grown in our homes. The spineless surface is usually peppered or flecked with white scales and you may be tempted to touch it to see if it is real. In its native habitat, central Mexico, it has attractive 2 inch yellow flowers in the summer. The plant's maximum height indoors is almost 2 feet with a diameter of 8 inches. Bishop's cap is excellent for a sunny

*Astrophytum myriostigma*

window. When desired, it can be moved to provide an accent piece in decorative arrangements.

CULTURE—*Light:* During the winter, provide full sun. During the summer, an east window may be best. *Temperature:* Keep cool (50 to 60°F) during the winter. Normal home temperatures are acceptable the rest of the year. *Humidity:* Dry air presents no problem. *Water:* Plants require less water during winter dormant period, perhaps as little as once every two weeks. During the rest of the year, water when the top portion of the soil has become dry. *Fertilizer:* Fertilize with reduced rates every 5 or 6 weeks during spring, summer, and fall, but not during the winter. *Soil and repotting:* Use soil mix number 5. Repot when the plant is too large for its container, preferably in the spring. *Pruning and grooming:* An occasional shower will remove dust. *Propagation:* Seed for advanced gardeners; top cuttings of mature plants. *Pests:* An easy plant to keep pest free as insects have few hiding places.

# BEAUCARNEA
(Agavaceae)

***Beaucarnea recurvata***—Ponytail

Ponytails are fascinating plants with large swollen trunks. Not only is their shape different, they are one of the few tree forms in the lily family. The swollen trunk is used to store water and enables the plant to survive extended periods of drought in the deserts of Mexico. Although eventually reaching 30 feet, it grows slowly indoors and would take decades to outgrow most home locations. A tapering stem arises from the swollen base which is capped by a thick crown of gracefully arching dark green leaves which are ¾ inch wide and up to 6 feet long. If a suitable location can be found in your home, it makes a truly unusual conversation piece. Small ponytails can be used on low tables; larger ones serve well as floor plants.

CULTURE—*Light:* Select the highest light area in your home for a ponytail. Supplemental light will help keep it more attractive. However, if you move the plant outdoors in the summer, select a partially shaded location to prevent leaf burn. *Temperature:* Normal home temperatures are acceptable. *Humidity:* Low relative humidity is no problem. *Water:* Avoid overwatering. Allow top soil surface to dry between waterings. *Fertilizer:* During summer, fertilize once a month at reduced rates. Leach soil well twice a year to reduce soluble salt level. Use a minor element fertilizer once a year. *Soil and repotting:* Use soil mix number 5. Repot as needed to keep plant in balance with container size. *Pruning and grooming:* Remove old leaves when dry. Wash foliage once a month. *Propagation:* Seeds. *Pests:* Chewing insects when placed outdoors.

# BEGONIA
(Begoniaceae)

So many kinds of begonias are grown as indoor plants that an entire book could be written about them. All have succulent stems with enlarged nodes and usually unequal leaf development. They are classified according to the type of root structure each has. If you are interested in more information on begonias, contact the American Begonia Society (See Appendix).

*Beaucarnea recurvata*

***Begonia semperflorens cultorum***—Wax Begonia Classified as a fibrous rooted begonia, wax begonia usually is between 8 to 12 inches high and has fleshy, small 2 to 4 inch glossy green leaves which develop a reddish cast if grown in a high light area. The colors of the 1 inch flowers include white, pinks, and reds.

111

Although begonias have been grown indoors since the Victorian era, they are not suggested for the beginning indoor gardeners.

CULTURE—*Light:* A bright east or west window sill is ideal for wax begonias. When they are moved outside, keep them in partial shade. *Temperature:* If possible night temperatures should be between 50 to 55°F and day temperatures not over 75°F. *Humidity:* They do best if humidity is over 25%. *Water:* Water when the top surface of the soil has dried. *Fertilizer:* Use reduced rate twice a month. *Soil and repotting:* Use soil mix number 1; repot in the spring. *Pruning*

*Begonia semperflorens cultorum*

*Begonia x rex cultorum*

112

*and grooming:* Occasional pruning may increase flowering. Clean foliage as needed and remove old blossoms. *Propagation:* Seeds, divisions, or cuttings. *Pests:* Aphids, chewing insects, and mites.

**Begonia x rex cultorum —** Rex Begonia

Wax begonias are grown predominately for flowers whereas rex begonias are grown for their foliage. They are characterized by having their flower and leaf stems emerging from rhizomes which have shallow roots. Foliage patterns in reds, silver gray, and green are almost endless. 'Merry Christmas,' 'Mikado,' and 'Helen Teupel' are the best known varieties.

CULTURE—*Light:* Rex begonias need medium to high interior light but no direct sun. *Temperature:* Normal home temperatures are acceptable. *Humidity:* Use humidity-increasing techniques when humidity is below 25%. *Pruning and grooming:* Some indoor gardeners cut the flowers off so they will not detract from the foliage. Syringe foliage to remove dust. *Propagation:* Seed, cuttings, division, or leaf sections that include a major vein. Other cultural requirements are the same as for wax begonias.

# BILLBERGIA
## (Bromeliaceae)

"Vase plants" is one of the most common names for bromeliads, and most billbergias resemble narrow vases formed by the clustering of their spiny leaves in a tight rosette. The combined impact of attractive inflorescences and colorful foliage make them an enjoyable house plant. They are relatively easy to grow indoors. A number of billbergias are available so if you become interested in bromeliads, you will have a variety to choose from.

**Billbergia nutans —** Queen's Tears, Indoor Oats

Since *B. nutans* is one of the easiest billbergias to grow indoors, it is a good

*Billbergia nutans*

*Billbergia zebrina*

113

bromeliad to practice growing before attempting more difficult members of the bromeliad family. The rosette of 12 to 15 leaves is about a foot long, green on the upper surface and a dull red below. The inflorescence with blue-edged rose-colored sepals and blue-edged green petals surrounded by rose-colored bracts is quite

Bougainvillea sp.

spectacular. As with other bromeliads, once a particular rosette flowers, it dies, but a number of suckers or offshoots are formed. A container of queen's tears when in bloom makes an interesting display plant as the colorful inflorescence stays attractive for weeks.

CULTURE—*Light:* Place in medium to high light indoors, but avoid direct sun. *Temperature:* Normal home temperatures are acceptable. *Humidity:* Usually humidity is no problem. *Water:* Allow soil surface to dry between waterings. Keep leaf cups filled with water. *Fertilizer:* Use reduced fertilizer rates once a month. Apply to soil surface. *Soil and repotting:* Use soil mix number 3. Repot and divide when container is crowded. *Pruning and grooming:* Remove dead rosettes after they have flowered. Syringe plants to remove dust once a month. *Propagation:* From offshoots. *Pests:* Scale.

### *Billbergia zebrina*—Zebra Urn

Zebra urn is one of the more spectacular bromeliads. The roset's greenish bronze leaves are striped with silvery gray and grow upright forming an open cylinder. The pendulous inflorescence hangs gracefully with rose-colored bracts and violet flowers.

CULTURE—The requirements are the same as for *B. nutans* except that *B. zebrina* requires higher humidity.

# BOUGAINVILLEA
## (Nyctaginaceae)

*Bougainvillea spp.*—Bougainvillea

Experienced horticulturists who have traveled in tropical and suptropical America are familiar with bougainvillea, a late winter and early spring blooming shrub. However, its use as an indoor plant is relatively recent and results from our knowledge that it is a short day plant like poinsettias so it can be brought into flower whenever desired. Plants require about 2 weeks of long nights to induce flowering. The heart-shaped leaves resemble lilac leaves in color and texture. Three small yellow flowers are enclosed by

Be careful to avoid being scratched by the thorns. *Pruning and grooming:* Decide what growth form you want your plant to have and prune or train it as it grows. Give the plants a monthly shower. *Propagation:* Cuttings. *Pests:* Scales and chewing insects.

*Brassaia actinophylla*

three colorful bracts. Bract color includes crimson, scarlet, rose-red, and purple. Bougainvillea is quite versatile and can be trained on a trellis or as a standard, or grown as a hanging basket or as a pot plant for a sunny window.

CULTURE—*Light:* Bougainvillea needs a full sun location indoors for flower production. It can be moved outdoors in the summer in a partial shade area. *Temperature:* It does best in a cool location; 60°F night temperature, 75°F day temperature. Avoid temperatures below 45°F. *Humidity:* Mist new growth to prevent desiccation. *Water:* Allow soil surface to dry between waterings, *Fertilizer:* Apply fertilizer at reduced rates once every 3 weeks. *Soil and repotting:* Use soil mix number 1. Repot if necessary after flowering.

*Brassaia arboricola*

# BRASSAIA
(Araliaceae)

*Brassaia actinophylla*—Schefflera, Umbrella Tree, Octopus Tree

Schefflera is one of the most common trees used for interior decorative purposes. Native to Australian rain forests where it may reach 60 feet, it adapts to low humidity environments and low light areas amazingly well. Grown indoors for its striking lacquered-looking compound leaves with from 3 to 9 leaflets radiating from a petiole which may be up to 18 inches long. When detached and held upright, each compound leaf resembles a small parasol or umbrella. When small, scheffleras make excellent plants for almost any location in the home, but as they grow larger, they look best as floor plants in medium sized tubs.

CULTURE—*Light:* Although schefflera tolerates low light areas, it does better in medium light. Rather than move it outside in the summer, shift the plant to a higher light location indoors. Full sun will burn leaves produced in shaded locations. *Temperature:* Normal home temperatures are acceptable. *Humidity:* No special care is needed. *Water:* Allow top soil surface to become dry before watering again. Avoid overwatering as this may lead to root rot. *Fertilizer:* Fertilize with reduced rates once every 3 weeks. *Soil and repotting:* Use soil mix number 2. Repot when the plant becomes too large for its container. *Pruning and grooming:* In most homes plants will require pruning to keep them from outgrowing their locations. Cut stems just above a leaf. Plants may develop several trunks but will remain attractive. Wash leaves as needed to keep off dust. *Propagation:* Air layers or seeds. *Pests:* Mites and scales.

*Brassaia arboricola*—Dwarf Schefflera

A recent introduction, dwarf schefflera initially looks just as its common name implies. Closer inspection shows the deep green leaflets on the compound leaf to be thicker, stiffer with smooth margins. Native to Taiwan, it grows to be only 12 feet high, while *B. actinophylla* may reach 60 feet. An excellent small table or window sill plant, it also offers possibilities as a pseudo-bonsai.

CULTURE—Care is similar to *B. actinophylla.* If light intensities are too low, the petioles and internodes will become excessively long.

# CALADIUM
## (Araceae)

*Caladium spp.*—Caladium

The tremendous variation in foliage coloration in caladiums allows an indoor gardener to select whatever color is desired to enhance a plant grouping. Colors vary from almost pure white to deep crimson, and include purple, bronze, pink, and chartreuse. Most have distinctly marked veins, black petioles, and arrow shaped leaves. Size varies from 6 inches to over 2 feet.

Potted caladiums are sometimes bought

Caladium
Freida Hemple'

*Caladium 'Candidum'*

from the florist but most are purchased as tubers and are started in the home. Plant tubers about 1 inch deep in a flat or shallow pot in either peat or peat with a little added sand. Keep warm, preferably around 80°F; temperatures should not drop below 70°F. If temperatures are kept high, the caladiums will leaf out in 4 to 5 weeks. Usually plants can be transplanted into the desired pot size within 2 to 3 weeks.

Some of the more common cultivars are 'Candidum' which is white with green veins; 'Freida Hemple' which has a red center fading into green toward the leaf margin and scarlet veins; and 'Lord Derby' which has a transparent rose leaf with thin green veins.

CULTURE—*Light:* Caladiums prefer high light interiors, but avoid a full sun location. A northeast window is ideal. *Temperature:* Normal home temperatures are acceptable. *Humidity:* They prefer humidity over 50%. *Water:* Since the thin large leaves transpire a lot of water, check soil often. Avoid feast and famine watering with caladiums. Keep soil moist but not saturated. After an 8 month growth period, allow the foliage to die back and store the tubers at 65°F. Start new growth in 2 months. *Fertilizer:* Fertilize frequently, about once every 2 weeks, with dilute applications. *Soil and repotting:* Use soil mix number 2. Repot tubers after their dormant period. *Pruning and grooming:* Cut off dried leaves and syringe foliage once a month. *Propagation:* Cut dormant tubers so each peice has at least 2 or 3 eyes. *Pests:* Chewing insects, nematodes, and mites.

# CALATHEA
(Marantaceae)

*Calathea makoyana* — Peacock Plant

The green feather design on the upper leaf of a peacock plant almost looks too artificial to be natural. The pattern is repeated in shades of purple on the reverse side. It is hard to envision a plant of this elegance growing on a forest floor in Amazonian jungles, its native home. Basically the plant seems designed for use as an accent piece in formal room arrangement. The almost stemless plant usually grows no more than about a foot high and does better indoors than one would imagine.

CULTURE—*Light:* Calathea prefers medium to high interior light levels. Avoid full sun locations as foliage will burn. It will tolerate low light levels for short time periods. *Temperature:* Avoid cold locations; best temperatures are 65°F night and 75°F to 80°F day temperatures. *Humidity:* Maintain humidity over 25% for best growth. *Water:* Keep the soil moist but not saturated. *Fertilizer:* Fertilize with reduced rates every 3 weeks in a good light situation. *Soil and repotting:* Use soil mix number 2. Repot only when plants are crowded in the container. *Pruning and grooming:* Trim off old leaves. Cut leaves can be used in floral arrangements. *Propagation:* Division. *Pests:* Mites.

*Calathea makoyana*

# CALCEOLARIA
(Scrophulariaceae)

*Calceolaria crenatiflora* — Slipperwort, Pocketbook Plant

Slipperwort is an unusual flowering plant with swollen flattened pouchlike flowers spotted with red or crimson. The 2 inch yellow-orange flowers mound above the 6 inch succulent-green leaves. Usually bought as a gift plant during the winter, its flowering can be prolonged indoors to perhaps a month by keeping it in a cool room (45° to 50°F) at night. Slipperwort is a spectacular plant which should be enjoyed for its flowers and then discarded when it is through blooming. Plants with a number of unopened buds will have the longest flowering time in your home.

CULTURE—*Light:* Place in bright light but avoid full sun locations. *Temperature:* Locate where the temperatures are lowest (45° to 60°F) for longest life. *Humidity:* Use humidity-increasing methods. *Water:* Keep soil moist. In a warm location, plant may need water twice a day.

# CAMELLIA
## (Theaceae)

*Camellia japonica*—Camellia

Camellia is a beautiful flowering shrub from the mountains in China that can be grown indoors if a cool, bright, light area can be found. A wide variety of cultivars are available with single or double flowers in shades of pink, white, and red. 'Debutante' seems to be one of the better cultivars for

*Calceolaria crenatiflora*

indoor use. It is a real accomplishment to be able to grow camellias indoors successfully and therefore I would recommend it only to those experienced gardeners seeking a challenge.

*Camellia japonica*

119

CULTURE—*Light:* East or west window areas offer the best light. Avoid full sun locations. *Temperature:* Maintain at 55° to 60°F night and 65° to 70° day temperatures. *Humidity:* Keep humidity high, over 50% if possible. *Water:* Use rain water if possible; tap water increases the soil pH. Keep soil moist. *Fertilizer:* Use an acid-forming fertilizer at dilute rates. Use a minor element fertilizer once a year. *Soil and repotting:* Use soil mix number 1. Camellias do not do well if frequently repotted so keep them in the same container for several years. Repot after flowering. *Pruning and grooming:* Keep plant pruned back to 3 or 4 feet. *Propagation:* Cuttings. *Pests:* Scales, aphids, and chewing insects.

# CAMPANULA
## (Campanulaceae)

*Campanula isophylla* —
Star of Bethlehem, Italian Bellflower

If you have a cool, sunny room in your home during the winter, try growing Italian bellflowers. The thin cascading stems have 1 to 2 inch heart-shaped, grayish-green downy leaves. Pale blue flowers appear in late summer through fall on thin stems. Campanula can be used for hanging baskets or trailing window sill plants. Cuttings taken in spring can be used in outdoor planter boxes for late summer color.

CULTURE—*Light:* Full sun or bright diffuse light is needed. *Temperature:* Campanula needs a cool indoor location (50° to 60°F). Warmer temperatures suppress flowering. *Humidity:* Usually humidity is no problem if plants are kept cool. *Water:* Allow top soil surface to dry before watering again. *Fertilizer:* Use reduced rates every 4 weeks. *Soil and repotting:* Use soil mix number 5. Do not repot but take cuttings. *Pruning and grooming:* Pinch plants back to increase branching. Syringe foliage to remove dust. *Propagation:* Cuttings. *Pests:* Mites.

*Campanula isophylla*

Carissa
grandiflora

# CARISSA
(Apocynaceae)

*Carissa grandiflora* —Natal Plum

Although natal plum grows 5 to 7 feet in its native habitat in South Africa, two cultivars, 'Boxwood Beauty' and 'Bonsai,' make excellent flowering house plants which can be turned into pseudo-bonsai since even without pruning the plants seldom exceed 2 feet. The 1 to 2 inch white flowers stand out against the deep green 1 inch leaves. The fruits can be eaten and taste like cranberries.

CULTURE—*Light:* Place in full sun or bright light indoors. Put in partial shade if taken outdoors. *Temperature:* Natal palm tolerates temperatures from 40° to 90°F. *Humidity:* It needs no special care. *Water:* Top surface of soil should dry out between waterings. *Fertilizer:* Use reduced rates and fertilize every 6 weeks; increase if you note deficiency symptoms. Apply minor element mix once a year. *Soil and repotting:* Use soil mix number 1. Repot when needed. If

growing as a pseudo-bonsai, do not increase pot size. *Pruning and grooming:* Give it a monthly shower to remove dust. *Propagation:* Cuttings. *Pests:* Scales.

# CHAMAEDOREA
(Palmae)

*Chamaedorea elegans*—Parlor Palm

Parlor palm is a small, single trunked palm which is widely used in dishgardens and terrariums, as well as small individual potted specimens. Slow growing indoors, it may achieve 3 to 4 feet or so in a decade. Usually 4 to 6 featherlike dark green fronds are clustered at the top of the plant. With proper care, these plants will last for years indoors.

CULTURE—*Light:* Use in low to medium interior light. If placed in full sun, the foliage will burn. *Temperature:* Keep above 50°F. Grows best with night temperatures of 65°F and day temperatures of 80°F. *Humidity:* Average home conditions will cause no damage. *Water:* Allow soil surface to dry thoroughly and then water well. *Fertilizer:* Apply reduced rates every 3 to 6 weeks.

Chamaedorea
elegans

Chamaedorea
erumpens

# CHLOROPHYTUM
## (Liliaceae)

*Chlorophytum comosum*—Spider Plant

There are several cultivars of spider plant sold as graceful hanging baskets or pot plants. Most have some degree of white variegation in the foliage. 'Vittatum' has green leaves with a white stripe down the center, and 'Variegatum' has white borders on green leaves. Long arching stems bearing white flowers which later develop small plantlets emerge from the center of the mound of foot long linear leaves. This response is controlled by photoperiod, with flowers formed in short days, and leaves produced in long days,

Spider plant stands a great deal of abuse.

CULTURE—*Light:* Place in medium to high light. Avoid full sun. *Temperature:* It will tolerate temperatures down to 40°F and up to 90°F. *Humidity:* During periods of low humidity, plants may brown on tips. Avoid placing in drafts. *Water:* Although it will withstand some neglect, spider plant will grow better if soil is kept uniformly moist. Leaf tips turn brown if the soil dries excessively. *Fertilizer:* Apply reduced rates once a month. *Soil and repotting:* Use soil mix number 2. Repot when plants are crowded. *Pruning and grooming:* Remove faded foliage. Syringe foliage once every 2 weeks. *Propagation:* Division or small root leaflets on flowering stems. *Pests:* Scale.

*Chlorophytum comosum*

*Soil and repotting:* Use soil mix number 2. Repot as needed to keep plant in balance with the container. *Pruning and grooming:* When old fronds have dried up, remove them. Palms have only one growing point and will die if you cut off the top. *Propagation:* Seeds, but they take several months to germinate. *Pests:* Scale, mites, and mealybugs.

*Chamaedorea erumpens*—Bamboo Palm

Bamboo palm is a clump growing palm with several thin canes or trunks in a container. It reaches a height of 5 to 6 feet indoors. Most bamboo palms sold are the cultivar 'Fairchild' which has two broad leaflets on the tip of each frond. Bamboo palm adds an oriental touch when used as a low table or floor plant.

CULTURE—Same as *C. elegans* except plants can be divided when repotted. Cut the soil ball in half and you will have twice the number of bamboo palms.

*Chrysalidocarpus lutescens*

CULTURE—*Light:* Place in medium to high interior light. A location by an east or west window is ideal. Avoid extended full sun locations as foliage will bleach. *Temperature:* Normal room temperatures are acceptable. *Humidity:* Keep relative humidity above 30% if possible. *Water:* Maintain a moist soil, do not allow to become dry. *Fertilizer:* Use a reduced rate once a month. *Soil and repotting:* Use soil mix number 2. Repot every 2 to 3 years when the plant outgrows its container. *Pruning and grooming:* Remove dried old fronds. *Propagation:* Seeds or division of clumps in containers. *Pests:* Scales and mites.

# CHRYSANTHEMUM
(Compositae)

*Chrysanthemum morifolium* —Chrysanthemum

Potted chrysanthemums are so popular that almost everyone is familiar with some of the many flower colors and forms sold today. Although these perennials are easy for the florist to grow and flower, it is beyond the capabilities of most indoor gardeners to make them rebloom unless one has a greenhouse. Usually the easiest solution is to discard the plants after flowering. If you enjoy challenges you can take cuttings and grow mums indoors and see if you can produce flowers. Chrysanthemums are short day plants and between the end of March and the end of September will need long nights for approximately 8 weeks until flowers have started to open.

CULTURE—*Light:* Locate in south, east, or west windows indoors. *Temperature:* Night temperatures of 55°F, day temperatures of 70°F. *Humidity:* Use methods to increase humidity for plants purchased from a florist.

# CHRYSALIDOCARPUS
(Palmae)

*Chrysalidocarpus lutescens* —Areca Palm, Butterfly Palm

Areca palm, a clump growing palm, produces clusters of ringed bamboo-like canes that reach 30 feet in its native Madagascar. When potted in containers, it seldom exceeds 15 feet. The long arching leaves have almost 100 light green leaflets attached to a yellow midrib. Areca palm may be used as a low table plant when small and a floor specimen when larger. When the plant becomes too large for its location, divide the clump and keep the smallest portion. You can also use pruning shears and cut the largest cane off close to the soil line.

# CISSUS
## (Vitaceae)

***Cissus rhombifolia***—Grape Leaf Ivy

*Cissus rhombifolia*, a member of the grape family, makes a durable and long lived house plant. Grown as a hanging basket, its stems cascade over the side of the container displaying its quilted-looking, green, waxy leaves with their brownish lower leaf surfaces. It can also be trained to climb around a window or up a wall if its tightly clinging tendrils can find firm support.

CULTURE—*Light:* Locate in an east or north window since grape leaf ivy needs medium light to survive indoors.

*Chrysanthemum morifolium*

*Water:* Keep soil moist but not saturated. Most plants sold in florist's shops will require more water than your other indoor plants. *Fertilizer:* Use reduced rates once every 3 weeks. *Soil and repotting:* Use soil mix number 1. Repot in the spring. *Pruning and grooming:* Pinch terminal growth to induce bushiness. Remove side buds once flowers have been induced to increase flower size. *Propagation:* Cuttings. *Pests:* Aphids and mites.

Cissus antarctica

*Temperature:* Average home temperatures are acceptable. Avoid locations below 50°F. *Humidity:* It tolerates low relative humidity. *Water:* Allow upper soil surface to dry between waterings. *Fertilizer:* Use reduced rates once every 3 to 4 weeks. Use minor element fertilizer once a year. *Soil and repotting:* Use soil mix number 2. Repot as needed to balance plant and container. *Pruning and grooming:* Prune tips occasionally to stimulate branching. It can be kept cut back and trained as a pseudo-bonsai. *Propagation:* Use tip cuttings. *Pests:* Mealybugs, scale, and mites.

### Cissus antarctica —Kangaroo Vine

Kangaroo vine is more widely used in Europe than in the United States. Some growers feel it is called kangaroo vine because it grows by leaps and bounds but it can be kept under control with judicious pruning and training. Its 6 inch oval shaped, bright-green leaves with light reddish-brown veins make it an attractive plant to use on an open trellis to divide a room or to break up a bare wall. If grown as a hanging basket, pinch the young shoots back and the new shoots will trail over the side of the container.

CULTURE—Similar to *C. rhombifolia.*

Cissus rhombifolia

125

# CITROFORTUNELLA
(Rutaceae)

**Citrofortunella mitis** — Calamondin Orange

*Citrofortunella mitis*

Calamondins are one of the best citrus trees to grow indoors. Usually they are sold with small 1½ inch orange fruit on the ends of branches, which stand out against the dark green, shiny leaves. Although overbearing, the largest fruit set is in November and December when they look like small trees all decorated for Christmas. With dedicated care, calamondins will survive and bear fruit for years in your home. Remember that the flowers have to be pollinated in order to bear fruit so if you do not put your calamondin outdoors, transfer pollen from the anthers to the stigma with a small brush. The fruit is edible but it is too acid for most people although it can be used for flavoring like lemons or limes.

CULTURE — *Light:* A bright or sunny indoor location will keep the plant growing. If it is moved outdoors during the summer; place it in partial shade. *Temperature:* Surprisingly, citrus does best with cool temperatures, 50 to 60°F night temperatures and up to 70°F in the day. Avoid temperatures below 32°F. *Humidity:* Calamondins tolerate low humidity. *Water:* Do not allow the soil to become too dry. Strive for a reasonably moist soil. Foliage will be sparse with infrequent waterings. *Fertilizer:* Once every 3 to 4 weeks apply reduced amounts during spring, summer, and fall; in the winter, apply every 5 to 6 weeks. *Soil and repotting:* Use soil mix number 1. Shift up to a larger container as needed. *Pruning and grooming:* Prune to maintain desired height since calamondin will grow up to 12 to 15 feet if not pruned. Wash dust and grime off foliage when kept indoors. *Propagation:* Air layers. *Pests:* Scales, mites, and chewing insects.

126

# CLIVIA
(Amaryllidaceae)

### *Clivia miniata* 'Grandiflora' —Kafir Lily

Kafir lily has thick, deep green, straplike leaves up to 2 feet long which grow in 2 rows from thick fleshy roots. In the spring a 20 inch flowering stem has 10 to 20 lilylike 3 inch orange flowers. Under good growing conditions, flowers may last a month or longer indoors. An easy-to-care-for flowering house plant, it requires a dormant period during late fall and early winter.

CULTURE—*Light:* Place in high interior light but avoid prolonged full sun locations. *Temperature:* Normal home temperatures are acceptable but clivias do best with cool temperatures of 55° to 60°F during the late fall and early winter resting period. *Humidity:* Kafir lily tolerates home humidities. *Water:* During spring, summer, and early fall, water when top surface of soil is dry. Grow on the dry side during dormant period. *Fertilizer:* Use reduced rates every 3 weeks from late February through September. *Soil and repotting:* Use soil mix

*Clivia miniata* 'Grandiflora'

number 1. Repot only when the plant is cramped in its container. Disturb the roots as little as possible when repotting. Repot after flowering. *Pruning and grooming:* Remove dried flower stalks. Syringe foliage to remove dust as needed. *Propagation:* Division after flowering. *Pests:* Usually no problems indoors.

# CODIAEUM
(Euphorbiaceae)

### *Codiaeum variegatum* —Croton

Crotons have rather demanding requirements to be grown successfully indoors. Yet they remain a popular plant because of the unbelievable color range in their foliage. The thick, leathery leaves are seldom of any one particular color; slightly colored young green leaves develop intense reds or oranges as they mature. Their best indoor use is to provide color contrast in groupings with other plants. Since leaves produced indoors lack the luster of sun leaves, crotons should be taken outdoors when it warms up to develop good leaf color.

*Codiaeum variegatum*

127

CULTURE —*Light:* Indoors, locate crotons in the brightest spot with the most sun. Small plants should be placed on the window sill. In summer a southeast location outdoors or a partially shaded location will develop good foliage color. *Temperature:* Leaves drop off if temperatures go much below 45°F; cold air blasts also cause leaf drop. *Humidity:* They do best with high relative humidity. Use any recommended humidity-increasing technique. *Water:* Water plants to maintain a constant water supply in the soil. *Fertilizer:* Apply fertilizer at reduced rates every 3 weeks during spring, summer, and fall; once every 6 weeks during the winter. *Soil and repotting:* Use soil mix number 2. Repot when plants have outgrown their container. *Pruning and grooming:* Prune leggy growth back to produce a bushy plant. Crotons will grow to 8 feet tall without pruning. Wash or shower foliage to keep plant attractive. *Propagation:* Cuttings and air layers. *Pests:* Scales, mites, and aphids.

# COFFEA
## (Rubiaceae)

### *Coffea arabica*— Coffee

Coffee is another plant that can be grown as a small indoor tree or shrub. When the plant matures, white fragrant ¾ inch flowers are formed in clusters close to the leaf axils. The dark red fruits which follow take several months to ripen. Although flowering may be spasmodic in most homes, the thin, green, waxy leaves and delicate branches complement most decors. With proper cultural care, you can watch the plant mature from a small window sill plant to a charming floor plant.

CULTURE—*Light:* Place in high interior light, but avoid extended full sun locations. If placed outdoors during the summer, locate in partial shade. *Temperature:* Keep temperatures above 60°F; otherwise normal room temperatures are acceptable. When outside, bring in before night temperatures drop below 55°F. *Humidity:* It does better with increased humidity. *Water:* Allow top soil surface to dry between waterings. *Fertilizer:* Use reduced rates every 3 weeks. *Soil and repotting:* Use soil mix number 1. Repot when necessary. *Pruning and grooming:* You can control the type of plant that will develop. Pinching terminal when young will produce a shrub; allowing plant to elongate will produce a tree form. Shower or wash leaves once a month. *Propagation:* Fresh seeds or terminal cuttings. *Pests:* Scales and mealybugs.

*Coffea arabica*

*Coleus blumei*

# COLEUS
## (Labiatae)

*Coleus blumei* —Coleus

Coleus is an easy-to-grow plant which can brighten up any room. The colorful leaves range from almost black through shades of red, pink, green, yellow, and gold. If grown where the light is too low, the foliage color will fade. Height varies from 1 to 3 feet, making an attractive plant for the window sill or for a table.

CULTURE—*Light:* Place in medium to high interior light locations. North or east windows provide the ideal light in many homes. *Temperature:* Normal house temperatures are acceptable. Does best with 65°F night and 75° to 80°F day temperatures. *Humidity:* Normal home humidity is not a problem unless the plant is located too close to heat registers. *Water:* Lower leaves drop if the plant is allowed to wilt too often, but avoid overwatering. *Fertilizer:* Used reduced rates once each 3 weeks during spring, summer, and fall; every 5 to 6 weeks in the winter. *Soil and repotting:* Use soil mix number 1. Repot as needed to maintain balance between pot and plant. *Pruning and grooming:* Pinching will increase branching and fullness of the plant. Shower to keep leaves clean. *Propagation:* Cuttings or seeds. *Pests:* Aphids and mites.

# CORDYLINE
## (Agavaceae)

*Cordyline terminalis* —Ti Plant

Over the years commercial plant growers have developed a wide variety of ti plants with different color foliage ranging from black-green to light pink. Most ti plants have leaves about 18 inches long and about 1 inch wide. The long leaves are used by Polynesian natives to make hula skirts and thatch roofs. Not the best of indoor plants because they require bright light, high humidities, and cool temperatures for best leaf color development. Usually lower leaves drop indoors and the plant will have a terminal cluster of leaves and a bare stalk.

CULTURE—*Light:* The ti plant needs bright interior light. East window sun will not burn foliage, but sun through a south window might. *Temperature:* Best leaf color occurs with 55° to 60°F night and 75°F day temperatures. *Humidity:* Keep humidity above 25%. *Water:* Allow top soil surface to dry between waterings. *Fertilizer:* Use reduced rates every 4 or 5 weeks. *Soil and repotting:* Use soil mix number 2. Repot in spring or summer. *Pruning and grooming:* Remove older dried leaves and wash or wipe leaves on plant once a month. Plant top can be removed to induce branching. *Propagation:* Stem or terminal cuttings, air layers, or seeds. *Pests:* Mites and scales.

# CRASSULA
## (Crassulaceae)

*Crassula argentea*—Jade Plant, Chinese Rubber Tree

Jade plant looks like a miniature tree, with a thick brown stem and dark green, thick fleshy 1 inch leaves on the numerous branches. Its beauty is best appreciated if it is not grouped with other indoor plants. You may be rewarded with star-shaped, white flowers in spring. Although it grows 10 feet tall in its native South Africa, it can be kept at any desired height over 8 inches by pruning. Most indoor gardeners have better luck growing the plant in a container that almost seems too small. Leaves will develop a reddish margin in high light locations. Jade plant is an easy-to-grow, attractive specimen plant for window sill or table. It is an excellent plant for a bonsai effect.

CULTURE—*Light:* Jade plant can be grown from low light interiors to full sun locations. If light intensity is too low, the plant becomes leggy. *Temperature:* Avoid locations where temperatures are below 50°F; otherwise normal room temperatures are acceptable. *Humidity:* No special care is needed. *Water:* Adjust water frequency to the demands of the plant. Too little or too much water causes leaf drop. Thick leaves indicate ample water; thin, wrinkled leaves indicate less than adequate water. Avoid overwatering. *Fertilizer:* Use reduced rates once every 3 weeks. *Soil and repotting:* Use soil mix number 2. Mature plants do not require repotting more than every 3 to 4 years. Young plants may need repotting every year in the spring. *Pruning and grooming:* Jade plants may require occasional pruning to keep them in balance with their containers and locations. *Propagation:* Cuttings root easily, even in water. *Pests:* Usually not bothered by insects.

*Cordyline terminalis*

*Crassula argentea*

# CROCUS
(Iridaceae)

*Crocus spp.* —Crocus

During those gray winter days in January and February, nothing is as cheerful as spring bulbs flowering indoors. Crocus offers a variety of colors and most home gardeners are successful in having the bulbs flower. If you purchase potted crocus ready to bloom from a bulb specialty company or from a florist, just follow their instructions. Otherwise treat bulbs as suggested below.

FORCING

Select large crocus bulbs for forcing. After purchase, store bulbs between 55 to 65°F for several weeks and then pot them in soil mix number 1 or other porous soil mix. When

*Crocus sp.*

planting, cover so only the tip of the bulb is visible when you are finished. Leave about an inch of room between bulbs. The potted bulbs should be placed where the temperature can be kept between 35° to 50°F for about 8 weeks. A good root system must be formed before the plants are brought indoors. Keep soil moist during rooting period. Planting dates can be staggered so that bulbs will be in flower from December through the end of February. Potted bulbs can be placed outside but they should be protected from freezing as this prevents development. If you are using outdoor cooling, it will usually take almost 12 weeks for roots to develop adequately. Place in a cool location when you bring them indoors (55 to 60°F) until the flowers have colored. After flowering, bulbs can be planted in the garden for bloom the next year.

CULTURE—*Light:* High interior light area is best. *Temperature:* After forcing regime is complete, cool temperatures (55 to 65°F) prolong flower life. *Humidity:* Maintain humidity over 25%. *Water:* Keep soil moist. *Fertilizer:* None required. *Soil and repotting:* Plant in garden when the foliage has withered. *Pruning and grooming:* Trim dried foliage before planting in the garden. *Propagation:* Young corms formed after flowering. *Pests:* Usually none indoors.

*Crossandra infundibuliformis*

# CROSSANDRA
(Acanthaceae)

### *Crossandra infundibuliformis* — Crossandra

If you want a plant that has attractive foliage and flowers, crossandra is a good choice. It combines attractive 3 to 5 inch, glossy, deep-green foliage with salmon pink flowers 1 to 2 inches wide. Given reasonable care, crossandra will bloom all year. The flowers can be used as cut flowers for table decorations.

CULTURE—*Light:* Place in high interior light but avoid hot sunny areas since too much sun makes the leaves bleach. An easy window location is ideal. *Temperature:* Do not let temperatures drop below 55°F at night. Normal home temperatures are acceptable. *Humidity:* Maintain relative humidity above 25%. *Water:* Use room temperature water to keep soil moist. *Fertilizer:* Use reduced rates every 3 weeks during spring, summer, and fall. Decrease frequency in winter. *Soil and repotting:* Use soil mix number 1. Repot in early spring. *Pruning and grooming:* Pinch back plants to induce bushiness. Crossandra may need some pruning to keep it from outgrowing locations. *Propagation:* Seeds germinate at minimum temperatures of 75° to 80°F. It takes about 8 months for a plant grown from seed to bloom. Cuttings can also be taken. *Pests:* Mites are a common pest.

# CRYPTANTHUS
(Bromeliaceae)

*Cryptanthus bivittatus 'Minor' —*
Dwarf Rose Stripe Star

Dwarf rose stripe star is an appropriate name for this small terrestrial bromeliad from Brazil. It has short stems and 3 to 6 inch wavy, spiny leaves which form a flat rosette of attractively colored leaves against the ground. Colors vary with cultivars; 'Starlite' has olive green edges and rose pink centers, 'Pink Starlite' has light pink leaves with green centers, and other cultivars are striped with creams, pinks, and brown-greens. Whitish flowers which are almost hidden by the leaves sometimes appear. This plant is more commonly known as *C. roseus pictus* in the horticultural trade. A good window sill or table plant, it seldom grows more than a couple of inches high.

CULTURE—*Light:* Place in high light locations such as east windows. Avoid hot sunny locations. *Temperature:* Normal home temperatures are fine. *Humidity:* Plants do better with provisions for increasing the humidity. *Water:* Water plant to keep rosette moist. Allow top soil surface to dry before watering again. *Fertilizer:* Use reduced rates ever 5 to 6 weeks. *Soil and repotting:* Use soil mix number 3. Repot if necessary in the spring. *Pruning and grooming:* Give plants a syringing once every 3 weeks. *Propagation:* Offsets that form on the plant. *Pests:* Scales.

# CYRTOMIUM
(Polypodiaceae)

*Cyrtomium falcatum
'Rochfordianum'* —House Holly Fern

Holly fern is the ideal plant for all those people who want to grow ferns successfully indoors. The shining, leathery, dark green leaves with their saw-toothed edges resemble holly leaves. It reaches a maximum height of about 15 inches and a spread of about 3 feet indoors. Holly fern tolerates most indoor conditions and makes a good table plant. Few ferns are as long lived indoors.

*Cryptanthus bivittatus 'Minor'*

133

*Cyrtomium falcatum*
'Rockfordianum'

CULTURE—*Light:*
Place in medium to high
interior light. Avoid
prolonged full sun
locations.
*Temperatures:* Holly
fern can take temperatures down to 28°F,
but grows best with 60°F night and 75°F
day temperatures. *Humidity:* In contrast to
most ferns, it needs no special measures.
*Water:* Avoid overwatering but do not let the
soil dry excessively. *Fertilizer:* Use reduced
rates every 5 to 6 weeks. *Soil and repotting:*
Use soil mix number 6. Repot in the spring
when needed. *Pruning and grooming:*
Remove old fronds and clean foliage to keep
it glistening. *Propagation:* Divide large
clumps. Although holly fern can be grown
from the spores which form on the underside
of the leaf, it takes 3 or 4 years for a mature
plant to develop from spores. *Pests:* Chewing
insects and mites.

# DAVALLIA
(Polypodiaceae)

*Davallia fejeensis* —Rabbit's Foot Fern
As might be suspected from the species
name, *Davallia fejeensis* is native to the Fiji
Islands where it grows on tree branches and
trunks. The dark green, lacy, triangular
fronds arise directly from the creeping,
wooly, tan stem that resembles a rabbit's foot.
Rabbit's foot fern can be used in a hanging
basket, in a small pot plant for
window sills or tables, and in
terrariums.
CULTURE—*Light:* Locate in medium to
high interior light but avoid full sun locations.
Plants seem to do best in east and north
windows or on north porches during the
summer. *Temperature:* Tolerates normal
home temperatures but protect against
temperatures below 55°F. *Humidity:* During
periods when humidity is below 50%, protect
from desiccation. *Water:* Keep growing media

*Davallia fejeensis*

moist but do not overwater. *Fertilizer:* Use reduced rates every 5 to 6 weeks. Rabbit's foot fern has shallow roots and they are easily burned. *Soil and repotting:* Davallia will grow on a tree fern slab or use soil mix number 3. Repot as desired to balance plant and container. *Pruning and grooming:* Cut off faded fronds; syringe foliage once every 2 weeks. *Propagation:* Division of creeping rhizome. You will need to fasten the rhizome to the soil surface with a bent wire until new roots form. *Pests:* Scales and mites.

# DIEFFENBACHIA
## (Araceae)

Dieffenbachias have been nicknamed "Dumb Cane" because the leaf sap contains calcium oxalate crystals which when eaten cause swelling in the mouth and throat and inability to speak. Most dieffenbachia have large green upright stems with broad variegated leaves. Although native to the Amazonian jungles, the plants tolerate low humidity interiors. Widely used and worthwhile plants, most dieffenbachias tend to drop their lower leaves and leave a bare stem. Group dieffenbachias with other plants to screen the bare stems. They have been used indoors since the Victorian era.

*Dieffenbachia amoena —*
Giant Dumb Cane
The largest and tallest of the dieffenbachias used indoors, giant dumb cane may reach 6 feet and has leaves with elongated cream marks along the lateral veins. Usually it is used as a tall floor plant. 'Tropic Snow,' a highly colored cultivar with more yellow in the foliage and thicker leaves, is now available. Most foliage plant buyers feel it does even better indoors than giant dumb cane.
CULTURE—*Light:* It tolerates low to high interior light. Avoid full sun locations. *Temperature:* Keep night temperatures above 55°F as leaves of dieffenbachia are killed at that temperature. *Humidity:* It needs no special care. *Water:* Avoid overwatering or underwatering. *Fertilizer:* Apply once every 3 weeks at reduced rates.

*Soil and repotting:* Use soil mix number 2. Repot in spring if needed. *Pruning and grooming:* Wash or clean foliage as needed. When the plant gets leggy, air layer the top. When the top is removed, new growth emerges farther down on the old stem. *Propagation:* Stem sections, air layers, or cuttings. *Pests:* Mites, scales, and mealybugs.

Dieffenbachia amoena

Dieffenbachia 'Exotica Perfection'

Dieffenbachia maculata 'Rudolph Roehrs'

135

*Dizygotheca*
*elegantissima*

## Dieffenbachia 'Exotica Perfection'

'Exotica perfection' is a cultivar of unknown origin which differs from other dieffenbachias in suckering from underground stems in containers. It never grows much over 3 feet in height. Leaves are 6 to 8 inches long, and highly variegated with no particular pattern. 'Exotica perfection' is widely used in dishgardens and in small containers as a table or desk plant.

CULTURE—Similar to *D. amoena* except that it can be propagated by division.

## Dieffenbachia maculata 'Rudolph Roehrs' —Gold Dieffenbachia

A beautiful cultivar of *D. maculata* introduced 40 years ago by Mr. A. B. Graf, a well-known horitculturist. Young leaves are a translucent yellow that darkens with age to a chartreuse green. The midrib and leaf margins are green.

CULTURE—Similar to *D. amoena*. It grows well indoors but it should have medium light or higher to keep variegation attractive.

# DIZYGOTHECA
## (Araliaceae)

### Dizygotheca elegantissima — False Aralia, Spider Aralia

False aralia grows to a height of 25 feet in the New Hebrides where it is a native and changes the size and shape of its leaves while becoming mature. When young, *D. elegantissima* has a compound leaf composed of 7 to 11 narrow, gracefully dropping, lobed leaflets which become much wider as the plant matures. Normally grown as a single trunked container plant, it is an extremely distinctive looking plant. The foliage has a dark gray cast when viewed at a distance and stands out from other plants. Aralia is a long lived, elegant indoor floor plant.

CULTURE—*Light:* Locate close to an east or west window or other areas to provide the medium to high light intensity false aralia requires. *Temperature:* It adapts to normal room temperatures but avoid placing in locations below 55°F. *Humidity:* Provide a humid climate during periods of low relative humidity. Leaf tips turn brown when the room air is dry. *Water:* Allow top surface to dry between waterings. *Fertilizer:* Use reduced fertilizer rates every 3 weeks during spring, summer, and fall; every 5 to 6 weeks during winter. Use minor element fertilizer once a year. *Soil and repotting:* Use soil mix number 2. Repot young plants as needed. Older plants may need repotting once every 2 years in the spring. *Pruning and grooming:* Pinching or cutting terminal will increase branching. Mature plant will have to be pruned back to keep it from outgrowing its location. *Propagation:* Seeds, air layers, or cuttings. *Pests:* Scales and aphids.

# DRACAENA
## (Agavaceae)

Dracaenas that are commonly used indoors are superficially a diverse group of plants. Most do extremely well in low light areas and last for years indoors. Many are woody shrubs with leaves clustered on the stem in a rosette growth pattern. If you have room for only one large floor plant, try a dracaena.

### *Dracaena angustifolia honoriae*— Narrow-leaved Pleomele

Narrow-leaved pleomele has deep green, 18 inch long and 1 inch wide, tapering leaves. The gracefully arching leaves are crisply edged with cream yellow on new growth which fades to an ivory white with age. Indoors the plant slowly grows to a height of 4 to 6 feet with branching stems and long lasting closely arranged leaves. Pleomele is one of the more colorful plants for medium light areas. It can be used as a table plant when small, and as a low table or floor plant when taller.

CULTURE—*Light:* Locate in medium to high interior light. Avoid prolonged full sun locations. *Temperature:* Normal home temperatures are acceptable. *Humidity:* Maintain humidity above 25% for best-looking plants. *Water:* Allow top surface of soil to dry between waterings. *Fertilizer:* Use reduced

rates every 5 to 6 weeks. *Soil and repotting:* Use soil mix number 2. Repot older plants in the spring of the year; younger plants as needed. *Pruning and grooming:* Young plants should be pinched to increase branching. Syringe foliage to wash off dust. *Propagation:* Stem cuttings. *Pests:* Mites.

### *Dracaena fragrans* 'Massangeana'— Corn Plant

Used as an indoor plant for over 100 years, corn plant is extremely durable indoors. The 2 foot, yellow striped leaves are clustered in a rosette at the top exposing a brown barked stem covered wtih ridged leaf scars. The ½ inch fragrant whitish flowers are in a series of roundish clusters, borne on a terminal inflorescence that may be up to 2 feet in length. The flowers open only at night and exude a sticky sap.

CULTURE—Similar to *D. deremensis* but yellow coloration fades unless plant is placed in a medium or higher interior light.

### *Dracaena marginata*—Marginata, Red-margined Dracaena, Madagascar Dragon Tree

Dracaena angustifolia honoriae

Marginata is a favorite dracaena with interior decorators. Bare gray stems have a dense rosette of terminal, narrow, dark green leaves up to 20 inches long with red edges. Frequently it is used as a 4 to 6 foot tall floor plant with bent or curved stems, and short branches.

CULTURE—Similar to *D. deremensis*.

### *Dracaena sanderana*—Ribbon Plant

Ribbon plant is the smallest of the commonly used dracaenas. It grows with a single stem with 5 to 8 inch, narrow, medium green leaves with cream white borders. The green portion of the leaf sometimes looks as if it has a thin layer of white paint on it. It is widely used in dishgardens and terrariums or as multiples in small containers.

CULTURE—Similar to *D. deremensis*.

### *Dracaena surculosa*—Gold Dust Dracaena

*Dracaena surculosa* is a thin wiry stemmed plant with 2, 3, or 4 petiolules and yellow spotted, 2 to 4 inch elliptic leaves emerging from each node. The cultivar *D. surculosa* 'Florida Beauty' has leaves almost covered with yellow markings over the deep green leaves. As the leaf matures, the color fades to a whitish cream. *D. surculosa* grows to about 2 to 4 feet tall in a container. A useful window sill plant or a table plant. Cut foliage lasts a long time in cut arrangements.

CULTURE—Similar to *D. deremensis* but rapidly elongating stems growing from roots sometimes need pruning to keep them in balance with their container or location.

*Dracaena deremensis*
'Warneckii'

*Dracaena fragrans*
'Massangeana'

*Dracaena sanderana*

Dracaena
deremensis
'Janet Craig'

Dracaena
surculosa

Dracaena marginata

### Dracaena deremensis 'Janet Craig'

'Janet Craig' has solid, deep green leaves up to 2 feet long. It grows to a height of 15 feet in tropical Africa, but usually does not attain that height indoors. With age lower leaves die back, exposing a woody trunk

CULTURE—*Light:* Low to high interior light indoors; avoid full sun locations as foliage will burn in full sun. *Temperatures:* Normal room temperatures are acceptable. Avoid locations where temperatures fall below 55°F. *Humidity:* No problem with normal home relative humidity. *Water:* Allow top soil surface to dry between waterings. Use rain water, deionized water or water from a dehumidifier if possible as dracaenas are sensitive to fluorides in the water. *Fertilizer:* Use reduced rates every 3 to 5 weeks depending on growth rate. Use a minor element fertilizer once a year. *Soil and repotting:* Use soil mix number 2 but adjust soil pH to 6.5 which will prevent possible fluoride damage. *Pruning and grooming:* Remove dried leaves, and clean foliage every 3 or 4 weeks. *Propagation:* Stem cuttings and air layers. *Pests:* Mites and scales.

### Dracaena deremensis 'Warneckii'

The 12 to 18 inch linear leaves are faintly striped with white with 2 distinct milk white stripes close to the leaf's margin. With age some of the lower leaves will die back, exposing a woody trunk.

CULTURE—The same as *D. deremensis* 'Janet Craig.'

139

Dyckia
brevifolia

# DYCKIA
(Bromeliaceae)

*Dyckia brevifolia* —Miniature Agave

Dyckia brevifolia is a terrestrial bromeliad with thick, narrow leaves arranged in a dense rosette. The stiff, pointed leaves are striped with close white lines on the lower surface. Its common name suggests that it looks more like an agave than a bromeliad. The foot-long flower stem develops in the center of the leaf rosette and has short-stemmed yellow-orange flowers at the top. It tends to sucker and fill the pot with small plants under good growing conditions. Good as a sunny window plant or for arrangements with other succulents.

CULTURE—*Light:* Full sun or high light indoors is needed. *Temperature:* Native to southern Brazil, it tolerates temperatures down to 35°F. It grows well with 60° to 65°F night temperatures and 80°F day temperatures. *Humidity:* Dyckia does well in low humidity areas. *Water:* Avoid over-watering. Allow top soil surface to become dry between waterings. *Fertilizer:* Use reduced rates every 5 to 6 weeks. *Soil and repotting:* Use soil mix number 2. When container becomes crowded with maturing dyckia clumps, divide and repot. *Pruning and grooming:* Spray foliage once every 3 weeks to remove dust. *Propagation:* Offsets or seeds. *Pests:* Usually pest free.

# EPIDENDRUM
(Orchidaceae)

*Epidendrum atropurpureum* —Spice Orchid

Spice orchid grows on tree trunks and branches with green tear-drop shaped pseudobulbs bearing 2 or 3 green leaves which are 12 to 15 inches long. The fragrant flowers which give the plant its common name have dark brown and green petals and sepals and a white lip. Fifteen or more may be on one flower stalk. Spice orchid needs a rest period after flowering in the spring. It is easier to grow than most indoor gardeners realize. It is a good small window sill plant as it seldom grows over 30 inches high.

CULTURE—*Light:* The plant requires an east or west window location, but avoid prolonged full sun exposure. *Temperature:* Average home temperatures are acceptable. It grows better with night temperatures of 55° to 60°F and day temperatures of 70° to 75°F. *Humidity:* Keep humidity above 30%. *Water:* Use room temperature water as needed to maintain a moist soil. *Fertilizer:* Use about ¼ ounce of liquid 10-10-10 per gallon of water and fertilize once every 6 weeks if plants are growing in osmunda fern. *Soil and repotting:* Use soil mix number 4. Repot after flowering and before new growth starts. *Pruning and grooming:* Remove dried leaves; wash foliage to keep free from dust. *Propagation:* Division of the pseudobulbs. *Pests:* Scales and mites.

Epidendrum
atropurpureum

# EPIPHYLLUM
## (Cactaceae)

***Epiphyllum* hybrids** —Orchid Cacti

Orchid cacti are found in tropical rain forests in Central and South America, where they grow on the forest floor or above the ground on tree trunks and branches. Breeding programs have produced hundreds of cultivars of *Epiphyllum*. The spectacular foot-wide flowers may be bluish, red, pink, yellow, or white depending on the cultivar. The flattened, green stems are spineless and may be over 2 feet long. An easy plant to grow indoors; some people have kept potted plants for over 25 years. It usually flowers in the spring.

CULTURE—*Light:* Provide a high interior light location, an east window or north sunporch. Move the plant outdoors in the summer and place in partial shade. Avoid full sun locations. *Temperature:* Keep in a cool location during the winter, 45° to 55°F. Normal home temperatures are acceptable the rest of the year. *Humidity:* Epiphyllum may require misting when temperatures are high and humidity is low.

*Water:* Water when the top surface of the soil has dried during spring, summer, and fall. During the winter, water no more than necessary to keep stems from shriveling. *Fertilizer:* Use reduced rates every 2 weeks during spring, summer, and fall. No fertilizer should be applied during resting period. *Soil and repotting:* Use soil mix number 1. Small plants can be repotted as needed in the spring. Older plants need repotting only once every 2 or 3 years. *Pruning and grooming:* Remove faded flowers and give plants a shower. *Propagation:* Root cuttings in spring and summer. *Pests:* Mealybugs.

*Epiphyllum hybrid*

141

# EPIPREMNUM
(Araceae)

*Epipremnum aureum* —Golden Pothos, Hunter's Robe

Formally known as *Scindapsus aureum,* Golden pothos is similar to the climbing philodendrons in the way it grows. Native to Pacific Islands where it is called 'Taro Vine,' it forms thick woody stems with large perforated, yellow-streaked leaves. However, immature plants purchased in the store have heart-shaped, medium green leaves streaked with yellow. Usually pothos is sold either as a small potted plant or as a totem pole. Pothos can be trained to climb an indoor trellis or to form a frame around a window. It tolerates as much abuse as *Philodendron scandens oxycardium.* Several plants together make an attractive hanging basket. Forms variegated with white are also available; the most common is 'Marble Queen.'

CULTURE—*Light:* Locate in low to high interior light intensity. Avoid prolonged full sun locations. *Temperature:* Normal home temperatures are acceptable. Avoid temperatures below 50°F. *Humidity:* Usually normal humidities are no problem. *Water:* Allow soil surface to dry between waterings. *Fertilizer:* Use reduced rates every 5 to 6 weeks. *Soil and repotting:* Use soil mix number 2. Repot older specimens in the spring of the year. *Pruning and grooming:* Pinch younger plants to induce branching. Syringe leaves to remove dust. *Propagation:* Stem cuttings. *Pests:* Mites.

# EPISCIA
(Gesneriaceae)

*Episcia cupreata* —Flame Violet

Even without their exquisitely marked foliage, flame violets would be grown for their brilliant orange-red axillary flowers displayed on the cascading stems. This growth habit makes them excellent hanging basket plants, where trailing stems hang gracefully over the pot's edges. Depending on the cultivar, the simple, opposite, green leaves may be marked with patterns of metallic silvers, rich browns, and coppers. The plant can be adapted to most home environments, blooming in spring and summer. Flame violets are attractive small pot plants or almost any size hanging basket.

CULTURE—*Light:* High interior light intensities are needed if you want your plants to flower. Avoid full sun locations. If hanging baskets are placed outside during the summer, locate in partial shade. *Temperature:* Native to the American tropics, flame violets go dormant below 50°F.

*Epipremnum aureum*

*Episcia cupreata*

*Humidity:* Needs almost 50% relative humidity so it will require measures to increase relative humidity during winter months. *Water:* Use room temperature water, 65° to 75°F, and avoid getting it on the foliage. Keep soil moist but not saturated. *Fertilizer:* Use reduced rates every 3 weeks. *Soil and repotting:* Use soil mix number 7. Repot when necessary. *Pruning and grooming:* Remove faded flowers and leaves. *Propagation:* Leaf cuttings, stem cuttings, or runners. Start new plants every 2 or 3 years to replace less attractive older plants. *Pests:* Mites, mealybugs, and sometimes thrips.

# EUPHORBIA
## (Euphorbiaceae)

### *Euphorbia milii splendens* —
Crown-of-Thorns

Crown-of-thorns is an interesting plant with its thick, branching, gray stems covered with sharp spines. Bright coral-red bracts subtending the small, greenish-yellow flowers appear during late winter and early spring and spasmodically in the summer. Small 1 to 2 inch dull green leaves appear on new stem growth and fall off as the growth matures. Branches are often not strong enough to support their weight and assume a weeping character. Some indoor gardeners provide support with a trellis. An excellent plant for warm sunny locations.

CULTURE—*Light:* Place in full sun locations only. Warm south windows are the best location. *Temperature:* Keep plant above 60°F for best results except during a winter rest period when temperatures should be between 50° and 60°F. *Humidity:* Low relative humidities do no damage. *Water:*

*Euphorbia pulcherrima*

Allow soil to become dry before watering again; avoid overwatering. *Fertilizer:* Use reduced rates every 5 or 6 weeks. *Soil and repotting:* Use soil mix number 5. Repot older specimens only once every 3 or 4 years. *Pruning and grooming:* Prune plant back every spring leaving only the strongest branches on the plant. Rinse stems and foliage once a month to remove dust. *Propagation:* Allow stem cuttings to dry before propagating. *Pests:* Usually no problems.

### *Euphorbia pulcherrima* —Poinsettia

Traditions and legends have interwoven poinsettias with the Christmas holidays. Although millions of these plants are used indoors, in most cases they should be thought of as temporary residents in our homes, to be appreciated for their fiery red bracts and small yellow flowers during the cold winter days. The new cultivars and commercial growing practices have produced plants that can easily remain attractive until the end of January. A family friend once kept her poinsettia with leaves and bracts through the 4th of July! A variety of bract colors including scarlet reds, pinks, and whites are now available. Poinsettias must be given short days (no light at night) from October 1 until bract color is well developed. When in flower poinsettia is an attractive house plant but I recommend that most indoor gardeners purchase plants from a florist every year.

CULTURE—*Light:* Poinsettias need high interior light to maintain foliage. *Temperature:* Avoid locating plants where temperatures fluctuate markedly. Normal room temperatures are acceptable. *Humidity:* Plants bought from a florist need a relative humidity of about 50%. *Water:* Leaves may drop if soil is kept too dry, but avoid overwatering. *Fertilizer:* Do not fertilize newly purchased plants for about 2 months. Then use reduced rates once every 2 to 3 weeks. *Soil and repotting:* Use soil mix number 1. Repot after flowering is completed. *Pruning and grooming:* Cut the plants back in the spring to induce new growth. Poinsettias grow to a height of 10 feet and will require pruning to keep them in balance with their location. *Propagation:* Stem cuttings. *Pests:* Mites and scales.

*Euphorbia milii splendens*

# FATSHEDERA
(Araliaceae)

*Fatshedera lizei* –
Botanical Wonder Plant

   The common name, botanical wonder plant, is applied to *F. lizei* because it is a cross between two different family genera, *Hedera helix hibunica* (a type of English ivy) and *Fatsia japonica* (Japanese aralia). Desirable characteristics of both parent plants have been combined to produce a hardy and durable house plant. The alternate, lobed, medium green leaves are attached to a woody stem which will grow to about 5 feet before it can no longer support itself and arches over.

*Fatshedera lizei*

Kept pruned back, it can be developed into a 2 to 3 foot pseudo-bonsai. *F. lizei* is also attractive as a window plant or a low table plant. It is an easy-to-grow plant for most indoor gardeners.

   CULTURE—*Light:* Place in medium to high interior light but avoid prolonged full sun exposure. *Temperature:* It will tolerate temperatures down to 30°F. It grows best in cool locations, with night temperatures of 55° to 60°F and day temperatures of 65° to 70°F.

*Humidity:* It tolerates normal home humidities. *Water:* Allow top soil surface to become dry between waterings. *Fertilizer:* Use reduced rates every 2 weeks. *Soil and repotting:* Use soil mix number 2. Repot when needed. *Pruning and grooming:* Pinch plants to induce branching. Prune back in spring to keep plant in balance with its container. Wash plants once a month as needed. *Propagation:* Stem cuttings. *Pests:* Mites, mealybugs, and scales.

*Fatsia japonica*

cool locations. It also does well as an outside patio plant during frost-free weather.

CULTURE—*Light:* Place in medium to high interior light locations. Avoid prolonged full sun locations. Outside place in partial shade. *Temperature:* Although it will take temperatures down to 30°F, more ideal temperatures are 55°F night and 70°F day. *Humidity:* Humidity-increasing measures during dry winter weather will keep foliage more attractive. *Water:* Water when top surface of soil is dry. *Fertilizer:* Use reduced rates every 3 weeks. Use minor element fertilizer once a year. *Soil and repotting:* Use soil mix number 2. Smaller specimens should be repotted when they are too large for their containers. Repot larger specimens in the spring every 2 or 3 years. *Pruning and grooming:* Tips should be pinched to increase branching. Leaves should be sponged or washed with a moist cloth. *Propagation:* Fresh seeds or cuttings can be used to propagate *F. japonica*. *Pests:* Aphids, mites, and scales.

# FATSIA
(Araliaceae)

*Fatsia japonica* —Japanese Aralia

A large spectacular indoor plant, fatsia should be used only where there is enough room to properly display its shiny, deep green 5 to 9-lobed leaves which may be up to 15 inches wide. In its native Japan, fatsia may grow to be 15 feet tall. Given good growing conditions, it forms small white flowers in terminal clusters on the thick, green stem. Japanese aralia should be grown as a large floor plant. Use as a tropical-looking plant in

# FICUS
(Moraceae)

Ficus is a large genus of plants, perhaps encompassing 800 species of woody plants from tropical and subtropical countries. Many of these can be grown as indoor plants, and several make excellent indoor plants. Most of the common ficus used indoors are large tropical trees in their native habitat and require pruning and shaping to keep them from outgrowing their locations.

## Ficus benjamina—Benjamina, Weeping Fig

A widely used indoor tree, benjamina has 2 to 5 inch, glossy green leaves with an elongated tip which curves gracefully downward. It forms aerial roots in moist, humid environments but it seldom does this indoors. The small leaves and willowy branches seem balanced with a mature height of 6 to 12 feet, making it a perfect indoor tree. It does well when confined to small containers and can be grown as a pseudo-bonsai if kept pruned back and properly trained.

CULTURE—*Light:* Benjamina can be placed in low light to full sun locations. Generally the higher the light, the more leaves on the plant. Leaves will burn if moved from a shaded location to full sun. Leaves will drop if abruptly moved from high to low light. *Temperature:* It will withstand temperatures to 45°F, but does better if kept above 55°F. Normal home temperatures are just about ideal. *Humidity:* Normal home humidity range poses no problems. *Water:* Allow top surface of soil to dry between waterings. *Fertilizer:* Use reduced rates every 3 weeks when the plant is growing. Use a minor element fertilizer once a year on mature specimens. *Soil and repotting:* Use soil mix number 2. Repot smaller specimens

*Ficus elastica 'Decora'*

as needed, larger specimens once every 2 or 3 years. *Pruning and grooming:* Cut plant back as needed to keep it in balance with its location and container. Wash or shower foliage once a month to keep natural leaf sheen evident. *Propagation:* Stem cuttings. *Pests:* Mites and scales.

## Ficus elastica 'Decora'—
### Rubber Plant

Over a century of use as an indoor plant has proven the durability of the rubber plant to endure low light levels, low humidities, and sometimes infrequent care by neglectful gardeners. Although it grows to over 80 feet high in its native India, occasional pruning keeps it small enough to be used indoors, even as a window sill plant. Occasionally, the lower leaves drop, and the indoor plant owner is left with a bare stem and a few upper leaves. The best remedy is to air layer the upper portion. New growth will develop on the lower portion of the plant. The reddish tinge you notice in plant stores will fade in low light areas. Rubber plant can be trained as a pseudo-bonsai.

CULTURE—Similar to *F. benjamina.*

*Ficus benjamina*

# FITTONIA
## (Acanthaceae)

Fittonia is a small, creeping, weak-stemmed herb with large, opposite, oval leaves with distinct markings on the foliage. It never grows much higher than 4 to 5 inches as the hairy stems cannot support themselves beyond this height, and cascade over and root at the nodes. The paper-thin leaves of fittonias need high humidity to remain attractive indoors. Usually they are used as terrarium plants for this reason. Short lived flowers are in narrow spikes with greenish bracts.

### *Fittonia verschaffeltii*
—Red-nerved Fittonia

Red-nerved fittonia has dark olive green leaves, 3 to 4 inches long, covered with a network of red veins.

CULTURE—*Light:* Place in medium to high indoor light levels. Avoid full sun locations. Leaf color will be better in higher light. *Temperature:* Normal home

*Ficus lyrata*

### *Ficus lyrata*—Fiddle-leaf Fig

*Ficus lyrata* is an impressive and striking indoor tree from West Africa where it grows to about 40 feet. The stiff 1 to 2 foot leaves are shaped like a violin with yellowish veins against a lustrous green background. The combination of large leaves and rough scaly bark makes this a very rugged-looking plant. It is normally used as a floor plant.

CULTURE—Similar to *F. benjamina*. Usually it is propagated only from air layers.

### *Ficus pumila* 'Minima'—Dwarf Creeping Fig

Creeping fig is a vining ficus with dark green, closely spaced, quilted ½ inch leaves. An excellent plant for cool locations, creeping fig will tolerate temperatures below 32°F for short periods of time. A very versatile plant, dwarf creeping fig can be used in a hanging basket, treated as a totem pole subject, trained on an indoor trellis, or developed into a pseudo-bonsai.

CULTURE—Similar to F. benjamina except it can stand cool temperatures and should not be grown in full sun locations.

*Ficus pumila* 'Minima'

Fittonia verschaffeltii argyroneura

Fittonia verschaffeltii

temperatures are acceptable. Avoid temperatures below 55°F. *Humidity:* Fittonia needs a high humidity. It does best if grown in a terrarium or home greenhouse. *Water:* Soil surface should not dry excessively. It grows best in a moist but not saturated soil. *Fertilizer:* Use reduced rates every 4 weeks. *Soil and repotting:* Use soil mix number 2. Repot when necessary. Older plants may lose their attractiveness and new plants should be started. *Pruning and grooming:* Wash foliage with tepid water once every 2 weeks. Prune flower spikes off when they appear. *Propagation:* Stem cuttings any time. *Pests:* Aphids and sometimes mealybugs.

### *Fittonia verschaffeltii argyroneura* —Silver-nerved Fittonia

*F. verschaffeltii argyroneura* is very similar to *F. verschaffeltii* except that the nerves are marked with white instead of red. Some indoor gardeners feel this variety grows faster and is easier to maintain indoors than the red-nerved fittonia.

# FUCHSIA
## (Onagraceae)
### *Fuchsia hybrida* —Fuchsias

Fuchsias are a diverse group of plants ranging from plant forms ideally suited for hanging baskets to tree forms. Most cultivated forms are derived from species found in the American tropics but a few are native to New Zealand. Although their growth habits may differ, all have showy 2 inch long flowers with colored recurved sepals above the petals which may be an entirely different color. Flower color depends on the cultivar, and includes white, pink, red, violet, purple, and blue. Many of the cultivars selected are ideally suited for hanging baskets with cascading branches covered with spectacular flowers. Some are suitable for standards. Fuchsia can add much to the home but they are not recommended for the beginning home gardener. If you would like more information than can be given here, contact the American Fuchsia Society (See Appendix). Fuchsias flower most prolifically during the long summer days.

CULTURE—*Light:* High interior light is needed inside; partial shade outside. *Temperature:* Fuchsias grow best with cool temperatures, and most cultivars should have 55° to 60°F night temperatures and 65° to 70°F day temperatures. *Humidity:* They

Fuchsia hybrid

# GUZMANIA
## (Bromeliaceae)

Guzmanias are bromeliads which grow on tree trunks and are native to tropical rain forests in Central and South America. The leaf rosette is composed of smooth edged leaves about 12 inches long. The flower spike emerges from the center of the rosette carrying a spectacular inflorescence which may remain colorful for months.

### *Guzmania lingulata* 'Major'—Scarlet Star

Scarlet star has green leaves clustered in a rosette and a striking inflorescence with 12 to

Guzmania monostachia

require 50% relative humidity for best growth. Group fuchsias and protect from drying winds. *Water:* Do not let the soil dry excessively during the growing season. Reduce watering frequency during the dormant season from October until March when they are kept in a cool, frost-free location. *Fertilizer:* Use reduced rates every 2 weeks when the plants are in active growth. Do not fertilize while they are dormant. *Soil and repotting:* Use soil mix number 1. Repot before active growth in the spring. *Pruning and grooming:* Prune branches back when repotting in the spring and leave about 6 inches of old growth. *Propagation:* Rooted cuttings. *Pests:* Aphids.

15 scarlet recurved bracts. Bract size varies from 1 to 5 inches with the lower bracts the longest. In the center, small yellow-tipped, red bracts surround whitish flowers. It is easy to maintain for several months indoors while in flower but somewhat difficult to grow in most homes for extended time periods. Few plants can command as much attention as scarlet star when it is in flower. It is ideal for use as a table plant when in flower.

CULTURE—*Light:* Place in high interior light, but avoid prolonged full sun locations; partial shade if placed outdoors.
*Temperature:* Normal home temperatures

Guzmania lingulata 'Major'

are satisfactory. Avoid temperatures below 55°F. *Humidity:* Maintain relative humidity above 50%. *Water:* Keep rosette filled with water. Use rain water or distilled water. Soil should be watered when top surface dries out. *Fertilizer:* Use dilute rates every 4 weeks; apply to soil media. *Soil and repotting:* Use soil mix number 3. Repot young bromeliads when necessary. *Pruning and grooming:* No pruning is needed until plant has finished flowering, then remove parent plant after it has withered. When offshoots are large enough to handle, they can be repotted. *Propagation:* Offshoots or seeds. *Pests:* Scales.

## Guzmania monostachia
—Striped Torch

Striped torch grows about 1 to 2 feet tall with smooth-edged, leathery, yellow-green leaves that may be up to 18 inches long, arranged in a spreading U-shaped rosette. The torchlike inflorescence emerges from the center of the rosette with white flowers contrasting with brown-striped, scarlet-red bracts. Bract color varies somewhat with plant selection and some *G. monostachia* have red and white bracts. It is best used as a decorator item when in flower.

CULTURE—Similar to scarlet star.

# GYNURA
## (Compositae)

### Gynura aurantiaca 'Purple Passion'

The iridescent purple green leaves of *G. aurantiaca* almost look artificial. The sheen comes from the purple hairs on the 3 to 5 inch green leaves with purplish veins. A rapid grower from Java's jungles, purple passion makes a beautiful hanging basket with its colorful foliage cascading gracefully over the sides of the container. If you enjoy watching your plant grow, this plant is one to buy. Used as a ground cover in an indoor planter, it spreads extremely fast under good growing conditions. Some indoor gardeners like the contrast provided by the small orange dandelion-like flowers that form spasmodically, but other gardeners remove them.

*Gynura aurantiaca 'Purple Passion'*

CULTURE—*Light:* Place in medium to high interior light, but avoid full sun locations. Partial shade outdoors. Purple color in leaf hairs fades in low light areas. *Temperature:* Normal home temperatures are acceptable; temperatures below 55°F reduce growth. *Humidity:* Use humidity-increasing measures during dry periods. *Water:* Allow top surface of soil to dry between waterings. *Fertilizer:* Use reduced rates every 4 weeks. *Soil and repotting:* Use soil mix number 2. Repot as needed to retain balance between plant and container. *Pruning and grooming:* Prune plants back when they get leggy. Wash foliage once a month to reduce dust on plant. *Propagation:* Take stem cuttings to propagate new plants once a year. *Pests:* Mites.

# HAWORTHIA
## (Liliaceae)

**Haworthia subfasciata**—Little Zebra Plant

*Haworthia subfasciata* is one of the more common of the many haworthias or wart plants grown indoors. The thick, succulent, 2 to 4 inch, deep green leaves are spotted with raised white dots which tend to be grouped into bands on the lower leaf surface. It is an excellent plant for dry terrariums or simulated miniature desert scenes. The rosette of thick leaves tapering to a sharp point look like many native desert plants. If grown in good light, a long slender flower stalk which may be over 20 inches long will bear scattered small white flowers with green stripes. An easy plant for the beginner, *H. subfasciata* withstands considerable neglect and makes a good window sill plant.

CULTURE—*Light:* East or west windows provide adequate light. Plants in south windows may burn. *Temperature:* Normal home temperatures are acceptable. *Humidity:* Native to dry regions in South Africa, *H. subfasciata* needs no special treatment. *Water:* Allow top surface of soil to become dry before watering again. *Fertilizer:* Use reduced rates every 5 to 6 weeks. *Soil and repotting:* Use soil mix number 5. Older specimens should be repotted in early summer. Younger specimens whenever needed. *Pruning and grooming:* No pruning needed; shower leaves once every 3 to 4 weeks. *Propagation:* Use offsets which emerge from between leaf bases. *Pests:* Usually no major problems.

*Haworthia subfasciata*

# HEDERA
## (Araliaceae)

*Hedera helix* —English Ivy

Literally hundreds of different cultivars of English ivy are available to be grown as indoor plants. Great diversity exists in leaf shape, but most ivies have a 5-lobed, deep green leaf with greenish white veins. Indoors, it is usually grown as a window plant or hanging basket where its stems can gracefully trail over the side of the container. If some support is provided, it will climb by means of small suction roots on its stem. Most indoor gardeners do not know that they are growing

*Hedera helix*

the juvenile form of English ivy and if they grow their plant long enough (15 years) and keep it pruned back, it changes from being a trailing vine to a small upright shrub. To learn more about English ivies, contact the American Ivy Society (See Appendix).

CULTURE—*Light:* Place in medium to high interior light indoors such as an east or north window. When it is taken outside for the summer, locate in partial shade. *Temperature:* Ivies do best where it is cool, 55 to 60°F night and 65 to 70°F day temperatures seem best when grown indoors. *Humidity:* Dry air may present problems, and ivies should be grown where humidity can be over 30%. *Water:* Allow top surface of soil to dry between waterings. *Fertilizer:* Use dilute rates once every 4 to 5 weeks. *Soil and Repotting:* Use soil mix number 1. Repot younger specimens when needed, older plants in spring before new growth starts. *Pruning and grooming:* Pinch tip to induce branching and create a fuller plant. Wash foliage once every 2 to 3 weeks. *Propagation:* Stem cuttings. *Pests:* Mites and scales.

# HEMIGRAPHIS
## (Acanthaceae)

### *Hemigraphis alternata* 'Exotica'
—Waffle Plant

Waffle plants are fast growing, trailing plants, rooting when their stems touch the soil surface. Their common name originates from their puckered leaves with scalloped margins which look as if they had been placed in an old waffle iron. Both the 2 to 3 inch leaves and the stems have a deep purple cast to them. The cluster of small white flowers are very distinctive against the purple foliage. Waffle plants form mounds about 6 inches high in containers. Recommended for arranging in a basket or in 3 to 5 inch containers where its stems cascade gracefully over the sides.

CULTURE—*Light:* Place in low to high interior light locations. Do not place in full

153

sun. If the light is too low, purple color in foliage will fade. *Temperature:* Normal home temperatures are acceptable. Avoid areas below 55°F. *Humidity:* During periods of low relative humidity, use humidity-increasing measures. *Water:* Allow top surface of soil to dry between waterings. *Fertilizer:* Use reduced rates every 3 to 4 weeks. *Soil and repotting:* Use soil mix number 2. Repot when necessary. *Pruning and grooming:* Prune older stems back to induce new, colorful growth. *Propagation:* Stem cuttings or division of established plants. *Pests:* Mites, aphids, and scales.

*Hemigraphis alternata 'Exotica'*

# HIBISCUS
## (Malvaceae)

*Hibiscus rosa-sinensis*—Chinese Hibiscus

Hibiscus is widely grown in tropical and subtropical portions of the world for its beautiful 4 to 5 inch funnel shaped, flaming red flowers with protruding yellow stamens and pistils. Even without the flowers, the plant's glossy, deep green leaves would make it worth growing. Hibiscus are rather versatile and can be trained in small tree forms, kept severely pruned back and developed into pseudo-bonsai, trimmed as a large window sill plant, or used as a floor plant near

*Hibiscus rosa-sinensis*

a large window. It makes a great patio plant in the summer in partial shade.

CULTURE-*Light:* Place in full sun locations for best flowering. In less than full sun, the plant gets leggy. Outside place it in partial shade. *Temperature:* Keep hibiscus in rooms that do not exceed 75° in the winter. Avoid temperatures below 50°F. *Humidity:* Keep humidity above 25% during periods of low relative humidities; otherwise buds may drop. *Water:* Allow soil surface to dry before watering again but large plants in small containers may need water twice a day. *Fertilizer:* Use reduced rates every 2 to 3 weeks. *Soil and repotting:* Use soil mix number 1. Repot in the spring. *Pruning and grooming:* Prune plants back in the spring. If trained as a pseudo-bonsai, prune when needed. Syringe foliage as needed to remove dust. *Propagation:* Terminal cuttings. *Pests:* Aphids and mites.

# HIPPEASTRUM
(Amaryllidaceae)

*Hippeastrum* **hybrids**—Amaryllis

Amaryllis is one of the showiest of indoor bulbs used for forcing during the northern winters. Either before, after, or while the long, green, strap-shaped leaves emerge, a hollow flowering stalk with 2 to 6 flowers appears. Colors of the 8 to 12 inch flowers include solid white, oranges, pinks, reds, and stripes. Few plants can surpass the beauty of an amaryllis in full bloom. With proper care, your amaryllis will bloom year after year indoors.

CULTURE—*Light:* Place in high interior light locations but avoid full sun. During the summer, place your potted amaryllis outside in a partial shade location. *Temperature:* Normal home temperatures are acceptable. Amaryllis will tolerate temperatures around freezing but will not grow. It needs cool storage temperatures (50° to 55°F) from October until December or January. Basement temperatures may be ideal. *Humidity:* When young leaves and flowering shoot are emerging, daily misting will help prevent desiccation. *Water:* During the

dormant period, allow the soil to become dry; but during growing period, water when the top surface of soil becomes dry. *Fertilizer:* Fertilize after flowering every 3 to 4 weeks with reduced fertilizer rates. *Soil and repotting:* Use soil mix number 1. When potting or repotting amaryllis, keep 1/3 to 1/2 of the bulb above the soil. After several years in the same container, small side bulblets may form. At this time, the plant should be repotted and the bulblets removed. *Pruning and grooming:* When the plant is allowed to die back in the fall, the dried leaves should be cut off. Keep foliage clean by showering. *Propagation:* Use seed or the side bulblets. *Pests:* Chewing insects.

Hippeastrum hybrid

# HOWEA
(Palmae)

*Howea forsterana* —Kentia Palm

Kentia palms are native to a small island west of Australia where they grow to 60 feet high. Yet because of their slow growth indoors and their graceful, deep green, featherlike fronds which arch upward and then curve downward, they are one of the popular palms for indoor use. Usually kentias are sold with 3 to 5 plants per pot to give the illusion of a multiple-trunk palm. Large plants are ideal for creating a tropical effect in a large room. Smaller plants can be used as low table plants for a number of years before they outgrow their locations.

CULTURE—*Light:* Kentias tolerate low to high interior light locations. Avoid full sun locations. *Temperature:* Normal home temperatures are acceptable. *Humidity:* Fronds are less likely to develop brown tips if relative humidity is increased. *Water:* Allow top surface of soil to dry between waterings, but avoid letting soil become too dry. *Fertilizer:* Use reduced rates every 5 weeks. *Soil and repotting:* Use soil mix number 2. Repot as needed to balance plant with container. *Pruning and grooming:* Old dried fronds should be cut off. Give plants a shower once a month. Do not cut back the growing tip or the plant will die. *Propagation:* Seed, but it is difficult to obtain. *Pests:* Scales and mites.

# HOYA
(Asclepiadaceae)

*Hoya carnosa* 'Variegata' —Wax Plant

Hoyas are thick, stiff leafed, climbing vines from Asia. They are grown both for their attractive green foliage bordered with cream white margins and for the clusters of 12 to 15, ½ inch, waxy, fragrant flowers that develop on small, knotty, flower spurs. Hoya should not be moved when buds are setting as a change in light intensity may cause bud abortion. As the vines grow, they can be trained to frame windows or to grow on a small indoor trellis. Vines can reach up to 8 or 10 feet if desired. Their slow growth makes them ideal for dishgardens. Wax plant is a long lived and durable house plant.

CULTURE—*Light:* Locate in medium or high interior light. Diffuse sunlight is probably the best light for wax plants. *Temperature:* Normal home temperatures are acceptable, but wax plants grow best with temperatures about 50° to 55°F night, and 60° to 65°F day temperatures. *Humidity:* It

*Howea forsterana*

*Hoya carnosa 'Variegata'*

tolerates low relative humidity. *Water:* Allow top surface of soil to become dry between waterings. During winter dormant periods water just to prevent leaf shriveling. *Fertilizer:* During spring, summer, and fall, use reduced rates every 3 to 4 weeks. Use minor element fertilizer once a year. *Soil and repotting:* Use soil mix number 2 or 5. Hoyas should be repotted only when absolutely necessary. *Pruning and grooming:* Prune to increase branching. Do not cut flowers as flowers form year after year on the same spur. *Propagation:* Stem cuttings or air layering. *Pests:* Mealybugs and scales.

# HYACINTHUS
## (Liliaceae)

*Hyacinthus orientalis* —Hyacinth

Hyacinths are popular outdoor spring flowering bulbs that can also be used to brighten homes during the gray winter period from January through March. The large bulbs produce thick, upright growing, strap-shaped leaves. The inflorescence merges from the bulb's center bearing clusters of fragrant bell-shaped flowers, which may be white, deep blue, light blue, pink, or red. Read the section on forcing bulbs on page 131 for additional information. Forced hyacinth bulbs cannot be forced again but should be planted outside in a bulb bed or discarded.

CULTURE—*Light:* The bulb should be kept in the dark until the flower buds are above the leaves. Then place in a high light area. *Temperature:* Normal home temperatures are acceptable but flowers last longer if kept cool at night (45 to 50°F). *Humidity:* No special provisions are necessary. *Water:* Flowers may not develop if soil is allowed to dry excessively. *Fertilizer:* Not needed during forcing period. *Soil and repotting:* Use soil mix number 1. Plant outdoors when through forcing. *Pruning and grooming:* Rinse foliage if dust accumulates. *Propagation:* It is easier to purchase new bulbs than to try to propagate them. *Pests:* Usually none when grown indoors.

*Hyacinthus orientalis*

157

*Hydrangea macrophylla*

# HYDRANGEA
(Saxifragaceae)

*Hydrangea macrophylla* —Hydrangea
Hydrangeas are usually received as gift
plants or bought for Easter or Mother's Day.
The large, circular flower cluster is composed
of 1 to 2 inch flowers whose color depends on
soil pH. Blue flowers are formed when the pH
is below 5.5 and pink flowers are formed
when the pH is 6.5 or higher. Flowers will last
for 4 to 6 weeks with proper cultural care.

When through blooming, the plants can be
transplanted outdoors in the southern portion
of the United States. If you enjoy a challenge,
you can try to have your hydrangeas bloom
the next spring. Prune the flowering shoots
back to about 6 inches, and place outside in a
partially shaded location. After the first frost,

158

move the plant to a cool (40 to 50°F), dark location until after the first of the year. The soil must be watered during dormancy to prevent stem desiccation and plant death. Place in a bright, warm area indoors but avoid prolonged full sun locations. The flowers formed will not be commercial quality but they will brighten your home.

CULTURE—*Light:* Place in high interior light. Avoid bright sun when flowering. *Temperature:* Normal home temperatures are acceptable except during dormancy. *Humidity:* Keep humidity above 25%. *Water:* Plants transpire lots of water and wilt easily. They may require watering twice a day when in active growth. Use a minimum amount of water during dormancy. *Fertilizer:* Use reduced rates every 2 weeks when in active growth. Control soil pH with aluminum sulfate or iron sulfate if blue flowers are desired. *Soil and repotting:* Repot after flowering; use soil mix number 1 for blue flowers and soil mix number 5 for pink flowers. *Pruning and grooming:* After flowering, cut shoots back to 6 inches. Wash foliage. *Propagation:* Stem cuttings in the spring. *Pests:* Aphids, thrips, mites, and scales.

# IMPATIENS
## (Balsaminaceae)

### *Impatiens wallerana* 'Variegata'
—Busy Lizzie Impatiens

Few plants are more dependable than impatiens in producing continual flowers indoors. The milky green, 1 to 2½ inch leaves, bordered with white, are complemented by flat spurred, light pink flowers. Growing to a height of about 12 to 18 inches, they are ideal table or window sill plants. Plants can be grown indoors during the winter and cuttings taken for spring outdoor plantings. Over 200 years' use as an indoor flowering plant suggests Impatiens' durability and attractiveness. It is recommended as a plant for beginners.

CULTURE—*Light:* Place in low to high interior light. Avoid full sun locations. Number of flowers increases with the amount of light. *Temperature:* Normal home temperatures are acceptable. *Humidity:* Usually it is no problem. *Water:* Allow top surface of soil to dry before watering. *Fertilizer:* Use reduced rates every 3 to 4 weeks during spring, summer, and fall. During the winter, apply every 5 to 6 weeks. *Soil and repotting:* Use soil mix number 1. Repot when needed to balance plant and container. *Pruning and grooming:* Pinch back to induce branching. Wash foliage every 2 weeks. *Propagation:* Stem cuttings. *Pests:* Aphids and mites.

*Impatiens wallerana 'Variegata'*

159

Justicia brandegeana

# JUSTICIA
(Acanthaceae)

**Justicia brandegeana**—Shrimp Plant

If you are looking for a flowering plant that will provide color indoors with a minimum of care, grow a shrimp plant. The colorful inflorescence is a terminal spike up to 4 inches long composed of small short lived white flowers and long lasting reddish-brown overlapping bracts. The attractive inflorescence complements the medium green 2½ inch opposite leaves. The shrimp plant will provide color throughout the year but will flower more profusely in spring and summer.

CULTURE—*Light:* Place in a full sun interior location for best appearance. *Temperature:* Normal home temperatures are acceptable. *Humidity:* Leaves curl up and drop off when humidity is too low. Use any convenient measures to increase humidity to prevent leaf drop. *Water:* If you let the soil dry excessively, the lower leaves will drop. *Fertilizer:* Use reduced rates every 2 or 3 weeks. *Soil and repotting:* Use soil mix number 1. Early spring is best for repotting. *Pruning and grooming:* In order to produce a compact shrimp plant, pinching back is

necessary. Prune plants in spring and fall. Remove withered bracts. *Propagation:* Cuttings or division. *Pests:* Aphids, chewing insects, and mites.

# KALANCHOE
(Crassulaceae)

**Kalanchoe blossfeldiana**—Christmas Kalanchoe

Kalanchoe is a small, compact, succulent plant with deep green, 1 to 3 inch leaves. A short day plant, it is covered with scarlet red flowers during the Christmas holidays. Usually no more than 8 to 10 inches high, it makes an ideal, small, flowering plant during the winter. Christmas kalanchoe can be kept flowering any time during the year by subjecting it to approximately 6 weeks of short days.

Kalanchoe blossfeldiana

CULTURE—*Light:* Place in high light locations indoors. It is a good plant for an east, south, or west window sill. *Temperature:* Normal home temperatures are acceptable. Avoid locations below 55°F. *Water:* Allow top soil surface to dry between waterings. *Fertilizer:* Use reduced rates every 3 or 4 weeks except during the winter, when you should apply fertilizer every 5 or 6 weeks. *Soil and repotting:* Use soil mix number 1. Repot in the spring. *Pruning and grooming:* Pinch growing tip of young plants to increase bushiness. Prune back old flowering stems. Shower the thick, succulent leaves every 2 to 3 weeks. *Propagation:* Stem cuttings or seeds. *Pests:* Usually no problems in the home; chewing insects outside.

*Lilium longiflorum*

# LILIUM
## (Liliaceae)

### *Lilium longiflorum* —Easter Lily

The Easter lily is so closely associated with Easter that almost all the millions of Easter lilies produced in this country are sold for Easter sales. Most plants sold today are either *L. longiflorum* 'Ace' or 'Nellie White.' Both of these cultivars are under 2 feet in height and have 3 to 8 blossoms per plant. The flowers are 5 to 8 inches long and 4 to 5 inches across. When the flowers are through blooming, continue normal watering procedures until the foliage dies back. Then plant the bulb about 6 inches deep in your garden. There it will flower next year in July. Remember when buying lilies to choose a plant with the greatest number of unopened buds.

CULTURE—*Light:* Place in high interior light. A sunny south window is perfect. *Temperature:* Lilies keep best in the home with 50° to 60°F night temperatures. Flower life is shortened at higher temperatures. *Humidity:* Normally it is not a problem. *Water:* Keep the soil moist, but do not overwater. *Fertilizer:* No fertilizer is needed. *Soil and repotting:* Not required with bought plants. *Pruning and grooming:* Cut off old flowers and stems before planting outside. *Propagation:* Seeds. *Pests:* Aphids.

161

*Maranta
leuconeura
kerchoviana*

*Maranta leuconeura
erythroneura*

# MARANTA
## (Marantaceae)

Marantas are low growing, herbaceous plants seldom exceeding 10 inches in height. Their extreme popularity results from their distinctly marked foliage and the habit of folding their leaves upward at night. Their common name, prayer plants, is given because of this characteristic. Small white or purplish flowers occasionally emerge from the leaf axils. When repotting any of the marantas, you will notice round swellings on the roots. This is not a disease or insect damage but small tuberlike swellings which are used to store excess photosynthates.

### *Maranta leuconeura erythroneura* — Red Nerve Plant

The zig-zag, succulent branches of red nerve plant bear 3 to 5 inch leaves that look artificial with their raised crimson veins against the deep lustrous green background with pale green interconnected splotches along the midrib. As the plant grows, the weight of the leaves pulls the stem down and the foliage trails gracefully over the side of the container. Although very exotic-looking, red nerve plant grows well inside. It can be used as a small totem subject, in hanging baskets, or as a small table plant.

CULTURE—*Light:* Medium to high interior light levels are needed by the plant. Avoid full sun locations. *Temperature:* Normal home temperatures; avoid locations colder than 50°F as foliage may be injured. *Humidity:* Use humidity-increasing measures during the winter. *Water:* Allow top surface to dry between waterings but do not neglect watering the plant. *Fertilizer:* Use reduced rates every 3 to 4 weeks during spring, summer, and fall, and every 5 to 6 weeks during the winter. *Soil and repotting:* Use soil mix number 2. Repot when needed to balance plant with container. Superphosphate in mix will cause leaf edges to turn brown. Adjust soil pH to 6.5. *Pruning and grooming:* Cut some of the stems bearing older, less attractive foliage off the plant once every 6 months to permit fresh new growth to develop. Rinse leaves off once every 3 weeks. *Propagation:* Division or cuttings. *Pests:* Mealybugs.

### *Maranta leuconeura kerchoviana* — Prayer Plant

You have often seen prayer plant advertised in magazines. It is very similar in its growth to red nerve plant except that the leaves are thinner and marked with pairs of dark brown spots on either side of the midrib. Each of the major lateral veins is embossed on the light green leaf blade.

CULTURE—Similar to *Maranta leuconeura erythroneura.*

# MONSTERA
(Araceae)

*Monstera deliciosa* —Philodendron pertusum, Cut-leaved Philodendron

In its native habitat on the Yucatan Peninsula of Mexico, monstera is a woody vine, climbing high in the trees with leathery, dark green, perforated leaves that may be 3 feet long. Because it has adapted to the deep shade of the jungles, it endures low light levels in our homes. The species name *deliciosa* is derived from the fruit which when ripe tastes like a pineapple-banana. Monstera is an ideal plant for low light areas. It can be allowed to grow around doorways and large windows.

Monstera deliciosa

CULTURE—*Light:* It tolerates low to high interior light. Avoid full sun locations. *Temperature:* Normal home temperatures are acceptable. Temperatures below 50°F stop plant growth temporarily. *Humidity:* It endures low relative humidities. *Water:* Allow top surface of soil to become dry before watering again. *Fertilizer:* Use reduced rates every 3 to 4 weeks. *Soil and repotting:* Use soil mix number 2. Repot if needed in the spring before new growth begins. Be sure to pack soil firmly around totem pole. *Pruning and grooming:* Wash foliage with a moist cloth as needed to remove dust from the foliage. Do not cut off aerial roots. *Propagation:* Air layers or stem cuttings. *Pests:* Mites and mealybugs.

# NARCISSUS
(Amaryllidaceae)

**Narcissus** hybrids —Daffodils, Narcissus

Although narcissus species are divided into 11 horticultural classes for floral characteristics, they can be divided into 2 groups for winter forcing, hardy narcissus and half-hardy narcissus.

Half-hardy narcissus for easy indoor forcing include *N. tazetta* cultivars and *N. poeta*. Their multiple flowers bring the promise of spring into your home during the long winter days. Cultivars which force well indoors are 'Soleil d'Or' with yellow flowers, 'Chinese Sacred Lily' with creamy white petals and yellow centers, 'Paper White' with all-white flowers, and 'Geranium' with white petals and an orange cup.

The bulbs should be potted in a shallow bowl filled with pebbles and water. Use a container at least 4 inches deep and large enough to hold more than one bulb. Fill one half of the container with pebbles and put bulbs in, then add pebbles to cover ⅓ of the bulb. Add water to fill container a little over half full. Place in a dark, cool location (about 50° to 55°F) until bulb growth is about 2 or 3 inches tall, then bring indoors and acclimatize them to bright light over a period of 5 days,

Narcissus
hybrid

colorful of the easy to grow indoor bromeliads. It has spiny margined, green leaves striped with creamy yellow. Leaves grow almost perpendicular to the water-holding rosette formed by the leaf bases. When tricolor flowers, the center of the rosette and the youngest leaves turn brilliant red and small purplish flowers emerge just above the water level in the rosette. The colorful display lasts for several months and makes tricolor a truly spectacular plant for interior use. After flowering, the rosette dies but offshoots develop from the base of the plant.

CULTURE—*Light:* Use in medium and high light interiors. Avoid full sun locations. *Temperature:* Normal home temperatures are acceptable. Avoid locations below 50°F. *Humidity:* Keep rosette filled with water and tricolor will adapt to most homes. *Water:* Keep leaf rosette filled; allow top surface of soil to dry between waterings. *Fertilizer:* Apply reduced fertilizer rates once every 2 or 3 weeks. *Soil and repotting:* Use soil mix number 3. Repot younger specimens as needed. It takes 2 or 3 years to produce flowering specimens in the home. *Pruning and grooming:* After the flowering rosette has died back, it should be removed and the offshoots repotted. *Propagation:* Offshoots formed after the plant has flowered. *Pests:* Scales.

finally placing them in a south window. Soil can be used instead of pebbles but if you use soil, ⅓ of the bulb should be covered. Use a container with good drainage. After forcing, the bulbs can be planted outdoors in areas where winter temperatures do not go below 20°F for extended time periods.

To force hardy narcissus indoors, see the discussion on page 131.

# NEOREGELIA
## (Bromeliaceae)

### *Neoregelia carolinae* 'Tricolor' — Tricolor Bromeliad

Neoregelia is a bromeliad which grows on tree trunks and branches and is native to tropical Brazilian rain forests. It is the most

Neoregelia carolinae
'Tricolor'

# NEPHROLEPIS
(Polypodiaceae)

A small book could easily be written describing the many cultivated species and cultivars of nephrolepis and their uses in enhancing our environment. Widely distributed in the tropics and subtropics, they are used for interior and exterior landscaping purposes.

### Nephrolepis exaltata 'Bostoniensis'—Boston Fern

Boston fern was discovered in a Boston nursery in 1894, and since then has been one of the most popular ferns for indoor use. The long, narrow, green fronds may reach 3 feet in length, with flat leaflets crowded on either side of the midrib. Cut fronds can be used in floral arrangements. Boston fern looks best in the home in a medium or large container with the fronds seeming to flow over the container's side.

CULTURE—*Light:* Boston fern needs medium to high interior light. Avoid full sun locations. Place in partial shade outside. *Temperature:* Although it tolerates a wide temperature range (32° to 95°F), it grows best at 60°F night and 75°F day temperatures. *Humidity:* Fronds remain more attractive when humidity is kept above 35%. Continual drafts dry fronds. *Water:* Allow top surface of soil to dry slightly between waterings. *Fertilizer:* Use reduced rates every 3 or 4 weeks. *Soil and repotting:* Use soil mix number 6. Repot in the spring. *Pruning and grooming:* Cut off older fronds to allow younger, more attractive fronds to develop. Syringe the fronds once every 2 weeks to remove dust and maintain plant beauty. *Propagation:* Can be propagated by division or by runners which emerge from the crown of Boston fern. *Pests:* Scales, mealybugs, and whitefly.

### Nephrolepis exaltata 'Fluffy Ruffles'

'Fluffy ruffles' is the most common of the over 90 cultivars of Boston fern. Usually it is sold in small, 3 to 4 inch pots, with 8 to 10 inch fronds with small leaflets which are twisted and crowded on the midrib as if there were not room for all of them. Transplanted to a larger container, the fronds may reach 18 inches or more in length. It is best suited for use as a table, desk, or window sill plant.

CULTURE—Similar to Boston fern. If the foliage develops a gray cast, the soil has been too dry some time in the past.
past.

Nephrolepis
exaltata
'Bostoniensis'

Nephrolepis exaltata
'Fluffy Ruffles'

# NIDULARIUM
(Bromeliaceae)

### Nidularium innocentii nana— Miniature Birdsnest

Miniature birdsnest is a bromeliad which looks something like a small neoregelia. The spiny-edged leaves have a brownish green upper leaf surface. The leaf bases form a cup which should be kept filled with water. Before the white flowers open in the center of the rosette, the youngest leaves turn an orange-red. The striking color combinations capture attention wherever a flowering miniature birdsnest is located. Although not the easiest plant to grow indoors, its small size and spectacular color pattern recommend it for experienced indoor gardeners.

CULTURE—*Light:* Place in medium to

high interior light areas. Avoid prolonged full sun locations. An east window location could be ideal. *Temperature:* Normal home temperatures are acceptable. *Humidity:* Locate where it is easy to increase the relative humidity. *Water:* Always maintain water supply in the cup formed by the leaf rosette. Keep soil surface moist but do not overwater. *Fertilizer:* Use reduced rates every 4 to 5 weeks. *Soil and repotting:* Use soil mix number 3. Repot younger plants as needed. *Pruning and grooming:* Remove central rosette when it has died back. Pick out flowers as they fade, as decaying flowers in the leaf cup may create a stagnant odor. *Propagation:* Offshoots which develop when the plant has completed flowering. *Pests:* Scales.

# ONCIDIUM
## (Orchidaceae)

*Oncidium sphacelatum* —Golden Shower

The golden shower orchid is a spectacular plant when flowering. The arching, branched inflorescence may elongate up to 3 to 5 feet and be filled with 1 inch yellow, brown-spotted flowers. Not really that difficult to grow indoors, it makes a good orchid for the beginning orchid grower.

CULTURE—*Light:* Place in high interior light intensity. An east window or bright diffuse sunlight would be ideal. *Temperature:* Normal home temperatures are acceptable. *Humidity:* Mist during periods of low relative humidity (under 25%). *Water:* Allow soil surface to dry between waterings. Reduce

*Nidularium innocentii nana*

166

*Oncidium sphacelatum*

given the name good luck plant because of its resemblance to a large four-leaved clover. The ¾ inch, yellow-throated rosy red flowers are borne in a cluster of 5 or more which emerge above the leaves. A white-flowered form is also available. Oxalis is an easy-to-grow flowering plant for sunny window sills. Start plants in the fall for winter bloom. After blooming, plants should be allowed to go dormant for a month or so.

CULTURE—*Light:* Oxalis needs high interior light. *Temperature:* Normal home temperatures are satisfactory. *Humidity:* It tolerates normal home humidities. *Water:* Allow top surface of soil to dry between waterings. After flowering, water just enough to keep soil slightly damp during resting period. *Fertilizer:* Apply dilute fertilizer every 5 to 6 weeks when plants are growing. *Soil and repotting:* Use soil mix number 1. Separate bulbs and repot after plant has gone dormant. *Pruning and grooming:* Cut off old flowers as they start to fade so plants will continue to flower. Rinse foliage every 3 weeks to remove dust. *Propagation:* Small bulblets separated from larger bulbs when repotting. *Pests:* Aphids.

*Oxalis deppei*

water during dormant season after new growth has matured. *Fertilizer:* Use about ¼ ounce of a liquid 10-10-10 per gallon of water, and fertilize once every 6 weeks if plants are growing in osmunda fern. *Soil and repotting:* Use soil mix no. 4. *Pruning and grooming:* Remove flower stalks after fading. Syringe foliage once every 3 weeks. *Propragation:* By division; seed and meristemming are extremely difficult for most indoor gardeners. *Pests:* Scales and mites.

# OXALIS
## (Oxalidaceae)

*Oxalis deppei* —Good Luck Plant
   Good luck plants from Mexico are charming plants with compound, clover-like leaves about 2 inches across. It has been

Paphiopedilum hybrid

green. Both of these terrestrial orchids can be grown as indoor orchids with most indoor gardeners reporting better luck with *P. x maudiae*. If you would like to grow something different inside, try one of these orchids. They are often sold as cypripediums.

CULTURE—*Light:* Locate in medium to high interior light levels. Avoid full sun locations. *Temperature:* Normal home temperatures. *Humidity:* Use humidity-increasing measures during the winter when humidity is below 25%. *Water:* Allow some drying of the soil surface between waterings, but soil should be kept fairly moist at all times. Reduce frequency of applications after repotting. *Fertilizer:* Use about ¼ ounce of a liquid 10-10-10 per gallon of water, and fertilize once every 6 weeks if plants are growing in osmunda fern. Leach container occasionally to avoid salt build-up. *Soil and repotting:* Use soil mix number 4. Repot every 2 or 3 years after flowering. *Pruning and grooming:* If desired, flowers can be cut to use in floral arrangements. Keep foliage clean with showers. *Propagation:* Division. *Pests:* Scales.

# PAPHIOPEDILUM
## (Orchidaceae)

**Paphiopedilum** hybrids —Ladyslipper Orchids

*Paphiopedilum* hybrids are among the most desirable of indoor orchids because they combine long lasting flowers and distinctive foliage in addition to making good house plants. Their thick, broad, strap-shaped leaves have a marbled or mottled green and brown upper surface while the under surface is purplish. The flowers are typical of ladyslipper or moccasin flower, with pouch-shaped lip. *P. x maudiae* has green and white flowers that last 3 months or more, and may bloom in both the spring and fall. *P. x harrisianum* has red flowers marked with

# PEDILANTHUS
## (Euphorbiaceae)

**Pedilanthus tithymaloides 'Variegatus'** —Ribbon Cactus, Redbird Cactus, Devil's Backbone

Pedilanthus is an easy-to-grow houseplant that does well in all but low light areas in the home. The alternate leaves vary from 2 to 4 inches in length and have irregularly defined cream colored margins on new foliage, changing to milk white as the foliage matures. Some selections have rose tints in the foliage. Green stems often have a zig-zag growth

Pedilanthus tithymaloides 'Variegatus'

habit. If plant is moved outside in the summer, many of the older leaves will fall off. If plants are subjected to cold temperatures (35°F) during the winter, small red flowers appear in the spring.

CULTURE—*Light:* Place in medium to high light interiors. An excellent window sill plant for all exposures. It may be used as a table plant near large windows. *Temperature:* Normal home temperatures are acceptable; will tolerate temperatures down to 35°F. *Humidity:* During periods of low relative humidity, mature leaves may fall. *Water:* Allow top surface of soil to dry between waterings. If the plant is underwatered, the leaves will go limp. *Fertilizer:* Use reduced rates every 4 to 5 weeks. *Soil and repotting:* Use soil mix number 5. Repot as plant growth dictates. *Pruning and grooming:* Cut tip back to induce branching. Plant sap is reported to cause skin irritations on sensitive people. Rinse foliage to remove dust. *Propagation:* Stem cuttings. *Pests:* Scales and mites.

an inner horseshoe-shaped marked circle. Plants vary in height from 1 to 6 feet depending on cultural practices and cultivars. Geraniums are dependable flowering plants for sunny windows.

CULTURE—*Light:* Place in high interior light with a full sun location if plants are to flower. *Temperature:* Although they do better wtih cooler temperatures, normal home temperatures are acceptable. *Humidity:* Geraniums tolerate dry air. *Water:* Allow top surface of soil to dry between waterings. *Fertilizer:* Use reduced rates every 3 to 4 weeks. *Soil and repotting:* Use soil mix number 1. Spring is the best time to repot. *Pruning and grooming:* To have plants flower during the winter, remove flower buds on plants indoors until sometime in October. Rinse foliage as needed to remove dust. *Propagation:* Cuttings. *Pests:* Mites, mealybugs, and whitefly.

# PELARGONIUM
## (Geraniaceae)

### *Pelargonium hybrids* —
Geraniums

Geraniums are extremely popular flowering plants, for both indoor and outdoor use. An almost endless variety of species and cultivars are available from 3 inch miniatures with brightly colored foliage to large, almost continually flowering pot plants. Contact the International Geranium Society to find out more about this fascinating group of indoor plants (See Appendix). The geraniums most widely grown indoors are cultivars of *Pelargonium hortorum*. The plant usually has green upright stems and roundish leaves with

*Pelargonium hybrid*

169

# PEPEROMIA
## (Piperaceae)

Peperomia is another plant group that offers a wide selection of plants that can be grown in the average home. Over 20 different kinds are available. Although superficially dissimilar, they are all relatively small, semi-succulent plants with firm thick leaves which may have fascinating foliage patterns. The white flowers are formed on an upright growing catkin.

*Peperomia caperata*

*Peperomia obtusifolia 'Variegata'*

25%. *Water:* Allow soil surface to dry between waterings. Plant is susceptible to root rot so avoid overwatering. The petioles become limp when plant is underwatered. *Fertilizer:* Use reduced rates every 3 or 4

***Peperomia caperata***—Emerald Ripple

The common name, emerald ripple, aptly describes this plant as its heart-shaped leaves are a deep, dark, almost black-green and the leaf surface is interestingly corrugated and rippled. The light colored petioles contrast nicely with the leaves. Leaves emerge from a short stem and radiate out to a distance of about 4 inches. It is an excellent plant for a 4 to 6 inch pot or in a terrarium planting. Mature plants form a mound of green leaves about 4 to 5 inches high.

CULTURE—*Light:* Locate in medium to high interior light. *Temperature:* Normal home temperatures. *Humidity:* Emerald ripple grows better when humidity is above

*Peperomia obtusifolia*

weeks. *Soil and repotting:* Use soil mix
number 2. Repot when necessary to balance
plant and container. *Pruning and grooming:*
You can cut off flower stalks if you prefer.
Rinse foliage over 2 to 3 weeks. *Propagation:*
Division or stem cuttings. *Pests:* Sometimes
mites can be a problem.

### *Peperomia obtusifolia*—
Baby Rubber Tree

*Peperomia obtusifolia* has thick, glossy
green, oval, sturdy leaves with red flecked
petioles. The leaves may be up to 3 inches
wide. When the reddish-green stems grow to
about 12 to 14 inches, they no longer can
support the combined stem and leaf weight
and then lean horizontally. It tolerates
interior environments extremely well but it is
subject to root rot if it is overwatered.

CULTURE—Similar to *Peperomia
caperata*. Older prostrate stems may be cut
off.

### *Peperomia obtusifolia*
'Variegata'—Variegated Peperomia

*Peperomia obtusifolia* 'variegata' has
irregular cream-colored margins with light
green leaves and reddish stems and petioles.
Stems are no stronger than the baby rubber
plant's and with maturity become prostrate.
Pinch plants to induce branching and fullness.
Remove older stems if desired. Propagate by
cuttings.

CULTURE—Similar to *Peperomia
caperata*.

# PHILODENDRON
(Araceae)

Philodendrons are one of the most widely
used foliage plants. Of the 200 types of
philodendrons found in the Central and South
American jungles, over 100 have been used
as house plants. Philodendrons can be
grouped into 2 categories, vining
philodendrons and nonclimbing or
self-heading philodendrons. Vining
philodendrons tend to be more widely used
because their smaller size makes them more
versatile for indoor use.

*Philodendron scandens
oxycardium*

*Philodendron hybrid*

*Philodendron bipennifolium*

171

Philodendron
'Burgundy'

Philodendron
'Emerald Queen'

Philodendron
'Florida'

### Philodendron scandens oxycardium—Heart-leaf Philodendron

More *P. oxycardium* (also called cordatum in the United States and scandens in Europe) is sold every year than any other indoor plant. The glossy green, heart-shaped leaves are almost perfectly symmetrical in outline. It endures low light, drought, and infrequent care. The leaves can be one foot in length but usually are between 2 to 5 inches. Available in all sizes from "thumb" pot size to 10 foot high totem poles. *P. oxycardium* can be used in hanging baskets, as trailing pot plants, trained on a trellis or totem, or in dishgardens. Few indoor plants are easier to grow and are more tolerant of a beginner's mistakes.

CULTURE—*Light:* Place in low to high interior light intensity. If the light intensity is too low, the leaf size becomes progressively smaller. Avoid full sun locations as the leaves will burn. *Temperature:* Normal home temperatures are acceptable. Avoid temperatures below 50°F. *Humidity:* Usually it is no problem in most homes. *Water:* Allow top surface of soil to become dry between waterings. *Fertilizer:* Use reduced rates every 4 to 5 weeks. Increase or decrease applications as needed. *Soil and repotting:* Use soil mix number 2. Repot older plants in the spring. *Pruning and grooming:* Plant can be pinched back to increase branching. Wash foliage as needed to keep leaves attractive. *Propagation:* Stem cuttings. *Pests:* Mites.

### Philodendron bipennifolium—Fiddle-leaf Philodendron

Fiddle leaf is a climbing philodendron usually sold as a totem pole or a small specimen in a dishgarden. The olive gray-green, 5 to 12 inch leaves, shaped somewhat like a fiddle, are attached to a thick stem which becomes somewhat woody with age. Fiddle leaf is a very durable plant indoors.

CULTURE—Similar to *P. oxycardium.* The stems are less flexible than *P. oxycardium's;* and when plants have lost their lower leaves, cuttings should be taken to start new plants. This will stimulate new growth on the older mature plant.

## Philodendron hybrids

Extensive breeding programs in Florida and elsewhere have produced a number of excellent philodendrons for interior use. The goals have been to produce plants that would endure low light conditions while providing colorful and attractive foliage. A number of plants are available and are excellent indoor plants having thick leathery leaves and good keeping qualities.

CULTURE—The culture for these hybrids is similar to *P. scandens oxycardium.*

### Philodendron 'Burgundy'

'Burgundy' has thick, 12 inch, arrow-shaped, reddish-green leaves with red stems.

### Philodendron 'Emerald Queen'

'Emerald Queen' has 12 to 18 inch, arrow-shaped, bright green leaves.

### Philodendron 'Florida'

'Florida' has deep green, 6 to 8 inch, anchor-shaped, indented foliage with red warty petioles.

### Philodendron 'Red Emerald'

'Red Emerald' has 12 to 15 inch, arrow-shaped, dark reddish-green leaves with red stems and petioles.

### Philodendron 'Prince Dubonnet'

'Prince Dubonnet' has 8 to 15 inch, dark green leaves with reddish under-surfaces.

### Philodendron selloum —Selloum

Native to Brazil, selloum forms a woody trunk when mature and may reach 8 feet or more in height. However, it grows slowly and it would need years before it reached such height indoors. It does require a lot of room for proper display indoors as each leaf may exceed 4 feet in length. Smaller specimens make durable floor plants for low light areas. Selloum is best used as a specimen plant where the medium green, deeply lobed leaves can impart a tropical setting. Unlike most other philodendrons, selloum is not cold sensitive and will stand leaf temperatures down to 30°F without showing cold damage.

CULTURE—Similar to *P. scandens oxycardium.*

Philodendron 'Red Emerald'

Philodendron 'Prince Dubonnet'

Philodendron selloum

# PHOENIX
(Palmae)

*Phoenix roebelenii*—Pigmy Date Palm, Dwarf Date Palm

   *Phoenix roebeleniis* are small feather palms with gracefully arching 2 to 5 foot long fronds. With proper care, they can be kept indoors for over a quarter century. Slow growing outdoors where they seldom exceed 10 feet, they add only a few inches a year indoors. The flexible, pendulous fronds become stiff toward the base where they develop spines. As the tree matures, the 3 to 5 foot trunk is covered with distinctive knobs which are leaf base remnants. The dwarf date palm is considered by many interior designers to be the most graceful of all indoor palms. It is best used as a medium-to-tall floor plant.

   CULTURE—*Light:* Medium to high interior light levels are needed. *Temperature:* It tolerates temperatures from 32° to 98°F so normal home temperatures are just about perfect. *Humidity:* It tolerates occasional periods of low humidity. *Water:* Allow top surface of soil to dry between waterings. *Fertilizer:* Use reduced rates every 5 to 6 weeks. *Soil and repotting:* Use soil mix number 2. Repot in the spring as needed. Be careful of the spines near the base of the fronds. *Pruning and grooming:* Cut off old fronds when they have withered. Rinse foliage as needed. *Propagation:* Seeds. *Pests:* Scales.

# PILEA
(Urticaceae)

   Pileas are a group of low growing, tropical and subtropical, herbaceous plants which seldom exceed 12 to 15 inches in height. All produce relatively small, greenish axillary flowers. They grow best in moist soils and are widely used as terrarium plants.

*Pilea cadierei*—Aluminum Plant

   The aluminum plant, native to Vietnam, has swollen nodes with opposite, green leaves with raised areas between the veins covered with irregular silver markings. *P. cadierei* is a relatively fast growing, easy-to-grow plant. With maturity, the stems become prostrate. It makes an unusual looking desk or table plant. Aluminum plant grows well on north and east window sills.

   CULTURE—*Light:* Locate in medium to high interior light. *Temperature:* Normal home temperatures are acceptable. Avoid temperatures below 55°F. *Humidity:* It does best when humidity is over 50%. *Water:* The plant transpires a lot of water and will wilt easily. Keep soil moist but do not overwater. *Fertilizer:* Use reduced rates every 3 to 4 weeks. *Soil and repotting:* Use soil mix number 2. Repot as needed. *Pruning and grooming:* Cut old prostrate stems off if desired, or let them trail over the side of the container. Rinse foliage as needed to remove dust. Pinching may increase branching. *Propagation:* Stem cuttings. *Pests:* Usually no problems indoors.

*Phoenix roebelenii*

*Pilea cadierei*

*Pilea microphylla*

## PITTOSPORUM
(Pittosporaceae)

*Pittosporum tobira*—Japanese Pittosporum

Japanese pittosporum is another very versatile plant that can be grown indoors and outdoors in full sun or in deep shade. Pittosporum is a shrub with leathery, glossy, dark green, 2 to 4 inch leaves which are closely spaced and crowded together at the end of each branch. Pittosporum can be used as a low table plant or a small floor plant. It will have a spread as broad as it is high. One of the more unusual uses for Japanese pittosporum is as a pseudo-bonsai where the gray bark will contrast with the dark foliage, *P. tobira* 'Variegata,' a variegated species, is also available. It has irregularly defined cream white margins on grayish green leaves. Because of its wide tolerance range, pittosporum is recommended for beginners.

CULTURE—*Light:* Place in medium to high interior light locations. Although it will tolerate low light areas, it will not grow there. It can be placed in full sun locations.

### *Pilea microphylla*—Artillery Plant

Used as a house plant for decades, this delicate-looking, soft, herbaceous plant is called artillery plant because the pollen is forcefully expelled from the pollen sac leaving a cloud of pollen dust in the air. The bright green stem has small, opposite leaves, one ¼ inch, the other less than ⅛ inch. It can be used as a single potted specimen or in terrariums.

CULTURE—Similar to *P. cadierei* but humidity should be kept over 50%.

*Pittosporum tobira*

one side of flattish, basal, round leaves. In their native habitat, they grow on tree trunks and branches. Usually, commercially grown plants are produced on tree fern or cork slabs. The flat leaves are sterile but the horn-like leaves produce spores close to the leaf margins. The grayish green leaves reach a maximum length of about 3 feet. Staghorns can be used as hanging plants in north windows or other windows that are shaded.

CULTURE—*Light:* Place in medium to high light. Avoid locations with prolonged full sun as leaves will burn. *Temperature:* Normal home temperatures are acceptable. *Humidity:* Mist plant when relative humidity

*Temperature:* Normal home temperatures are acceptable. Pittosporum tolerates temperatures from 25° to 95°F. *Humidity:* Tender new growth may need misting during periods of low humidity. *Water:* Allow top surface of soil to become dry between waterings. *Fertilizer:* Use reduced rates every 4 to 5 weeks. *Soil and repotting:* Use soil mix number 1. Repot larger plants in the spring; smaller plants may be repotted as needed. *Pruning and grooming:* Pinch tips back to induce branching. Syringe foliage every 3 weeks to remove dust. *Propagation:* Stem cuttings or seed. *Pests:* Aphids, scales, and mites.

# PLATYCERIUM
## (Polypodiaceae)

*Platycerium bifurcatum—* Staghorn Fern

Staghorn ferns are rather fascinating plants with large antlerlike leaves emerging from

*Platycerium bifurcatum*

is below 15%. *Water:* Use warm water and soak the support the plant is growing on. Water twice a week in most locations. *Fertilizer:* Use reduced rates every 4 or 5 weeks. Apply to the support the fern is growing on. *Soil and repotting:* It does not need repotting, but it may need a new support with time. *Pruning and grooming:* Dried up basal leaves should remain on the plant. Hornlike foliage can be cut off when dried. Syringe foliage with tepid water only. *Propagation:* Cut off small plants called pups produced on other parts of the support. Small pups can be fastened to a porous support and new plants can be started. *Pests:* Under dry conditions, mites.

CULTURE—*Light:* Place in medium to high interior light. Adapts to shaded or full sun locations. *Temperature:* Normal home temperatures are acceptable but it tolerates temperatures from 25° to 95°F. *Humidity:* Usually there is no problem in the home. *Water:* Allow the top surface of the soil to dry between waterings. *Fertilizer:* Use reduced rates every 4 to 5 weeks. *Soil and repotting:* Use soil mix number 2. Repot older specimens in the spring, younger specimens as needed. *Pruning and grooming:* Pinch tip of young plants to induce branching. Prune or sheer plants to create desired shape. Syringe foliage to remove dust. *Propagation:* Seeds or cuttings. *Pests:* Usually no problem in homes.

# PODOCARPUS
(Podocarpaceae)

### *Podocarpus macrophyllus* 'Maki'—Podocarpus

Most people receiving a dishgarden or terrarium with a small podocarpus as a dominant feature do not realize this plant can grow to over 30 feet. The ¼ inch wide and 2 to 4 inch long, needlelike leaves are deep dark green on the older foliage and bright light green when young. Podocarpus adapts well to interior conditions and can be sheared, pruned, or trained as desired. It can be used as a pseudo-bonsai, a low table plant, a large floor plant, or a small window sill plant.

*Podocarpus macrophyllus 'Maki'*

*Polyscias fruticosa*

# POLYSCIAS
(Araliaceae)

*Polyscias fruticosa*—Ming Aralia

Ming aralia is one of the best plants for creating a pseudo-bonsai. As its common name suggests, the plant has a decided oriental appearance. The finely divided, lacy, compound leaves may be over 1 foot long and are attached to flexible, grayish-brown, twisted stems. Few indoor plants have the character that ming aralia does.

CULTURE—*Light:* Locate in medium to high interior light. Avoid prolonged full sun exposure. *Temperature:* Normal home temperatures are acceptable. Avoid locations where temperatures go below 50°F. *Humidity:* Use methods to increase humidity during periods of low relative humidity indoors. *Water:* Allow top surface of the soil to dry between waterings. Plants are subject to root rot if overwatered. *Fertilizer:* Use reduced rates every 4 to 5 weeks. *Soil and repotting:* Use soil mix number 2. Repot older specimens in the spring, younger specimens as needed. *Pruning and grooming:* Pinch growing tip when young to induce branching. Syringe foliage every 2 weeks. *Propagation:* Stem cuttings and air layers. *Pests:* Scales and mites.

# PTERIS
(Polypodiaceae)

*Pteris ensiformis* '**Victoriae**' —Victorian
Table Fern

As its common name suggests, table fern
was widely used during the Victorian era. Its
popularity has decreased since then as central
heating and the accompanying lower relative
humidity indoors have become universal.
However, given a little extra care,
Victorian table fern can enhance your
home with its silver and green fronds. The
6 to 14 inch fronds gradually bend as they
mature and arch gracefully over the sides
of the container. At infrequent intervals erect
spore-bearing fronds appear with the spores
arranged in rows next to the margin of
each leaflet. Victorian table fern is an
excellent fern for north window sills
with a humid microclimate. The silver
leaflets edged in green provide an
appealing focal point in a terrarium.

CULTURE—*Light:* Place in medium to
high interior light levels but avoid full sun
locations. *Temperature:* It tolerates normal
home temperatures. *Humidity:* Use
humidity-increasing methods to keep
humidity above 50%. *Water:* Allow soil
surface to dry between waterings; avoid
overwatering or underwatering. *Fertilizer:*
Use reduced rates every 5 to 6 weeks. *Soil
and repotting:* Use soil mix
number 2. Repot as
desired. *Pruning and
grooming:* Cut old
fronds off close to the soil
line to promote new
growth. Cut fronds
are excellent
for floral
arrangements.
*Propagation:*
Division or
spores. *Pests:*
Mites and
mealybugs.

Punica granatum nana

# PUNICA
(Punicaceae)

*Punica granatum nana*—Dwarf Pomegranate
Pomegranates have been grown by
gardeners for over 2,000 years in dry,
subtropical regions of the world. The dwarf
pomegranate may grow to 6 feet, but it is
usually much smaller indoors. The new stem
growth is square with a reddish cast bearing
opposite, glossy green leaves with a reddish
midrib. During the spring and early summer,
older specimens produce 1 inch scarlet
flowers at the end of terminal growth.
Flowering is followed by edible 2 inch,
orange-red fruit. An interesting
conversation plant, it can be trained to
produce an attractive pseudo-bonsai. The
larger cultivar, *P. granatum* can also be
grown indoors and trained as a bonsai.

CULTURE—*Light:* Locate in a window
with the greatest amount of sun. Growth and

Pteris ensiformis 'Victoriae'

179

flowering can be improved if plants are taken outdoors in the summer. *Temperature:* Normal home temperatures are acceptable. It will tolerate cold temperatures (28°F) but the plant will lose its leaves. *Humidity:* New growth should be misted during periods of low humidity. *Water:* Allow top surface of soil to dry between waterings. *Fertilizer:* Use reduced rates every 4 to 5 weeks. Use a minor element mix once a year. *Soil and repotting:* Use soil mix number 1. Repot older specimens once every 2 to 3 years in the spring. *Pruning and grooming:* Prune and train plant for desired effects. Pinch terminal shoots of young plants to induce branching.

Syringe leaves every 2 weeks. *Propagation:* Cuttings and seed. *Pests:* Scales are sometimes a problem.

# RHODODENDRON
## (Ericaceae)

### *Rhododendron* hybrids—Azaleas

Azaleas are usually bought or received as a flowering gift plant. They require constant care in the home to prevent leaf and bud drop. Provide a cool, bright location and use any convenient method to increase the relative humidity. Gift azaleas may require watering

Rhododendron hybrid

180

twice a day to prevent wilting. After the azalea has finished flowering, the indoor gardener has a choice: either discard the azalea (they can be planted outdoors in the southern United States) or accept the challenge of growing it and trying to have it flower next winter. To keep it, you should prune off some of the branches and remove dried flowers. Water as needed. After temperatures will not go below 30°F, the plants can be placed outside in a partial shade area. Bring the plant indoors before temperatures will go below 30°F. Place in a cool (45° to 55°F night temperatures), bright room until flowering begins. When flowering has begun, move the plant where you can enjoy the flower color.

CULTURE—*Light:* Place in a high interior light location; full sun indoors if temperatures are cool, otherwise diffuse sunlight. *Temperature:* Azaleas grow best in cool locations but they will tolerate normal home temperatures while flowering. *Humidity:* Keep humidity high for best growth. *Water:* Water as needed to keep soil moist; gift plants should be bottom watered or immersed. *Fertilizer:* Use reduced rates every 5 to 6 weeks. Use iron chelate if leaves begin to yellow. *Soil and repotting:* Use soil mix number 2. Repot after flowering. *Pruning and grooming:* Pinch new growth to increase branching. Syringe foliage as needed to remove dust. *Propagation:* Stem cuttings. *Pests:* Mites and aphids.

# SAINTPAULIA
## (Gesneriaceae)

**Saintpaulia hybrids**—African violets

Although African violets are the most popular indoor flowering plant, their cultural demands are rather exacting. Their popularity in spite of problems proves their value as indoor plants. African violets have been grown indoors for over 80 years. During that time period, several thousand cultivars have been developed. Generally they have a stemless rosette growth habit of thick, dark green, hairy leaves forming a mound 3 to 6

Saintpaulia hybrid

inches in height. Flower color depends on the cultivar and includes white, dark blue, violet, pink, and purple. Flowers may be single or double, usually with 2 to 6 flowers in a cluster. If you become interested in African violets, join the African Violet Society (See Appendix). African violets flower all year and while in flower can be used as decorator plants.

CULTURE—*Light:* Locate where they receive about 1,000 footcandles. A northeast window or shadowed east window is an excellent location. Avoid prolonged full sun locations. *Temperature:* African violets tolerate normal home temperatures. *Humidity:* Use methods to increase humidity. *Water:* Many growers use bottom watering to maintain a moist but not saturated soil. Use tepid water. *Fertilizer:* Use any of the special fertilizers for African violets which are on the market and use at recommended frequencies. Leach soil every 2 months if you use bottom watering. *Soil and repotting:* Use soil mix number 7. Repot in late spring. *Pruning and grooming:* Remove faded leaves. Use lukewarm water to wash dust off foliage as needed. *Propagation:* Division, leaf cuttings, or seed. *Pests:* Mites, mealybugs, and aphids.

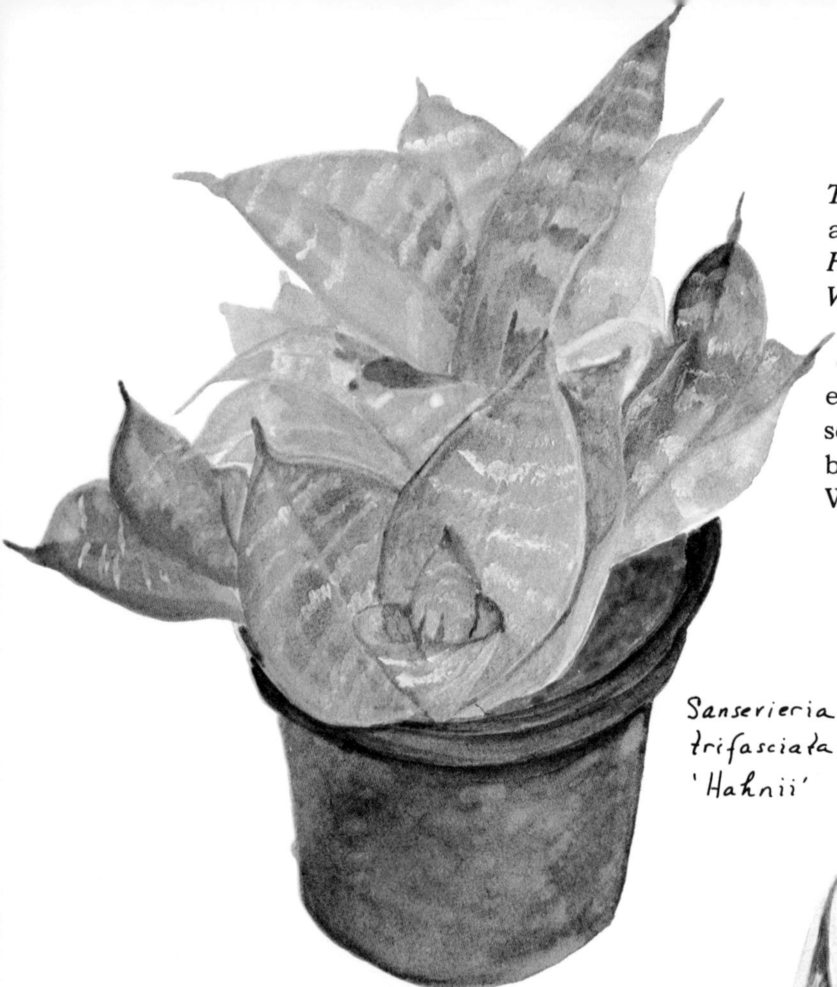

Sanserieria
trifasciata
'Hahnii'

*Temperature:* Normal home temperatures are acceptable; avoid locations below 50°F. *Humidity:* Grows well in low humidity areas. *Water:* Allow soil to dry between waterings. It will tolerate underwatering, but not overwatering. *Fertilizer:* Use reduced rates every 3 or 4 weeks. *Soil and repotting:* Use soil mix number 5. Repot when container becomes crowded. *Pruning and grooming:* Wash foliage occasionally. *Propagation:* Root

# SANSEVIERIA
## (Agavaceae)

Sansevierias are among the most durable of all indoor plants. They are essentially stemless plants with leaves emerging in an upright-growing rosette from a short, thick, underground rhizome. They tolerate a wide variety of soil types and light intensities, and are resistant to most pests. Although they tolerate tremendous neglect, even sansevierias can die from poor cultural care. Overwatering can induce root rot and sudden chilling to 45° to 50°F will cause dead areas on the leaf.

### Sansevieria trifasciata
**'Laurentii'** —Gold-banded Sansevieria

*Sansevieria trifasciata* 'Laurentii' is an erect-growing plant with gold-banded margins and sharp pointed leaves. New growth has silver and dark green horizontal bands which become less distinct with age. Mature foliage may be up to 4 feet in length.

CULTURE—*Light:* It can be grown in deep shade or full sun. Shade-acclimatized plants should not be placed in full sun.

Sansevieria
trifasciata
'Laurentii'

has 3 to 6 inch, silver and dark green horizontal banded leaves arranged in a rosette with the leaf bases forming a cup, similar to bromeliads. Once it reaches about 6 to 8 inches high, a new leaf rosette is produced from the thick underground rhizome.

CULTURE—Similar to S. *trifasciata* 'Laurentii' except that leaf cuttings can be used to propagate the plants. Do not keep water in the cup formed by the leaf bases.

### *Sansevieria trifasciata* 'Zeylanica'—Snake Plant

'Zeylanica' has erect swordlike leaves produced in clusters of 3 to 6 leaves from a horizontal rhizome. It is identical to S. *trifasciata* 'Laurentii' except that leaves lack the yellow leaf margin.

CULTURE—Similar to S. *trifasciata* 'Laurentii' except leaf cuttings can be used to propagate this plant.

# SCHLUMBERGERA
## (Cactaceae)

### *Schlumbergera truncata*— Christmas Cactus

Christmas cactus is a type of cactus which grows on tree trunks and branches with flattened, narrow stem sections with teeth

*Sanserieria trifasciata 'Zeylanica'*

divisions. Plant from leaf cuttings lose the yellow leaf margin. *Pests:* Seldom a problem.

### *Sansevieria trifasciata* 'Hahnii'—Birdsnest Sansevieria

Birdsnest sansevieria is a mutant form of S. *trifasciata* discovered in a nursery in 1939. It

*Schlumbergera truncata*

toward the end of each stem section. It needs short days to flower. Although it usually blooms sometime from Thanksgiving to Christmas, it can be brought into flower with 8 weeks of short days any time you desire. An easy-to-grow plant that tolerates considerable neglect, Christmas cactus makes an attractive basket plant with the light green stems cascading over the sides.

CULTURE—*Light:* Place in medium to high interior light intensities. Avoid full sun locations. *Temperature:* Normal home temperatures are acceptable. Avoid locations below 50°F. *Humidity:* Usually humidity causes no problems indoors. *Water:* Allow top surface of soil to become dry between waterings. *Fertilizer:* Use reduced rates every 4 to 5 weeks. Use a minor element fertilizer once a year. *Soil and repotting:* Use soil mix number 2. Repot mature specimens every 3 or 4 years. *Pruning and grooming:* Give the stems a shower occasionally to remove dust. *Propagation:* Stem cuttings. *Pests:* Mealybugs.

# SCINDAPSUS
## (Araceae)

*Scindapsus pictus*—Silver Pothos

The leaves are silver spotted and heart-shaped with one side larger than the other. Native to Indonesia where it may climb forty feet up a tree, Silver Pothos can be grown as a totem or grouped in a hanging basket. You can try this plant on a pedestal planter allowing the foliage to cascade over the sides.

CULTURE—*Light*: Locate in low to high interior light intensity. Avoid prolonged full sun locations. *Temperature*: Home temperatures (not below 50° F.) are acceptable. *Humidity*: Requires humid locations. *Water*: Let soil surface dry between waterings. *Fertilizer*: Use reduced rates every 5 to 6 weeks. *Soil and repotting*: Use soil mix number 2. Repot older specimens in spring. *Pruning and grooming*: Pinch younger plants to induce branching. Syringe leaves to remove dust. *Propagation*: Stem cuttings. *Pests*: Mites.

*Scindapsus pictus*

# SINNINGIA
## (Gesneriaceae)

*Sinningia speciosa*—Gloxinia

Gloxinias produce spectacular 3 to 6 inch, velvetlike flowers. Flower color varies with cultivars and colors include scarlet, violet, white, blue and white, red and white, and other shades. Flowers may be single or double, depending on the cultivar. Foliage somewhat resembles large African violet leaves but it is a lighter green. Plants may be bought in bloom at a florist or raised from dormant tubers. Dormant tubers usually can be started in 5 inch pots; larger tubers may require larger pots. The tuber should be planted right side up; the top of the tuber has a slight depression. When planting, leave the top portion of the tuber exposed. Water as needed to keep soil from drying out and keep temperatures between 70° to 80°F. After sprouting, move the plant to a bright area but not a full sun location.

CULTURE—*Light:* Locate plants where they receive about 1,000 footcandles. *Temperature:* Normal home temperatures are almost ideal. Avoid temperatures below 50°F. *Humidity:* Keep humidity above 50%.

*Water:* Use tepid water when watering plants. Allow soil surface to dry between waterings, but do not underwater. Gloxinias have fine roots which dry out easily. Stop watering when plant leaves wither after flowering. *Fertilizer:* Specialized fertilizers for African violets work well. Use at recommended or reduced rates. *Soil and repotting:* Tubers can be knocked out of the pot and stored at 55° to 65°F in sand that is kept slightly damp to prevent the tuber from shriveling, or the tuber can be left in its container and stored. Depending on cultivar, gloxinias need a 2 to 4 month dormancy period. *Pruning and grooming:* If tubers are knocked out of the pot, dried roots and leaves should be cleaned off the tubers. When the plants are actively growing, leaves should be syringed with warm water. *Propagation:* Seed, leaf cuttings, or stem cuttings. Seed takes at least 7 to 8 months in most homes to produce a flowering plant. *Pests:* Aphids.

Sinningia speciosa

185

# SOLEIROLIA
(Urticaceae)

**Soleirolia soleirolii** —Baby Tears

Baby tears is a charming plant with small, ¼ inch, thin, round, green leaves. The leaves are crowded so closely together that at a distance, the plant looks like moss. In its native Corsica, it forms low mats of greenery in moist areas. Baby tears is an excellent plant for terrariums, dishgardens, hanging baskets or ground cover plantings with other plants. It quickly forms a low growing mat about ½ inch high.

*Soleirolia soleirolii*

CULTURE—*Light:* Place in medium to high interior light. Avoid full sun locations. *Temperatures:* Normal home temperatures are acceptable. Avoid high temperature locations. *Humidity:* Keep relative humidity over 35% for best growth. *Water:* Soil should be kept moist but provide good drainage. *Fertilizer:* Use reduced rates once every 3 to 4 weeks. *Soil and repotting:* Use soil mix number 2. Repot when desired. *Pruning and*

*grooming:* Use tepid water to rinse foliage once every 2 weeks. *Propagation:* Divide mats of established plants. *Pests:* Normally no problems in the home.

# SPATHIPHYLLUM
(Araceae)

**Spathiphyllum 'Clevelandii'** —Peace Lily

Peace lilies have quilted, narrow, dark green leaves, 2 to 8 inches long. Complementing the graceful, flexed leaves is a striking inflorescence with a 4 to 6 inch wide spathe around a white flower spike. Both the spike and the spathe may turn green with maturity. Flowers remain attractive for extended time periods both on the plant and as cut flowers. An excellent plant for low

*Spathiphyllum 'Clevelandii'*

*Spathiphyllum 'Mauna Loa'*

*Soil and repotting:*
Use soil mix number 2. Repot as
needed to keep plant in balance with
container. *Pruning and grooming:* Trim
occasional brown leaf tips. Wash foliage
to remove dust as needed. *Propagation:*
By division. *Pests:* Aphids.

### Spathiphyllum 'Mauna Loa'

'Mauna Loa' is a hybrid with leaves similar
to S. 'Clevelandii' but the leaves are about half
as broad as they are long. It also has a larger
white spathe that may be up to 6 inches long.
The number of flowers is increased if the
plant is placed in higher light intensity areas.
If potted in a large container, 'Mauna loa'
may reach 24 inches. It does equally well in a
smaller container.

CULTURE—Similar to S. 'Clevelandii'.

light areas, it can be
moved about to bring life
and color to dark corners.

CULTURE—*Light:* Peace lily tolerates low
to high interior light. Avoid full sun locations.
If the light intensity is too low, the plant will
not flower. *Temperature:* Normal home
temperatures are acceptable. *Humidity:*
Increase indoor humidity during winter to
avoid occasional brown leaf tips. *Water:* Keep
soil surface moist, but avoid overwatering.

*Syngonium podophyllum*

# SYNGONIUM
## (Araceae)

### Syngonium podophyllum
—Nephthytis

Syngoniums are viny plants from tropical America that have arrow-shaped leaves when young. As the plant grows, the new leaves develop lobes, and mature plants may have up to nine lobes per leaf. Usually nephthytis is sold and used indoors with less than 5 sections because distinctive markings on the foliage tend to fade with maturity. It makes an excellent totem pole subject in low light areas and can also be trained to climb an indoor trellis. The two most common cultivars are 'Emerald Green' with all-green quilted leaves and 'Green Gold' with cream yellow markings over and radiating out from the midrib.

CULTURE—*Light:* Nephthytis tolerates low to high interior light. *Temperature:* Normal home temperatures are acceptable. Avoid temperatures below 50 °F. *Humidity*: Normal home humidities cause no problems. *Water*: Allow top surface of soil to dry out between waterings. *Fertilizer:* Use reduced rates every 2 or 3 weeks. *Soil and repotting:* Use soil mix number 2. Repot as needed to keep plant in balance with container. *Pruning and grooming:* Pinch growing tip to induce branching. Prune plant as needed to keep it in shape. Syringe foliage as needed to remove dust. *Propagation:* Stem cuttings. *Pests:* Mites can be a problem when humidity is low.

# TULIPA
(Liliaceae)

*Tulipa spp.*—Tulips

Tulips are another spring bulb that can be forced in pots for early bloom indoors. If you have purchased potted tulips from a bulb specialty company or from a florist, follow their instructions until plants are showing color. If you would like to prepare your own tulip pots for indoor bloom, follow the instructions for forcing spring flowering blubs indoors on page 131. Only the early tulips can be easily forced indoors; most bulb specialty companies will list tulip cultivars that are suitable for flowering indoors. Once tulips are forced, proper cultural care is needed to extend flower life and to keep the bulbs healthy for subsequent outdoor planting.

CULTURE—*Light:* Keep potted bulbs in the dark until buds are visible, then place in a bright indoor location. Full sun in a cool location is acceptable. *Temperature:* After forcing regime is completed, plants last longer if kept in cool (55° to 65°F) locations. *Humidity:* Locate where humidity is over 25%. Avoid drafty locations indoors. *Water:* Keep soil moist indoors. *Fertilizer:* None needed indoors. *Soil and repotting:* After flowering, plant in the garden or discard. *Pruning and grooming:* Trim dried foliage from plant prior to planting in the garden. *Propagation:* Bulblets on side of the bulb. *Pests:* Usually no problems in the home.

Vriesea x mariae

# VRIESEA
(Bromeliaceae)

Vrieseas are a group of epiphytic bromeliads whose smooth edged, flexible leaves are arranged so the leaf bases form a water-holding cup. Species are easily crossed and many hybrids have been introduced by plant breeders. Almost all vrieseas have beautiful inflorescences and many have attractive variegated foliage.

Tulipa spp.

189

*Vriesea x mariae* —Painted Feather

Once you have seen the plant in flower, you feel the common name should be "Spectacular Painted Feather." The inflorescence is a long erect stem with large, showy yellow bracts with orange-red bases. Although the yellow flowers are short-lived, the inflorescence stays colorful for months. Even when not in flower, the plant is interesting as the flexible green leaves have pink overtones. Painted feather makes a beautiful display plant when in flower.

CULTURE—*Light:* Painted feather needs high interior light intensity but avoid full sunlight. *Temperature:* Normal home temperatures are acceptable. Avoid temperatures below 55°F. *Humidity:* Keep in areas where humidity can be maintained above 25%. *Water:* Keep rosette cup filled with water. Allow top soil surface to dry between waterings. *Fertilizer:* Use reduced rates every 3 to 4 weeks. Apply to soil

*Vriesea splendens*

190

surface. *Soil and repotting:* Use soil mix number 3. Repot younger plants as needed. Remove and pot offsets when they are large enough to handle. *Pruning and grooming:* After flowering, remove dried and withered foliage. Spray plants to remove dust as needed. *Propagation:* Remove offsets. *Pests:* Scale and thrips.

### *Vriesea splendens* —Flaming Sword

Flaming sword is named for the flaming red bracts arranged in terminal clusters on top of a long flowering stem. Each yellow flower is short-lived but they appear over an extended time period and provide contrast to the red bracts. The green, flexible foliage is crossbanded with brown stripes. The combination of attractive foliage and a brilliant colored inflorescence make this a must for bromeliad growers.

CULTURE—Similar to *Vriesea x mariae.*

# VANILLA
## (Orchidaceae)

### *Vanilla planifolia* —Vanilla

Vanilla is a vining, climbing orchid whose curved fruit has been used to make vanilla extract for over 2,000 years. The plant bears alternate, thick, fleshy, light green, 4 to 9 inch leaves on a thick, succulent stem. Two inch axillary flowers may be formed any time of the year. Vanilla can be trained on a trellis or grown on a totem pole. It makes an interesting conversation piece.

CULTURE—*Light:* Vanilla needs high interior light. Avoid prolonged full sun locations. *Temperature:* Normal home temperatures are acceptable. *Humidity:* Locate where humidity can be maintained above 25%. *Water:* Allow top surface of soil to dry between waterings. *Fertilizer:* Use about ¼ ounce of a liquid 10-10-10 per gallon of water and fertilize once every 6 weeks if plants are growing in osmunda fern. *Soil and repotting:* Use soil mix number 3. Repot specimens every 2 or 3 years. *Propagation:* Stem sections. *Pests:* Scales.

*Vanilla planifolia*

# ZEBRINA
## (Commelinaceae)

*Zebrina pendula* —Wandering Jew

Wandering Jew is a trailing plant that has worldwide distribution in subtropical and tropical areas. The greenish-purple stem bears thick leaves with two broad silver bands on a deep green background and deep purple underneath. Wandering Jew grows rapidly and makes an excellent hanging basket. Cuttings can be grown in water for short time periods. Sometimes it is used as a ground cover in large planters.

CULTURE—*Light:* Zebrina pendula tolerates low to high interior light intensity. If light is too low, foliage color will fade. *Temperature:* Normal home temperatures are acceptable. *Humidity:* Usually indoor humidities create no problems. *Water:* Allow top surface of soil to become dry. *Fertilizer:* Use reduced rates every 4 to 5 weeks. *Soil and repotting:* Use soil mix number 2. Repot as needed; start new plants when older plants become unattractive. *Pruning and grooming:* Pinch young plants to induce branching. Plants grow fast and require some pruning to keep them in check. Syringe foliage to remove dust. *Propagation:* Stem cuttings. *Pests:* Mites can be a problem when the relative humidity is low.

*Zebrina pendula*

# SOILS AND REPOTTING

A healthy and vigorous root system is needed for a plant to produce attractive foliage or flowers. Unfortunately, because it is difficult to inspect a plant's root system, many indoor gardeners forget that roots supply the aboveground portion of the plant with water, nutrients, and other essential materials for continual growth. Too often the expression, "Out of sight, out of mind," sums up some indoor gardeners' lack of concern for their plant's roots. To grow and maintain attractive indoor plants requires an ability to create the best possible environment for your plant's roots.

In most homes, overall plant growing conditions are less than perfect but you can partially compensate for this by using a soil mix that provides favorable conditions for root growth. Although plants differ in specific soil mix requirements, there are certain qualities a soil mix should have. It should be able to:

(1) Hold water.
(2) Retain fertilizer in a form available to the plants.
(3) Be porous enough to allow adequate soil aeration.
(4) Support growth of favorable micro-organisms.
(5) Be free from diseases, insects, and other pests.
(6) Provide mechanical support for the plant.

These six criteria of a good soil mix are extremely important when growing plants in containers because the roots are confined within a container, and most water and plant nutrients required by the plant have to be obtained from a limited soil volume. Consequently, a plant in a container needs a different soil mix than when it is grown outdoors. Actually an indoor gardener needs to provide a soil mix that drains better and provides better aeration than the soils the plants would grow in satisfactorily outdoors. Soils in containers do not drain as well nor are they as well aerated as the same soils in a garden plot. In addition, soil mixes need to be free of insects, diseases, and other pests to insure the best possible growth. Growing conditions are not as favorable indoors as outdoors and plants need protection from naturally occurring pests that they can tolerate outdoors.

This explains why plants will thrive outdoors in certain soils but when containerized in that particular soil mix they do poorly. Few native soils are really suited for use in containers because of the resulting change in soil aeration and drainage.

Plants growing in containers obtain water and plant nutrients from a limited soil volume and require a different soil mix than plants growing in soil.

## Soil Mix Components

When it is time to repot your plants or to pot recently propagated plants you will want to prepare your own soil mix. Many materials are available, and if you understand their qualities, you will be able to select the best combination for your plants.

*Garden Loam:* Most soil mix recommendations for indoor plants include a good garden loam as a part of the mix. With the urbanization of America, good loam soils are not available to most indoor gardeners even in those portions of the United States where these soils occur. Even those of us who are fortunate to have access to good garden loam soils will have to use some amendments to make them more suitable for growing plants indoors. Soil properties can be improved with several materials which can be purchased at local garden centers and plant stores.

*Potting Soils:* Many companies prepare and offer pre-mixed potting soils for indoor plants. They provide an excellent substitute for garden loam soil for those of us who live in urban areas where garden loam soils are unavailable. However, most of these have too fine a texture and do not provide enough aeration and drainage when used as the only component in a soil mix. Some specially prepared soil mixes for cacti and African violets may be acceptable to use as they have been prepared. Read the label and check the ingredients against recommended mixes for a specific plant. What pre-mixed potting soil does offer is a clean, sterilized or pasteurized soil that can be used as one part of most soil mixes you may prepare.

*Peat:* Probably the most widely recommended soil mix component is peat. Peat is partially decomposed plant material formed underwater in bogs and marshes. Most peat sold in garden supply stores is from Canada, Europe, or Michigan. Usually compressed when packaged, one 6 cubic foot bag fluffs out to about 18 cubic feet. Peat has great water and nutrient holding capacity while still providing adequate drainage and aeration.

*Bark:* Ground softwood pine bark (¼ to ½ inch particles) is a good soil mix component. Bark increases aeration when used in a soil mix. It also has good water and fertilizer holding capacity. Decay and oxidation occur slowly and bark will last about two years when used in a soil mix.

*Perlite:* Perlite is an excellent soil mix component because it increases both aeration and water holding capacity. The grayish white particles are produced by heating volcanic rock to over 1,500°F and are completely sterile because of the manufacturing process. After processing, perlite is graded into different sizes with finer material used for seed germination mixes and the coarser grades for soil mixes.

*Vermiculite:* Vermiculite is an inorganic mix component formed by heating mica to over 1,000° F. The expanded plates are stacked together in small packets. They increase the ability of a soil mix to retain both water and fertilizer. The coarser grades of vermiculite are best for soil mixes, and the finer grades for seed germination mixes.

*Manures:* Although manures are recommended in some soil mix recipes, the quality is quite variable from source to source. Most manures are much better suited for outdoor use.

*Milled sphagnum moss:* This is ground sphagnum moss and is widely used for seed germination as it contains a natural fungal inhibitor which prevents damping off. It is recommended for use in soil mixes for germinating seeds.

*Sand:* The only type of sand to use in a soil mix is the coarse or sharp builder's sand which is composed of much larger grains than beach sand. Some plant stores stock sand; in other areas a concrete or construction supply company may have to be contacted to purchase large-grain sand. Sand is used to increase aeration and drainage in a soil mix. Since it does not retain nutrients, do not use more than 50% in any soil mix except for propagation purposes.

● Memo
Other soil mix components can be used if they satisfy the six criteria of a good soil mix. For instance use gravel in place of sand for coarse porous soil.

*Leafmold:* Bags of decomposed leaves, branches, and rotten tree trunks scraped from a forest soil are sometimes sold as leafmold. Although it is often mentioned as an excellent component for soil mixes, its consistency and quality tend to vary. Plant growth in soil mixes using large quantities of leafmold may be erratic. If you can locate a source that is uniform in quality, it is a good amendment. Some indoor gardeners make their own leafmold by collecting leaves in the fall and composting them.

*Osmunda fiber:* One of the more widely recommended materials for use in orchid soil mixes is shredded masses of osmunda fern roots. Osmunda fiber is sold in three grades. The fine grade is used for seedlings.

*Fir Bark:* Another recommended material for use in orchid soil mixes is shredded Colorado fir bark. This material is also available in three grades with the finest grades for seedlings and the coarsest for large plants.

*Wood Shavings:* Wood shavings can be used as an organic component in soil mixes but usually they break down fairly fast and the soil level shrinks in the container quite noticeably. The best wood shavings to use are cypress wood shavings which resist decomposition. Add about 6 ounces of a 16-4-8 fertilizer per half bushel of wood shavings to prevent nitrogen depletion.

## Potting Soil Fertilizers

Recommended soil mixes usually specify certain fertilizers which should be added to supply required plant nutrients. Excluding the nitrogen, phosphorus, and potassium fertilizers, the following potting soil fertilizers are added to the soil mix and supply enough nutrients for one to three years depending on the plant and the location. Most indoor plants are repotted within that time period and fresh nutrients are supplied then.

*Dolomite:* Ground dolomitic limestone supplies both magnesium and calcium when used in a soil mix. Usually it is recommended at 2.5 to 3.0 ounces (1/5 to 1/4 cup per half bushel of soil mix). It can be used at higher concentrations if needed to increase the pH of the soil mix.

*Bonemeal:* Bonemeal is available in two forms, steamed and raw. Both are finely ground bones, with raw bonemeal having about 3% to 4% nitrogen and 20% phosphoric acid. Steamed bonemeal has about half the nitrogen, but about the same phosphorus analysis. The phosphorus in bonemeal becomes available slowly over an extended time period and many indoor gardeners use bonemeal. It is usually recommended at ¾ ounce (1½ tablespoons) per half bushel of soil mix.

*Superphosphate:* Superphosphate is probably the most widely used material to supply phosphorus in soil mixes. It is available in

● Memo

If you use a liquid fertilizer on a regular schedule, there is no need to add nitrogen or potassium to your soil mix.

two forms, either 20% or 45% phosphoric acid (called Treble Superphosphate). Because of the manufacturing process, it also supplies sulfur. It is not recommended for soil mixes for dracaenas, cordylines, and marantas because its fluoride content causes tip burn. The recommended rate is about 1½ tablespoons (¾ ounce) per half bushel of soil mix.

*Sulfur:* Wettable sulfur is a very finely ground sulfur which is used to lower soil pH. See suggested rates in soil pH discussion.

*Iron Sulphate:* Iron sulphate is used both to acidify the soil and to supply iron and sulfur to the soil mix. Mix one tablespoon to a gallon of water and use to water plants, or add to a half bushel of soil mix.

*Minor Element Mix:* Different manufacturers supply minor element mixes in different formulations. They may be water soluble powders, concentrated liquids, or even impregnated glass beads. Use the recommended rate or less as overapplication of minor elements will kill a plant.

*Nitrogen, Phosphorus, and Potassium Sources:* A variety of formulations are available, but the nutrient requirements of most indoor plants will be met if you add 3 tablespoons of a dry 6-6-6 or 8-8-8 fertilizer per half bushel of soil mix. Supplemental fertilizer will not be needed for 3 to 4 months after repotting your plants. At least two different manufacturers produce slow release fertilizers which look like plastic BB's. About 2 ounces per half bushel will supply enough fertilizer for about 3 to 9 months depending on the fertilizer release ratio.

## Soil pH

Soil pH is a measure of the acidity (sourness) or alkalinity (sweetness) of a soil or a soil mix. A pH of 7 is neutral, neither acid nor alkaline. Acid soils have a pH below 7.0 and alkaline soils have a pH above 7.0. Soil pH is important because it controls the availability of nutrients in the soil. Most indoor plants grow best with a pH between 6.0 and 6.5. Some plants as azaleas and camellias require a more acid soil and the pH should be kept between 4.5 and 6.0. Container soil sometimes becomes alkaline over a period of time if hard water containing dissolved calcium and magnesium salts is used. If an acid forming fertilizer is used, it will counteract the alkaline water and keep the soil pH acid. Some garden stores and supply firms (see Appendix) sell pH paper that can be used to determine the approximate pH of your soil mix. Adjust soil pH to 6.5 with dolomite to prevent fluoride induced tip burn on cordylines, dracaenas, and marantas. The pH of a soil mix can be increased by using dolomite. If the soil pH needs to be lowered, wettable sulfur or iron sulphate can be used. Use the suggested rate in Table 1 to adjust soil pH.

● Memo

Soil pH is important because it controls the availability of certain fertilizers to plants. Iron and manganese are the best examples of fertilizers that are unavailable at a pH over 7.

197

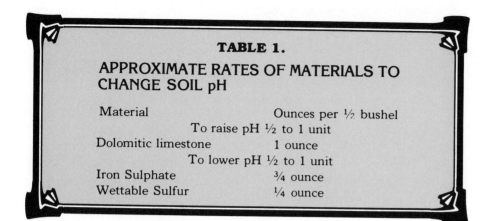

**TABLE 1.**

## APPROXIMATE RATES OF MATERIALS TO CHANGE SOIL pH

| Material | Ounces per ½ bushel |
|---|---|
| To raise pH ½ to 1 unit | |
| Dolomitic limestone | 1 ounce |
| To lower pH ½ to 1 unit | |
| Iron Sulphate | ¾ ounce |
| Wettable Sulfur | ¼ ounce |

# PREPARING SOIL MIXES

The easiest way to prepare soil mixes is to get all soil components together and select an appropriate mixing container. It may be a cardboard box, a large plastic wastepaper basket, or a bushel basket. The container should be large enough to make at least a half bushel at a time. If this is more than you need, the excess can be kept in a plastic bag. Soil mix recommendations are based on volume and not weight, so a garden trowel or a small shovel is ideal for most mixing operations. Scoop and add the quantities as suggested into the container. Continue until you have enough to take care of your required repotting. This should then be thoroughly mixed. If you have used garden soil or other unpasteurized mix components, the entire soil mix should be pasteurized. Pasteurization eliminates harmful organisms as weed seeds, nematodes, insect pests, and disease causing organisms, but does not kill all beneficial soil organisms. Sterilized soil has had all soil inhabiting organisms killed, and if a disease causing organism becomes established in the medium it has no biological competition and can spread extremely rapidly.

To pasteurize your soil mix, wet it throughly, put it in a covered roasting pan, and place it in an oven preheated to 200° F. Insert a meat thermometer into the center of the mix. When the middle of the mix has reached 175° to 180° F, bake for an additional half-hour. Do not let the temperature exceed 180° as the organic matter will burn at higher temperatures. Turn on the hood fan to dissipate objectionable odors. After ½ hour, remove the pan and uncover it. Allow the soil mix to cool and then store in a plastic bag (garbage can liner) so it will not dry out. Prior to pasteurization, superphosphate and dolomitic limestone can be added to the soil mix. Other fertilizer materials should not be added until after the soil mix has cooled.

● Memo

It is easier and safer to prepare large quantities of a soil mix than small quantities. And in the long run it takes less effort.

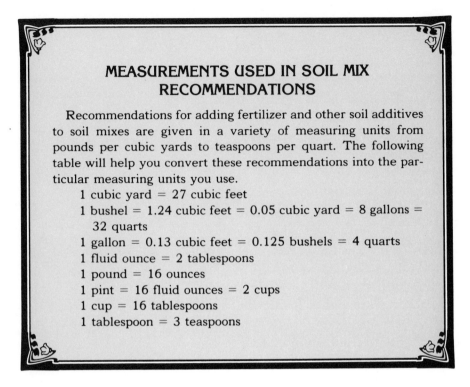

## MEASUREMENTS USED IN SOIL MIX RECOMMENDATIONS

Recommendations for adding fertilizer and other soil additives to soil mixes are given in a variety of measuring units from pounds per cubic yards to teaspoons per quart. The following table will help you convert these recommendations into the particular measuring units you use.

    1 cubic yard = 27 cubic feet
    1 bushel = 1.24 cubic feet = 0.05 cubic yard = 8 gallons = 32 quarts
    1 gallon = 0.13 cubic feet = 0.125 bushels = 4 quarts
    1 fluid ounce = 2 tablespoons
    1 pound = 16 ounces
    1 pint = 16 fluid ounces = 2 cups
    1 cup = 16 tablespoons
    1 tablespoon = 3 teaspoons

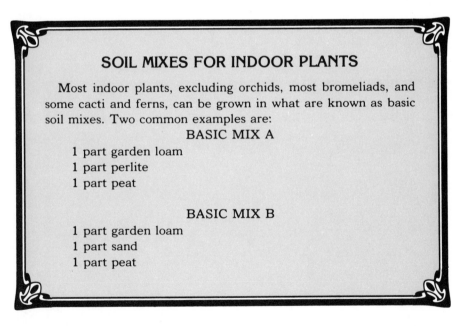

## SOIL MIXES FOR INDOOR PLANTS

Most indoor plants, excluding orchids, most bromeliads, and some cacti and ferns, can be grown in what are known as basic soil mixes. Two common examples are:

### BASIC MIX A

    1 part garden loam
    1 part perlite
    1 part peat

### BASIC MIX B

    1 part garden loam
    1 part sand
    1 part peat

● Memo
Store any excess soil mix in a container or plastic bag where it will not dry out. Dry soil mix is difficult to rewet.

If you have access to a good garden loam and are growing a variety of plants, these mixes will give satisfactory growth for most plants. However, you may live where it is not feasible to get a good garden soil. Many areas of the south and west have heavy clay soils with poor drainage and aeration properties, and some parts of the United States have sandy soils with poor physical and chemical properties. This problem can be solved by purchasing premixed potting soils from either a garden center or some other convenient retail outlet. Most of these potting mixes do not provide adequate drainage or aeration due to their fine texture, but they can be used as a substitute for good garden loam.

Although the basic mixes will grow a variety of indoor plants, growth can be improved by adding some nutrients to the soil mix which usually are not supplied by supplemental fertilization practices.

Each location in the United States has certain distinctive qualities and characteristics (light intensity, humidity, and water pH) which influence plant growth indoors. These influence what soil mix will work best in your area. Your cultural care practices also influence what soil mix will work best. If you like to water your plants frequently, a light, well-drained soil mix will give plant growth; however, if you water less often, a different soil mix will work best for you. Consequently any soil mix recommendation can only be considered as a starting point to determining what will make your plants grow best. Experiment with a number of different mixes and see in what soil mix your plants do best. Join a local garden club or plant society and find out what other gardeners are doing in your area.

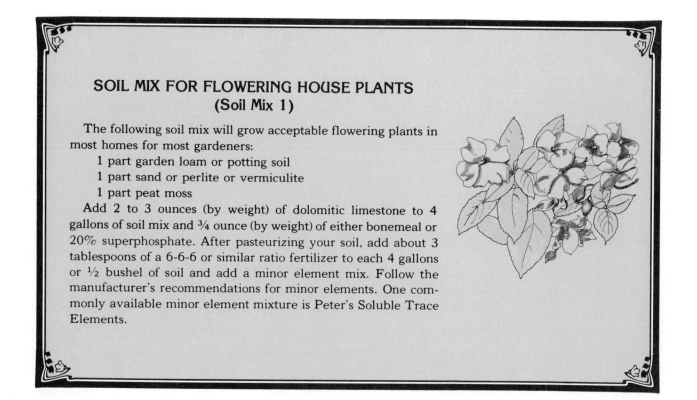

## SOIL MIX FOR FLOWERING HOUSE PLANTS
### (Soil Mix 1)

The following soil mix will grow acceptable flowering plants in most homes for most gardeners:

1 part garden loam or potting soil
1 part sand or perlite or vermiculite
1 part peat moss

Add 2 to 3 ounces (by weight) of dolomitic limestone to 4 gallons of soil mix and ¾ ounce (by weight) of either bonemeal or 20% superphosphate. After pasteurizing your soil, add about 3 tablespoons of a 6-6-6 or similar ratio fertilizer to each 4 gallons or ½ bushel of soil and add a minor element mix. Follow the manufacturer's recommendations for minor elements. One commonly available minor element mixture is Peter's Soluble Trace Elements.

## SOIL MIXES FOR FOLIAGE PLANTS
### (Soil Mix 2)

Although most foliage plants will grow satisfactorily in the soil mix recommended for flowering house plants, they will grow better if the soil mix contains a higher percentage of organic matter.

The following soil mix recommendations will provide a satisfactory potting soil for your foliage plants.

| | or | or |
|---|---|---|
| 1 part garden loam or potting soil | 1 part pine bark | 1 part sand |
| 1 part sand or vermiculite | 2 parts peat moss | 1 part pine bark |
| 2 parts peat moss | | 1 part peat moss |

Add 2 to 3 ounces (dry weight) of dolomitic limestone to 4 gallons (½ bushel) of soil mix. Some foliage plants (cordyline, dracaena, and marantas) suffer fluoride damage from fluorides in the water and the pH of the soil should be adjusted so it is no lower than 6.5. Superphosphate contains enough fluoride to cause foliar burn on sensitive plants. Research has not indicated whether or not bonemeal would cause fluoride damage.

After pasteurizing your soil, add 3 tablespoons of a 6-6-6 or other fertilizer ratio as 5-10-5 to each half bushel. Plastic coated fertilizers can also be used; most of them require about 2 ounces per half bushel. Add a minor element mix to the soil mix.

## SOIL MIXES FOR BROMELIADS
### (Soil Mix 3)

Bromeliads are plants from Central and South America which are either epiphytic (grow on tree branches or in crotches of trees) or terrestrial (grow in the ground). Although most of the bromeliads can be grown successfully in foliage plant mixes, most grow better in soil mixes recommended for bromeliads. Any mix for bromeliads must be well aerated and drained. The following mixes will produce good quality bromeliads.

| | or | or |
|---|---|---|
| 2 parts peat moss | | |
| 1 part perlite | 1 part peat | 1 part peat |
| 1 part fir bark | 1 part pine bark | 1 part pine bark |
| | | 1 part cypress shavings |

Add 2 ounces of dolomitic limestone to 4 gallons (½ bushel) of soil mix and a minor element mix. Dissolve 1 ounce of 10-10-10 water soluble fertilizer in 3 gallons of water. Use this solution after repotting and once a month to water the soil, and add a little to the water in the vase formed by the overlapping leaf bases.

## SOIL MIXES FOR ORCHIDS
### (Soil Mix 4)

Orchids have a great deal in common with bromeliads. They also grow as epiphytes on tree branches and in tree crotches and as terrestrials. A good soil mix for orchids should have excellent drainage and aeration. Some soil mixes that can be used are:

   3 parts osmunda tree fern fiber (moisten before using by
      soaking in water for 12 hours)
   1 part redwood bark
      or
   Tree fern slabs may also be used to grow epiphytic orchids.
      or
   5 parts fir bark
   1 part perlite

Add 1 ounce (dry weight) of dolomitic limestone per ½ bushel (4 gallons). Do not add fertilizer to the mix, but fertilize after the plants are potted. Use ¼ ounce of liquid 10-10-10 with minor elements per gallon of water and fertilize once every 6 weeks if the plants are growing in osmunda fern. If plants are growing in fir bark, use a liquid 30-10-10 with minor elements every 6 weeks instead of a 10-10-10.

## SOIL MIX FOR SUCCULENTS AND CACTI
### (Soil Mix 5)

Cacti and other succulents grow best in a well-drained and aerated soil. A good mix is:

   2 parts garden loam or potting soil
   2 parts sand
   2 parts peat
   1 part perlite (crushed charcoal can be substituted)

Add 2 ounces (dry weight) of dolomitic limestone to 4 gallons (½ bushel) of soil mix, 2 ounces (by weight) of bonemeal, and ½ ounce of superphosphate.

After pasteurizing your soil, add a minor element supplement. A water soluble fertilizer as Peter's Soluble Trace Elements can be used to effectively dispense the elements in the mix.

## SOIL MIX FOR FERNS
### (Soil Mix 6)

Ferns grow well in most recommended mixes with a high proportion of organic matter with good soil aeration and drainage characteristics. Consequently you could use any of the suggested foliage plant mixes. However, most ferns kept indoors grow better in the following mix:

1 part garden loam or potting soil
1 part peat moss
1 part pine bark
1 part coarse sand

Add 2 ounces (dry weight) of dolomitic limestone to 4 gallons (½ bushel) of soil mix and ½ ounce of either bonemeal or 20% superphosphate. After pastuerizing the soil mix, add minor elements to the mix. Use a dilute solution of Peter's Soluble Trace Elements and pour in the mix and stir well. Add 1 tablespoon of a 6-6-6 ratio or similar ratio to each half bushel of soil mix.

## SOIL MIX FOR AFRICAN VIOLETS
### (Soil Mix 7)

Any number of soil mixes for African violets exist and most of them will grow well-formed plants. African violets will grow in a variety of soil mixes that are well drained and aerated. Many African violet growers have found the following soil mix will produce excellent plants.

2 parts peat moss
1 part vermiculite
1 part perlite

Before pasteurizing the soil, add 2½ tablespoons of dolomite and 1½ tablespoons of 20% superphosphate to each half bushel. After pasteurization, add 3 tablespoons of a high phosphorus fertilizer as a 5-10-5 or similar ratio.

# Repotting

Repotting requires mastery of two indoor gardening skills: knowing when to repot and knowing how to repot. The best time to repot varies from plant to plant and decisions have to be made on an individual basis. Normally indoor plants do not require frequent repotting. The exceptions that prove the rule are recently propagated plants. They usually are potted in small containers to provide the best environment for rapid root growth, and may require repotting once a month for several months.

An established plant requires repotting when the plant has outgrown both its container and the amount of soil mix. An equilibrium exists between the volume of the soil mix in the container and the plant's requirement for water and nutrients. If you suspect a plant needs repotting, the easiest way to check is to knock the plant out of its container and check the plant's roots. If there is a solid mass of roots growing around the outside of the soil ball, the plant should be repotted.

You are probably wondering how often your plants should be checked to see if they need repotting. The answer is to let your plants tell you. There are certain clues or responses that you can use to guide you so you do not have to be continually checking the amount of root growth. Some reasons your plants may require repotting are: (1) The plant requires watering more than once a day. (2) Roots are growing out of the bottom of the drainage hole. (3) The plant has grown too large for its container and it is no longer in balance with the container. Most plants look best when they are no more than about 2 to 3 times taller than the diameter of the container. If a plant is growing in a 6-inch pot, it should be repotted if it exceeds 18 inches in height.

Soil mixes with a high proportion of organic matter oxidize and decay with time and the physical and chemical properties of the soil mixes change. Repotting is necessary to restore the desired soil environment for the roots.

Depending on these factors, repotting may be necessary every four months or only once every four years. Whatever the frequency, plants should be repotted when it least interferes with their natural growth pattern. Normally your plants become reestablished fastest if they are repotted when dormant but just before they start growing again. Therefore, most people suggest repotting in the spring, as the increased light intensities indoors and more favorable humidities stimulate a faster growth rate. Plants that grow slowly all year can be repotted when desired. Wait until indoor plants are through flowering before repotting.

Actual repotting is not difficult and I find it an enjoyable, relaxing experience. Probably the most difficult task is "knock-

Plants may be "knocked out" of their pots by tapping gently on a work bench, tabletop, or other firm object. Hold the soil ball and container as shown in the illustration.

A plant needs repotting if there is a solid mass of roots growing around the outside of the soil ball.

ing" the soil ball out of the container. First have the plant well watered so you lose as little soil as possible from the soil ball. To knock the soil ball out properly, place one hand over the top of the container and grasp the stem with the index and second finger. Turn the pot upside down, and tap the side of the container against a firm object. Usually the plant and soil ball will slide out. If the plant has been allowed to become "pot bound," it may be necessary to insert a wooden dowel in the drainage hole and push the soil ball out of the container. If it seems impossible to get the soil ball out of the container, the only solution is to break the container. Most containers for growing indoor plants are naturally sloped to aid in getting the soil ball out.

Usually when plants are repotted, a container that is one size larger will be more than adequate. Overpotting or using too large a container for the plant is not desirable as the excess soil volume stays moist for extended time periods and may create conditions favorable for root rot.

Once you have removed the soil ball and plant, you are ready to transfer it to a clean pot. If transferring to the same size pot, both the roots and tip should be pruned back to allow room for adding new soil and to maintain the root shoot ratio. Plants that have become "pot bound" should have the outer root mass cut off the root ball so that roots do not continue growing in a circular fashion.

Contrary to popular opinion, there is no reason to put pieces of broken clay pots or stones on the bottom of the container to improve drainage if the container has drainage holes. The only reason to use stones or pot pieces is to keep the soil mix from running through the drainage holes. If the soil has an adequate moisture level, there is no need to do this. The pieces of clay pots or stones only reduce the volume of the container. Add soil mix to the bottom of the container until enough height is reached so the transferred soil ball and plant is about ½ to 1 inch below the top of the pot lip. Then pack soil mix between the soil ball and the inside of the container, firming it with a wooden dowel or paint stick. When you are through packing the soil around the old soil ball, water the plant until the water drains through.

## Containers

Plants are amazingly adaptable and can be grown in a wide variety of containers. In fact, any shape or form and material you can imagine has probably been used by someone, sometime, to grow plants. Although a wide variety of containers are available for growing plants indoors, the easiest to obtain are the common pot sizes and shapes used by commercial nurseries. Clay pots are

A plant should be "in balance." The top plant is too small for its container, while the bottom plant is too tall. The middle plant is "in balance" with its container.

**205**

manufactured in standardized sizes and shapes. Pot size is designated by the top diameter of the container and may range from 2 inches to 10 inches or more. Certain names are applied to pots based on the relationship of height to top diameter. Standard pots are as high as wide, azalea pots are ¾ as high as wide, and bulb pots are ½ as high as wide. Orchid pots are basically azalea pots with slotted drainage holes extending from the bottom of the container up halfway to the rim. This is done to provide excellent drainage and aeration for orchid roots.

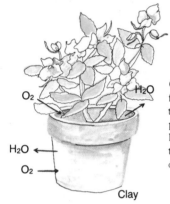

Clay allows water to evaporate from the side wall and oxygen to enter the soil mix. However, plants growing in clay pots have to be watered more often than plants in plastic, ceramic, or metal containers.

Clay

Plastic

The most common container for years was the clay pot, but in the past decade plastic pots have become widely used. Although most of the controversy over whether plastic or clay pots are better has been resolved, some indoor gardeners still are not sure which type of container to use.

Clay pots have several advantages for growing indoor plants which should be seriously considered. They are porous, allowing air to slowly diffuse through the sides of the container. Water also evaporates from the container walls, and plants in clay pots need to be watered more often than plants in glazed or plastic pots. Commercial growers prefer plastic pots to clay because of the weight difference which reduces transportation charges. In the home, however, the added weight of a clay pot is an advantage as plants are less likely to tip over. However, not everything is perfect, and clay containers will build up an accumulation of salts on the outside of the container, and the natural looking red color will be overlayed with a thin, white layer. In greenhouses these salts provide an excellent medium in which algae will grow, but in most homes it is too dry for algae growth. Used clay pots should always be soaked to remove soluble salts and scrubbed clean before being used again. As a general precaution against diseases, dip used pots for 30 minutes in a solution of 1 part bleach to 9 parts water after cleaning, and then dip in clean rinse water. This procedure should be followed for all your pots if you have had any problems with root rotting diseases.

Although I prefer the natural red tones of clay pots, some indoor gardeners paint them to match their decor. Most oil based paints will work well but the painting should be done and allowed to dry before using. Painting clay pots destroys the porosity of the clay, and they then have characteristics similar to plastic, metal, or glazed pots. If you are using this type of pot, be sure the soil mixes used are well drained and the plants are not overwatered. If you water your plants more than necessary, an unpainted, unglazed pot is ideal. However, if you prefer to water once or twice a week, plastic or glazed pots will suit your needs much better.

Although plastic pots come in a variety of colors and clay pots can be painted various colors, some indoor gardeners prefer containers which are more ornamental. Glazed pots are available in many shapes, colors, and designs. Remember that the container should complement the plant and not distract from it. When buying decorative containers, generally it is better to buy containers with muted designs for foliage plants and solid colored ones for plants which flower continuously. The easiest solution in using ornamental containers is to slip an already potted plant inside. If you plan to set clay or plastic pots inside decorative pots, make sure the container is bigger than the pot in which your plant is growing. Measure the height and width of the pot and make sure the pot will fit completely inside the decorative one. It is better to have the decorative container a bit too large than to have the clay pot you are trying to hide destroy the visual effect by revealing its rim over the edge of the decorative container. Provide for drainage as discussed in the watering section. This same procedure can be used when putting plants in metal containers or anything else that seems appropriate. If the plants are potted directly into glazed or metal containers, there is always a possibility of breaking or damaging the containers when repotting.

The latest addition to container variety is the hanging basket. They are made of many materials such as glazed pottery, metal, plastic, and wood. You can also buy decorative hooks in almost any style and of various materials as wrought iron, brass, and copper. The baskets can be suspended from hooks on macrame cords, chains, or braided ropes. Interesting window treatments can be developed by using materials which complement your decor.

Finding suitable containers for large plants can sometimes be difficult but more and more plant stores and garden centers are stocking large wooden tubs which work well with many interior decors. No matter what type of container is used, be sure you provide good drainage and that you protect your carpets and floors with an impervious catch basin.

● Memo

The smaller the container, the more often an indoor plant should be repotted. The larger the container, the less often is repotting required. Some indoor trees in a sufficiently large container will grow well for five years or longer without repotting.

# PROPAGATING INDOOR PLANTS

Horticulturally, plant propagation can be defined as increasing the number of plants from existing ones. Most indoor gardeners do not realize the true implications of that statement. With but a few exceptions, you can have three, four, or as many plants as you want by propagating your own. The ability to propagate plants is a skill that not all indoor gardeners have, and there is real satisfaction in being able to say that you have produced a certain plant in your collection.

Plants are propagated by two methods, sexual and asexual. Space prevents a revealing account of a plant's sex life, but the end result is one to several thousands of seeds depending upon the plant, and growing plants from seeds is known as sexual propagation. Asexual propagation involves using a vegetative part of the plant as a leaf, stem, or root to produce a new plant. Both methods possess advantages and disadvantages.

## Seed

Viable seed production indoors requires good growing conditions, and many indoor plants will produce seed only in the ideal conditions obtained in a greenhouse. For most indoor gardeners, it is easier to purchase seed from a reputable dealer than to prepare seed from one's own plants. Do not order seeds unless you intend to germinate them shortly after you receive them because many indoor plant seeds lose their ability to germinate within a short time period. African violets, begonias, coleus, gloxinias, palms, podocarpus, schefflera, and other indoor plants can be grown from seed.

Seeds have been germinated in all kinds of containers, but the most practical are shallow, flat containers not much deeper than 3 to 4 inches. Bulb pots, flat plastic trays, and wooden flats are used by many indoor gardeners. Small pots can be used for single large seeds. Whatever container is used, it should have good drainage.

A good soil mix is essential for successful seed germination. Seeds can be germinated successfully in a number of different mixes that are well drained and disease- and insect-free. Materials suitable for use include peat, perlite, vermiculite, coarse sand, milled sphagnum moss, and potting soils. Results with garden soils are usually not as successful because drainage and aeration properties are not favorable. If you are not sure that the mix is disease- and insect-free, the soil mix should be pasteurized. (See page 198.) If you have trouble with the soil mix flowing through the drainage holes, use a thin layer of peat moss over the bottom of the container. After pasteurizing and cooling the selected soil mix, fill the container about ½ to ¾ inch from the top. (I prefer using a mixture of 1 part peat moss and 1 part perlite.) Seeds may be planted in rows or sprinkled over the surface of the soil. Small seeds do not need to be covered, but larger seeds should have a thin layer of soil mix placed over them. If you plant small seeds, use an atomizer to rewet the soil surface. With larger seeds, a soda bottle fitted with a sprinkler cap works well.

After seeding, the container can be covered with glass or newspaper, or slipped inside a plastic bag.

Containers can be covered with glass or newspaper or slipped inside a plastic bag. As most seeds germinate best between 65° to 75° F, almost any indoor location can be used. When you see leaves emerging from the soil, remove the cover and locate the container in a bright light area, but avoid full sun locations. After the first set of leaves has fully expanded and the second set of leaves is beginning to unfold, the plants can be transplanted to small 2½ to 3 inch containers.

Seed propagation has advantages when you are attempting to produce a number of plants and do not mind any variability which may occur among the seedlings. However, if you want a duplicate of the original, most indoor plants have to be propagated by asexual or vegetative means.

## Division

A number of methods can be used to propagate indoor plants vegetatively but the easiest method is division. Plants which grow with creeping rhizomes, produce basal stems, or form clumps or tubers, can be propagated by division. The method is particularly successful because the divisions have either stored food or partially established root systems. Normally division is accomplished by removing the plant and its attached soil ball from the container and dividing the clump of plants into smaller groups or into individual plants. To survive, a division needs a viable

Seedlings can be transplanted after the first set of leaves has fully expanded and the second set of leaves is beginning to unfold. Use a small trowel or similar tool to remove the seedling to prevent root damage.

When propagating plants by division, make sure that each unit has functional roots and leaves.

root system attached to functioning leaves. If dividing flowering plants, wait until flowering has stopped. Plants that grow from bulbs or tubers form small additional bulbs or tubers which can be separated every couple of years. Clump or cluster palms as areca and bamboo palms can be propagated by division.

## Air Layering

Air layering is a method used to propagate plants while they are still attached to the parent plant. This method allows you to produce plants 6 to 8 inches tall with several large leaves because the parent plant provides nutrients and water during root formation.

Most indoor gardeners use this method for plants that have lost their lower leaves and are no longer attractive, but it can be used for plants that root extremely slowly from cuttings or plants that will not produce roots by any other method. Aglaonemas, dieffenbachias, crotons, ficus, and philodendron are just a few plants that may be propagated by air layers.

Two different procedures are used to produce air layers. The most common method uses a 45° upward or downward cut about halfway through the stem. Select actively growing stems that are between ¼ and 1 inch in diameter and make your cut 6 to 8 inches from the terminal. After making the cut, insert a wooden matchstick or toothpick in the cut to keep the surfaces apart to prevent the stem tissue from healing. The other method that can be used is called girdling. Girdling involves removing a ¾ inch ring of bark completely around the stem. After the bark ring has been removed, the fresh wood should be scraped with a knife to remove any plant tissue that would form new conductive tissue and prevent rooting. This method is usually more reliable but it is not as widely used as making a diagonal cut. For faster root formation, apply a rooting hormone to the cut or ringed area. Then place a large handful of moist sphagnum moss around the cut. Before using the sphagnum moss soak it in water and squeeze the excess water out by hand. Although the size of the moss ball will vary with the particular plant, it should be about 6 times as long as the diameter of the plant stem and ⅔ as wide as long. The moss ball can be wrapped with plastic film or aluminum foil which should be at least 2 inches larger than the moss ball. Cup the aluminum foil around the moss ball to hold the sphagnum moss in place. A moss ball wrapped with plastic film may need to be held in place with string. Commercial growers use aluminum foil for air layers because the young roots burn when plastic film is used in full sun locations. After wrapping a moss ball, seal it as completely as possible to prevent water loss. Check periodically to see if the moss ball is still moist; if it has started to dry, add water. If the moss dries out during rooting, the recently formed roots will die back. Air layering is not for the impatient indoor gardener as it may take 2 to 3 months for the root system to be large enough to support the mature, large leaves on the cuttings. When you can see that the roots have penetrated the moss ball, it is time to cut the rooted air layer from the parent plant. Make your cut below the new root system, being careful not to disturb the new roots. Pot the layered cutting immediately in the recommended soil mix. If the layered cutting has a number of large leaves, it may need special treatment to prevent wilting until the root system is able to supply the water requirements of the plant. Misting or other humidity increasing measures may be necessary for the first two weeks. Occasionally, more drastic measures may be needed to prevent wilting and one or two of the lower leaves should be removed.

In most instances the portion of the plant remaining after an air layer is made will be a leafless cane or woody stalk. You can either wait and let new growth emerge or you can make stem cuttings of dieffenbachias, aglaonemas, and similar plants. (See stem cuttings, page 213 ).

## Suckers and Offshoots

Several indoor plants produce either suckers or offshoots and these can be used to produce another generation of plants. Suckers are new plants which arise from roots below the soil level next to the parent plant. These can be removed with a sharp knife. Cut them as close as possible to the parent plant. Usually they do not have a viable root system, but initiate one within several weeks after removal from the parent plant. Some bromeliads and aloes produce suckers.

Offshoots are lateral growths that develop from the basal part of the stem. Haworthias and bromeliads are some of the plants that

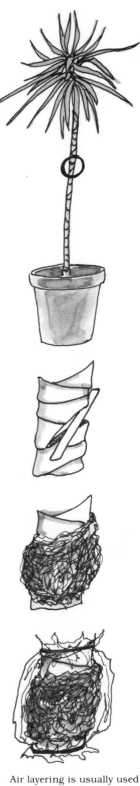

Air layering is usually used for plants that have lost their lower leaves:
(1) After making a diagonal cut through the stem, insert a small wooden stick to keep cut open.
(2) Wrap cut with sphagnum moss.
(3) Cover moss with aluminum foil or plastic film.

211

can be propagated by offshoots. Usually offshoots have started to form roots while still attached to the parent plant. Remove offshoots and pot them in the recommended soil mix. Recently potted offshoots and suckers should be located in an area of reduced light intensity for about 2 to 3 weeks before transferring to recommended light levels. During this period, the relative humidity should be kept over 60%. An easy way to do this is to place the recently potted plants in a small plastic bag with the top propped open. Spray the plants as needed to prevent wilting.

## Runners

Small plants produced at the end of specialized stems called runners can be used to propagate some indoor plants. These specialized stems develop from leaf axils at the base of the plants. Some common indoor plants propagated by runners are spider plants, flame violets, Boston ferns, and fluffy ruffles. Small pots filled with a suitable soil mix can be placed close to the parent plant. The young plantlets at the end of the aerial stem can be pegged down with a paper clip until the plant has rooted, usually within two weeks. Then cut the stem and you have a new plant.

If the plantlet at the end of the runner has already initiated a root system, the plantlet can be cut off before planting.

Suckers are new plants which arise from below the soil level next to the parent plant. Offshoots are lateral shoots that develop from the basal part of the stem.

## Cuttings

Although division, suckers, offshoots, and runners are easy methods of propagation, most house plants usually are propagated by cuttings. Several different types of cuttings are used; these include tip, stem, and leaf cuttings.

You will be more successful with cuttings from plants that are growing in your home. Cuttings taken from plants growing in low light areas or other areas where the plants are under stress will not root well because cuttings use stored food to initiate new roots.

### TIP CUTTINGS

Tip or terminal cuttings are cuttings that include a growing tip from the main shoot or one of the branches. The best length for tip cuttings is usually between 4 and 6 inches. Cuttings this size will usually contain the recommended minimum of two nodes. Best results are obtained when cuttings are taken from plants that are actively growing. Cut between two nodes (where the leaves emerge) when making the cutting. After removal, trim the cutting to ¼ inch below the bottom node, making a 45° angle cut.

Small plants produced at the end of specialized stems called runners can be used to propagate some indoor plants. The young plants can be pegged down in a small pot. After a new root system has formed, cut the connection between the plants.

Use a razor blade when working with herbaceous plants as aglaonemas, geraniums, peperomias. You may need to use a pruning shears on woody plants like camellia and ficus. Have your propagation facilities ready before taking cuttings so they will not wilt before propagation. If you are taking cuttings from a friend's plant, a plastic bag with a moist paper towel inside will keep the cuttings turgid. Basal leaves should be stripped off the cuttings so the stem can be placed about 1½ to 2 inches into the propagation medium. If taking a number of cuttings, place them so the leaves do not overlap each other by more than a third.

## STEM CUTTINGS

Stem cuttings always include some portion of a plant's stem. It may be a short stem section with one or two attached leaves called a single- or double-eye cutting, or a leafless stem cutting of plants as dumb cane and corn plant which are sometimes called cane cuttings.

*Single- or double-eye cuttings.* Single-eye cuttings are short stem sections with one leaf. The bud in the leaf axil is the part of the plant that will grow and produce a new plant. Double-eye cuttings have two leaves on the stem section. They usually grow a little faster because of the additional stored food in the longer stem section. Vining herbaceous plants as philodendrons and hoyas are usually propagated with single- or double-eye cuttings. Stem sections should be about 2 inches long for single-eye cuttings and about 3 inches long for double-eye cuttings. Insert the cuttings into the propagating medium until the bud is just slightly below the soil surface.

*Cane cuttings.* A number of indoor plants can be propagated by cutting the stem into sections. This method is called cane propagation because the stem sections used are leafless. Plants that can be propagated in this fashion are aglaonemas, cordylines, dieffenbachias, and some dracaenas. Aglaonemas and dieffenbachias can be propagated from cane sections having at least one bud per section. These stem sections should be laid horizontally in the propagation medium and just barely covered with soil. *Dracaena fragrans* should be propagated from stem sections at least one foot long. The sections should be placed vertically in the propagation medium. Six to twelve inch stem sections of cordyline and *Dracaena deremensis* 'Warneckii' can be placed vertically or horizontally in the propagation medium. Horizontal cane may produce more than one plant, whereas vertical cane will produce a single new plant.

Basal leaves should be stripped off the cuttings so they can be placed about 1½ to 2 inches into the propagation medium. A plastic bag placed around a pot makes a good propagation area for tip or terminal cuttings.

Cut between two nodes when making a stem cutting, and then trim the cutting to ¼ inch below the bottom node, making a 45° angle cut. In all three instances cuttings should be planted: (a) double-eye and depth cuttings; (b) single-eye and depth cuttings; (c) leaf petiole and depth cuttings.

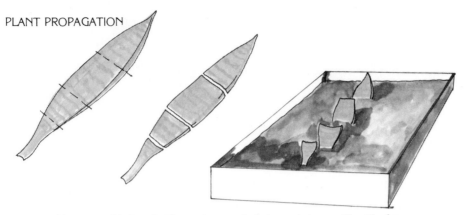

Use a razor blade or knife to cut sansevieria leaves into equal lengths for propagation purposes. Always insert the bottom of each section into the propagation medium.

## LEAF CUTTINGS

Some indoor plants can be propagated by using just one leaf from the plant. This provides a convenient way to produce new plants without ruining the appearance of the parent plant. Types of leaf cuttings include leaf-petiole, whole leaves without petioles, and leaf section cuttings. Variegated plants usually cannot be propagated by this method since the variegation will not be present in the young plants.

*Leaf-petiole cuttings and leaves without petioles.* Plants propagated by leaf-petiole cuttings usually have a fleshy leaf or petiole which contains enough stored food to start a new plant. Select healthy leaves on vigorous growth so rooting will occur faster. Diseased leaves will usually rot before producing new plants. Use a sharp knife or razor blade to remove the leaf. Trim the petiole so not much more than about 1½ inch is left. Insert the cutting into the propagation medium deep enough to support the leaf. New plants will be formed at the base of the petiole. Peperomia, hoya, begonia, kalanchoe, and African violets are a few of the plants that can be propagated by leaf cuttings. If the leaf does not have a petiole, new plants will be formed at the base of the leaf.

*Leaf sections.* Some plants will produce new plants from just a section of the leaf. Sansevieria is one of the best known examples of plants propagated by this method. A 12 inch leaf will yield 4 to 6 cuttings as each piece should be 2 to 3 inches long. Remember that each section of the leaf has a top and a bottom. Insert the bottom of each leaf section into the propagation medium.

Rex begonias can also be propagated from leaf sections. Cut the leaves into triangular-shaped pieces with each piece having a major vein. The pieces should be cut so the point of the triangle is the part closest to the parent plant. The point should be inserted into the propagation medium. The major vein should divide the triangle in two, and start at the tip end that is inserted into the soil.

Be careful not to injure newly formed roots when potting recently propagated cuttings.

Lay stem sections or cane cuttings horizontally in the propagation medium and barely cover for best growth.

214

# Germinating Fern Spores

Some of the more common indoor ferns (staghorn, Boston, fluffy ruffle) are propagated by division or runners. However, most true ferns can also be propagated by spores. Ferns are ancient plants, and coexisted with the dinosaurs. They evolved before seed plants and have a different method of sexual reproduction. Spores are usually formed on the underside of the leaf in either symmetrically arranged brown dots or in brown furry patches (staghorn fern is a good example). Spore bearing fronds should be cut off and allowed to dry for a few days. Then the spores can be shaken on a piece of white paper. As soon as they are collected, spores should be sprinkled on the surface of milled sphagnum moss in a well-drained container. Cover the top of the container with a piece of glass or clear plastic and place in a north window or other area where the light intensity is high enough to grow ferns. Use an atomizer and distilled or deionized water to mist the soil surface to keep the germinating spores from drying out. Always use a pasteurized soil mix for germinating spores as damping off can be a problem. Germinating spores should be maintained at temperatures between 70° and 80°F. In about a month or so the soil surface should be covered with small, green, heart-shaped structures that will produce young ferns. These heart-shaped structures are called prothallia. They need to be kept moist as a film of water is needed for fertilization to occur and to produce young ferns. The young ferns can be transplanted when they are 1 to 2 inches tall. Transplanting time depends on the fern species and may vary from 3 to 18 months. Most indoor gardeners have better success when several small ferns are transplanted together.

Rex begonias can be propagated from triangular shaped leaf sections. Insert the point of the triangle which was the part closest to the parent plant.

# Rooting Your Cuttings

Before taking cuttings, the indoor gardener should prepare a container using his or her preferred propagating mix. This will avoid unnecessary delays which may result in wilted cuttings.

Cuttings can be rooted in a wide variety of materials. Probably the most common method for beginning gardeners is a glass of water with the cuttings supported by their leaves or stems. Not all cuttings root satisfactorily in water, and the root systems formed in water are brittle and require an adjustment period when transferred to a potting mix before they can absorb adequate amounts of water to keep the foliage from wilting. Try rooting cuttings using other methods and see which you prefer. Use rooting hormones to shorten the length of time it takes to produce roots.

Spores are usually found on the underside of fern leaves either in symmetrically arranged brown dots or brown furry patches.

215

Although builder's sand, perlite, sphagnum peat, and vermiculite are satisfactory media for rooting cuttings, the best material seems to be a mixture of equal parts perlite and sphagnum peat. Amend this with 3 to 4 tablespoons of dolomite per half bushel of mix for best rooting. Strict sanitation is necessary if rotting of cuttings is to be avoided. If you are not sure that the propagating mix is disease- and pest-free, it should be pasteurized. (See instructions on page 198).

The type of container you will use will depend on the number of cuttings you are propagating and what is available in your home. Indoor gardeners have been successful using containers with or without drainage. The propagating mix should be kept moist but never be saturated with water. You can use quart or half gallon milk cartons, plastic gallon jugs with the tops cut off, clay bulb pans, plastic bags, regular clay pots, or any similar container. Whatever system you decide to use, there are several things to remember for your plants to root in the least amount of time. Since the cuttings do not have a root system to absorb water, the surrounding air should be humid to prevent wilting. Occasional mistings with an atomizer will be necessary to keep most cuttings from wilting. Place unrooted cuttings in an area with high light intensity, but avoid locations where full sun could burn the foliage. Temperatures should be kept between 65° and 80°F for best results.

Remember when placing plants in the propagating mix to space them so they can be removed without disturbing the root systems of the other cuttings. Usually they should be at least 1½ inches apart.

The question most commonly asked when propagating plants is, "How long before the cuttings will root?" This depends on the plant type and a whole host of other factors, but most indoor plants will have enough of a root system so they can be repotted in three to four weeks. Some plants may take up to 10 weeks before the roots are long enough for repotting. The cuttings should have roots almost one inch long before removing from the propagating mix. If you are really impatient, wait at least two weeks and gently remove one or more of the cuttings to see how long the young roots are. Once roots have been initiated, the number of mistings can be reduced to start adjusting the plant to the conditions in your home. Pot rooted cuttings at the same depth that they were placed in the propagating container, using a recommended soil mix. After you have potted your rooted cuttings, treat them the same way you would any newly purchased plant. (See directions on page 36).

Young ferns are produced from structures called prothallia. These young ferns can be transplanted when 1 to 2 inches tall.

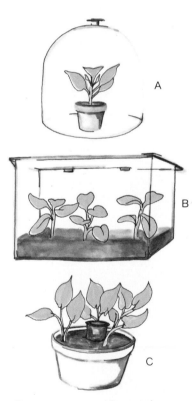

Common types of containers used to propagate cuttings: (a) a pot filled with selected propagation media and covered with a cake keeper may be used; (b) aquariums work well as propagating units because the top cover keeps the humidity high; (c) the pot within a pot method—to help keep the propagating media moist, the small inner plugged pot is filled with water.

# SPECIALIZED USES OF INDOOR PLANTS

Although many indoor plants are grown or used on window sills, they can be used to enhance our interior decor in other ways with only slightly more effort. Through the century and a half that plants have been used in interiors, a number of unusual or distinctive methods have been developed to display indoor plants. They can be arranged together to suggest tropical rain-forests or desert scenes in dishgardens or terrariums. Plants in containers can be hung from the ceiling or wall and the foliage and flowers allowed to cascade gracefully over the sides. Individual plants will grow into unusual forms or shapes by pruning and directing their growth to create plants that resemble ancient bonsai. Windows can become effective display areas with minor modifications. Any indoor area that receives adequate light can become an indoor garden spot.

## Hanging Baskets

A hanging basket is any container which can be suspended from a support and holds living plants. Their current popularity in our urban environment reflects their origin in the congested early middle eastern civilizations. Because they can be hung from a support, they convert space not used for other purposes into effective plant display areas. Being suspended in mid-air, people can easily observe the plant's flowers or foliage.

The basket may be a wooden box, moss-lined wire basket, ceramic container, plastic pot, or any other container suitable for plants suspended from a support. Hanging baskets can be used as transition plants between the outside and inside landscaping themes.

Almost all plants can be grown in hanging baskets, but cascading or trailing types and plants with colorful flowers or foliage look best. Table 1 on page 219 lists a number of indoor plants to use in hanging baskets. Choose plants for your hanging basket according to the size of the container and the light intensity where you will place the hanging basket. Aesthetically and culturally, it is better to have only one plant type in small hanging baskets. A mixture of plants can be used in large hanging baskets, but they should have the same cultural requirements so the basket will look attractive for the longest period of time. If you feel a certain area needs a hanging basket for aesthetic purposes but the light intensity is below recommended levels, you can have two baskets—one that you maintain in proper light intensity and one that is put on display. Rotate plants every two or three weeks to keep the plants healthy.

Although hanging baskets are very versatile, there are certain considerations which limit their use. Plants in hanging baskets normally use more water than plants in ground level containers because of the increased air movement. Hanging baskets in warm windy locations may require watering more than once a day. Most people find they have greater success with hanging baskets if they are located where they are easy to water, and in locations where they will not be overlooked when you water your plants. If plants are placed in a hard to reach location, a watering device is available that consists of a flexible plastic reservoir which is squeezed to force water through an extended tube with a curved ending.

Watering hanging baskets often presents a problem because no provisions have been made for the drainage water. Many containers that are aesthetically designed for use as hanging baskets need special handling to prevent the drainage water from ruining carpets and furniture or creating safety hazards if the water puddles on steps or walkways. Ingenious indoor gardeners have devised several methods to minimize these problems. One simple method is to detach the hanging baskets and water them where the drainage water will not create any problem. Another solution is to fabricate some sort of drainage facility that will catch and hold the excess water. Often this is difficult to do both aesthetically and functionally. The easiest solution is to use containers with a built-in shallow water collecting reservoir to catch the excess water. Some hanging baskets are constructed so the reservoir water covers the drainage holes. Fill the bottom of that container type with broken crocks or gravel to prevent the soil from being saturated after you water your plants.

When locating hanging baskets, a common mistake is putting

Use hanging baskets to effectively display your plants.

Two methods of providing drainage for hanging baskets.

them directly in the pedestrian traffic patterns where you, your family or guests may unexpectedly encounter them.

Hanging baskets are deceptively heavy when filled with moist soil and an abundance of plant material. The supports, whether they are brackets, hooks, masonry anchors or hollow wall anchors, must be strong enough to support the weight of the basket, soil, and plants. Nothing is more disheartening than discovering a smashed container with soil and plants scattered all over the floor. One other problem that some indoor gardeners have experienced with hanging baskets is that the ropes used to support hanging baskets rot and break if they become moist when the containers are watered. A simple solution to retain the decorative effect of the ropes is to reinforce them with clear nylon fishing line of the appropriate strength.

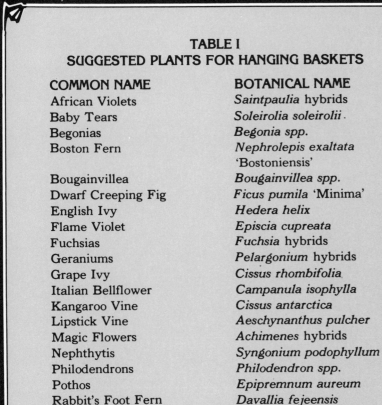

### TABLE I
### SUGGESTED PLANTS FOR HANGING BASKETS

| COMMON NAME | BOTANICAL NAME |
|---|---|
| African Violets | *Saintpaulia* hybrids |
| Baby Tears | *Soleirolia soleirolii* |
| Begonias | *Begonia spp.* |
| Boston Fern | *Nephrolepis exaltata* 'Bostoniensis' |
| Bougainvillea | *Bougainvillea spp.* |
| Dwarf Creeping Fig | *Ficus pumila* 'Minima' |
| English Ivy | *Hedera helix* |
| Flame Violet | *Episcia cupreata* |
| Fuchsias | *Fuchsia* hybrids |
| Geraniums | *Pelargonium* hybrids |
| Grape Ivy | *Cissus rhombifolia* |
| Italian Bellflower | *Campanula isophylla* |
| Kangaroo Vine | *Cissus antarctica* |
| Lipstick Vine | *Aeschynanthus pulcher* |
| Magic Flowers | *Achimenes* hybrids |
| Nephthytis | *Syngonium podophyllum* |
| Philodendrons | *Philodendron spp.* |
| Pothos | *Epipremnum aureum* |
| Rabbit's Foot Fern | *Davallia fejeensis* |
| Spider Plant | *Chlorophytum comosum* |
| Wandering Jew | *Zebrina pendula* |
| Wax Plant | *Hoya carnosa* 'Variegata' |

● Memo

Special wall mounts and wire clips permit almost any container 6″ or less in diameter to be converted to a hanging basket.

# Terrariums

If you have ever wanted to create your own miniature world, terrariums provide an excellent opportunity to allow your abilities free expression. Terrariums are miniature duplications of gardens or natural settings enclosed in glass or other transparent material. The enclosed container provides an opportunity to maintain high relative humidities and reduce drying drafts to a minimum. These conditions are ideal for many plants that otherwise could not be grown indoors.

Terrariums are another idea for using indoor plants that has come to us from the Victorian era. A British surgeon, Nathaniel Ward, discovered that plants would grow in an enclosed container. This gave him the idea to develop glass containers which he called Wardian cases to transport plants. His discovery was not only put to use to protect fragile plants transported from far corners of the world during trips back to England but also to display plants in Victorian drawing rooms. The past few years has seen a resurgence in terrariums of all shapes and sizes from round glass globes to large brandy glasses, square plastic cubes, large carboys and converted aquariums.

A well-planned terrarium can provide hours of enjoyment and last for a year or longer with simple care. There is more to making a terrarium than putting soil in a container and plants in the soil. Selecting the right container to use for a terrarium is the first decision you need to make. Choose a container that will be functional and look attractive where you intend to use it. However, do not select containers made of strongly colored glass because this will reduce the light plants receive. If you decide that you want to use a small bottle or a large vessel such as a carboy, remember that the larger the opening, the easier it will be to put the plants in the bottle.

After deciding what container to use, you have a basis for selecting what plant material to use. Choose plants that are in scale with the containers; small plants for small containers, large plants for large containers. Not all small plants stay small, so select plants that will not outgrow the terrarium in a short period. Plants selected should have similar light, water, and humidity requirements. For covered terrariums select plants that either prefer or tolerate high humidities. Plants that require a little more air circulation should be planted in round glass globes, brandy snifters, or other open terrariums.

Suggestions for plants to use in terrariums are listed in Table 2. Some of the slower growing woody plants as coffee and podocarpus will require an occasional pruning to keep them from outgrowing the terrarium. Mixing plants with different water, light,

Terrariums provide ideal growing conditions for many plants and require a minimum of maintenance.

Terrarium container designs are numerous.

fertilizer, and temperature requirements will shorten the aesthetic life of your terrarium. Always use disease and insect free plants to ensure your terrarium remains attractive for as long as possible. Plant selection will also depend on what you intend to use for a focal point in your terrarium. The terrarium focal point can be either a small figurine or a colorful plant. Most terrariums look best with only one dominant feature.

## TABLE 2
## SUGGESTED PLANTS FOR TERRARIUMS

| COMMON NAME | BOTANICAL NAME |
|---|---|
| African Violets | *Saintpaulia* hybrids |
| Aglaonema | *Aglaonema spp.* |
| Aluminum Plant | *Pilea cadierei* |
| Artillery Plant | *Pilea microphylla* |
| Baby Rubber Tree | *Peperomia obtusifolia* |
| Baby Tears | *Soleirolia soleirolii* |
| Caladium | *Caladium spp.* |
| Coffee | *Coffea arabica* |
| Dwarf Rose Stripe Star | *Cryptanthus bivittatus* 'Minor' |
| Emerald Ripple | *Peperomia caperata* |
| Flame Violet | *Episcia spp.* |
| Gold Dust Dracaena | *Dracaena surculosa* 'Florida Beauty' |
| Fluffy Ruffles | *Nephrolepis exaltata* 'Fluffy Ruffles' |
| Impatiens | *Impatiens wallerana* 'Variegata' |
| Natal Plum (Bonsai, Boxwood Beauty) | *Carissa grandiflora* |
| Nephthytis | *Syngonium podophyllum* |
| Parlor Palm | *Chamaedorea elegans* |
| Peacock Plant | *Calathea makoyana* |
| Podocarpus | *Podocarpus macrophyllus* |
| Prayer Plant | *Maranta leuconeura kerchoviana* |
| Rex Begonia | *Begonia sp.* |
| Red-nerved Fittonia | *Fittonia verschaffeltii* |
| Silver-nerved Fittonia | *Fittonia verschaffeltii argyroneura* |
| Victorian Table Fern | *Pteris ensiformis* 'Victoriae' |
| Wax Begonia | *Begonia semperflorens* |

Use a soil mix recommended for the plants you are using. If you mix a small quantity of soil, add about ½ teaspoon of a 10-10-10 and 2 teaspoons of dolomite for every 2 quarts of soil mix. Always pasteurize the soil to eliminate possible diseases and insects from your terrarium.

If you are making a terrarium in a bottle, you will need a few tools to successfully complete your planting. A long flat stick with

A few simple tools make terrarium building much easier.

221

an old teaspoon fastened on the end is useful for digging planting holes. Attach a short piece of heavy wire shaped like a hook to a long stick to place the plants in the bottle. Soil can be added with a paper funnel to prevent the soil from sticking to the bottle's sides.

Once you have mixed your soil, selected your container and plants, you are ready to build your terrarium. As most terrariums do not have drainage facilities, put a layer of pea-sized gravel in the bottom to act as a water reservoir. A general rule of thumb that many indoor gardeners have found useful is to use about ¼ inch of gravel for every inch of soil in the container. After leveling the gravel, add soil so the total volume of soil and gravel is about one quarter the container height. Before placing the plants in the terrarium, create your own miniature landscape. If the terrarium will be viewed mainly from one side, slope the soil to suggest a more natural scene. Terrariums that will be viewed from all sides usually look best if the soil is mounded in the center. Once you have formed the soil, decide where you want the plants to be installed. Then spoon out planting holes and install your plants. Sometimes when planting a narrow-mouthed bottle, some root pruning may be necessary to get the plant inside the bottle. Up to ½ of the root system may be removed without seriously harming the plant. The humid environment in the bottle garden will help keep the plant from wilting while new roots are forming. After placement in the planting hole, firm the soil around the plant's roots.

It is better to underplant than overplant as plants grow faster in the humid environment than most indoor gardeners anticipate. Make sure you have the plants established at the same depth as they were when growing in pots.

Usually when you are through planting, the sides of the container are streaked with soil. Wash this off by gently spraying with water. Rinse any soil off the plant foliage and put on the cover. The water used to clean the container and foliage usually adds enough water for plant growth. A covered terrarium is a closed system, and water transpired by the plant condenses on the container sides and returns to the soil. Additional watering may not be needed for six months or longer. Overwatering a terrarium may cause root rot, and the death of your plants. Water your terrarium only when the soil surface has dried.

After completing the terrarium, select a location compatible with the light requirements of the plants you have used. Never place a terrarium in full sun as the heat trapped inside the container will kill your plants. In most locations, terrariums will have to be turned frequently as the plants will grow toward the direction of the strongest light source.

• Memo

If you like ferns but you can't grow them properly try growing them in a terrarium. Usually the higher humidity in a terrarium will result in lush green growth.

Terrariums require a minimum of maintenance after planting, but remove dead leaves and prune overgrown plants so they remain in balance with the other plants. If the sides of the container become fogged, take the cover off for an hour or so. Do not be discouraged if your terrarium lasts only a few months, as it takes patience, practice, and perseverance to develop the indoor gardening skills to keep a terrarium growing for a year or longer.

If you are interested in crafts as well as plants, you may wish to investigate the use of sandcraft in your terrarium. Layering various colors of sand in a glass vessel creates patterns and pictures for the planting medium. Supplies are sold separately or in kits at many craft stores. After creating a sand design, you can plant your terrarium. Most sand terrariums look best when planted with a single specimen since the container design created by the colored sand is the focal point. Water carefully, perhaps with an eyedropper, so the sand design does not shift. Usually cacti and succulents are most compatible with the design and suggested watering practices.

## Dish Gardens

The term dish garden is applied to any grouping of small plants in an open shallow container. Basically there are two different types of dish gardens. One suggests a miniature landscape, and may be quite detailed with small figurines, ponds, rocks, and even miniature buildings. The other type is a combination of indoor plants which complement or contrast with each other. Most commercially prepared dish gardens are of this second type. Unfortunately, some of them are grossly overplanted, and will look attractive for only a few months. Dish gardens planted with just a few plants are easier to maintain and will be pleasing for a much longer time.

No matter what type of dish garden you decide to make, select plants with similar cultural requirements and for the light intensity of the location where the dish garden will be displayed. Many indoor gardeners prepare a sketch of their dish gardens to help in selecting plants. This gives them a better idea of how the plants and design will look once the dish garden is completed.

When considering what plants to use in your dish garden, do not overlook the cacti or succulents. You can make an interesting miniature desert scene in a large clay saucer with only a few cacti and small rocks, miniature pottery, or a ceramic donkey. Tropical scenes can be suggested with foliage plants and small palms; woodland scenes can be achieved with small woody plants. In many ways making a dish garden is similar to painting with living plants. Some plants that can be used in dish gardens are listed in Table 3.

Dish gardens can be very simple, with only one plant, very detailed with many plants, or of intermediate complexity.

223

Although any shallow container 3 inches or deeper can be used for a dish garden, the container should complement the plants to be used. For most dish gardens, a solid colored container seems best.

| TABLE 3 SUGGESTED PLANTS FOR DISH GARDENS | |
|---|---|
| COMMON NAME | BOTANICAL NAME |
| Aglaonemas | *Aglaonema spp.* |
| Aluminum Plant | *Pilea cadierei* |
| Ardisia | *Ardisia crenata* |
| Baby Doll | *Cordyline terminalis* |
| Birdnest Sansevieria | *Sansevieria trifasciata* 'Hahnii' |
| Bishop's Cap | *Astrophytum myriostigma* |
| Coffee Plant | *Coffea arabica* |
| Coleus | *Coleus blumei* |
| Dwarf Crown-of-Thorns | *Euphorbia milii splendens* |
| Dwarf Rose Strip Star | *Cryptanthus bivittatus* 'Minor' |
| Dwarf Creeping Fig | *Ficus pumila* 'Minima' |
| Emerald Ripple | *Peperomia caperata* |
| Exotica Perfection | *Dieffenbachia* 'Exotica Perfection' |
| Fiddle-Leaf Philodendron | *Philodendron bipennifolium* |
| Florida Beauty | *Dracaena surculosa* 'Florida Beauty' |
| Grape Ivy | *Cissus rhombifolia* |
| Gold-banded Sansevieria | *Sansevieria trifasciata* 'Laurentii' |
| Heart-leaf Philodendron | *Philodendron scandens oxycardium* |
| Jade Plant | *Crassula argentea* |
| Little Zebra Plant | *Haworthia subfasciata* |
| Miniature Agave | *Dyckia brevifolia* |
| Miniature Birdsnest | *Nidularium innocentii nana* |
| Nephthytis | *Syngonium podophyllum* |
| Parlor Palm | *Chamaedorea elegans* |
| Podocarpus | *Podocarpus macrophyllus* |
| Pothos | *Epipremnum aureum* |
| Rex Begonia | *Begonia x rex cultorum* |
| Rudolph Roehrs | *Diffenbachia maculata* 'Rudolph Roehrs' |
| Ribbon Plant | *Dracaena sanderana* |
| Schefflera | *Brassaia actinophylla* |
| Snake Plant | *Sansevieria trifasciata* 'Zeylanica' |
| Wax Plant | *Hoya spp.* |
| Weeping Fig | *Ficus benjamina* |

● Memo

Add small figurines or other ceramic pieces to your dish garden to enhance its aesthetic appeal.

Containers used for dish gardens usually do not have drainage holes and a half-inch or so of pea-size gravel is placed in the bottom of the container to act as a water reservoir. Use a soil mix recommended for the plants you select and partially fill the dish garden. Knock the plants out of their containers and position them in their intended locations. Add the rest of the soil mix to fill the dish garden about ¼ inch below the rim. Be sure the plants are planted no deeper than they were originally growing. If you are using rooted cuttings keep the roots spread apart. After all plants are in place, firm the soil around each plant and add enough soil to finish the plantings. If desired, slope or mound the soil slightly to suggest a natural landscape. Water the soil after planting. As dish gardens usually have no drainage holes any excess water should be drained by tilting the container on its side. Reread suggestions on page 40. Maintain your dish garden as you would any other indoor plant, following the suggested cultural practices found in the plant description section. Inspect your plants once a week for insect pests as insects spread rather quickly from plant to plant when they are grouped together.

Remember your dish garden is portable and can be used temporarily as a centerpiece or for other decorative purposes. However, the plants must receive adequate light to remain attractive. With proper care, many dish gardens last for 6 months or longer.

## Totems

Many indoor plants are climbing vines in their native habitat and produce aerial roots which cling to tree trunks providing support as the plants grow up the tree trunk. You can imitate nature in your home by placing a bark slab, a tree fern log, or a sphagnum moss wire log in a container and planting a climbing vine next to the support. Plants grown in this way are called totems. Indoor plants usually grown as small table plants can be converted to large floor plants by this method. Some plants suitable for this purpose are listed in Table 4 on page 226. Young plants make the best subjects for totems as they cling to the support as they grow. Use rooted cuttings, or recently potted plants in 3 or 4 inch containers. Determine the light intensity and other environmental factors of the location where you intend to use your totem and select plants that will grow under those conditions.

When building a totem, assemble all the materials you will need to complete it, including the container, plants, and the support. Select a container that is balanced with the height of your support, not your plants. A 6 inch pot for a 10 to 20 inch support, an 8 inch pot for a 20 to 30 inch support, a 10 inch pot for a 30 to 40 inch support, and a 12 inch pot for a 40 to 50 inch support. A large container is needed for aesthetic purposes and to provide

Many tropical foliage plants grow naturally as vines, climbing trees or other supports. A bark slab or moss-filled wire pole provides similar support in your home.

225

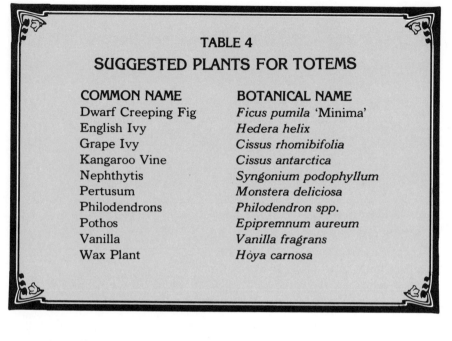

### TABLE 4
### SUGGESTED PLANTS FOR TOTEMS

| COMMON NAME | BOTANICAL NAME |
| --- | --- |
| Dwarf Creeping Fig | *Ficus pumila* 'Minima' |
| English Ivy | *Hedera helix* |
| Grape Ivy | *Cissus rhomibifolia* |
| Kangaroo Vine | *Cissus antarctica* |
| Nephthytis | *Syngonium podophyllum* |
| Pertusum | *Monstera deliciosa* |
| Philodendrons | *Philodendron spp.* |
| Pothos | *Epipremnum aureum* |
| Vanilla | *Vanilla fragrans* |
| Wax Plant | *Hoya carnosa* |

enough soil volume to maintain the plants when they have reached the top of the support. If you can not obtain a bark slab or tree fern log of the appropriate height, make a support from ¼ inch hardware cloth, filled with sphagnum moss (see illustration at right). Place the support for the vine in the container in an upright position. The support may be positioned either to one side of the container or placed in the middle depending on whether plants will be planted on one side, or on both sides of the support. Cover the bottom of the container with 2 to 4 inches of the recommended soil type for your plant. Hold the support and pack the soil mix firmly around it with your hands or a wooden dowel. Then place the plants in the container and firm the soil gently around the roots. Always be careful to set the plants at the same depth they were originally growing. Finish adding soil, leaving enough space between the top of the container and the soil surface to act as a water reservoir. Several methods are used to fasten the vines to the totem pole. On bark slabs or tree fern logs use plastic coated wire or string, on sphagnum moss filled wire logs use hairpins or staples at 6-inch intervals. As the plants grow, aerial roots fasten themselves to the totem pole and no additional support is necessary. Maintain the plants as suggested in the plant description section. If cultural conditions are favorable, each new leaf on the vine will usually be a little larger when it fully expands than the leaf just beneath it. When the plants have grown to the top of the totem pole, you can either cut the growing tip off to induce additional branching or bend the vine and weave the new growth into the older foliage.

After securing totem support, fill with sphagnum moss, secure to container and attach vine with staples or hairpins.

Bonsai is an ancient practice of dwarfing trees and other woody plants so they can be grown in small containers. Started by the Chinese, bonsai has been developed to its highest form by the Japanese. Special practices are used to keep the plants small and to maintain an ancient appearance. Some bonsai in Japan are reported to be more than 100 years old, but most specimens are less than 50 years old. Traditional bonsai plants are meant to be grown outdoors and are only brought inside for brief display periods.

Bonsai are especially appealing because of their ruggedness and appearance of antiquity. Similar effects can be created with a number of indoor plants that develop a woody trunk. The name that seems most appropriate for these plants is pseudo or false bonsai. Some indoor plants that develop character and can be used for pseudo-bonsai are listed in Table 5.

● Memo
Sometimes misshappen or stunted plants can be selected from a greenhouse or plant store; they will only need a little pruning or training to convert them into a pseudo-bonsai plant.

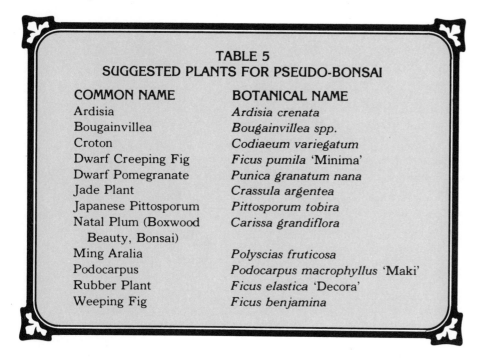

### TABLE 5
### SUGGESTED PLANTS FOR PSEUDO-BONSAI

| COMMON NAME | BOTANICAL NAME |
|---|---|
| Ardisia | *Ardisia crenata* |
| Bougainvillea | *Bougainvillea spp.* |
| Croton | *Codiaeum variegatum* |
| Dwarf Creeping Fig | *Ficus pumila* 'Minima' |
| Dwarf Pomegranate | *Punica granatum nana* |
| Jade Plant | *Crassula argentea* |
| Japanese Pittosporum | *Pittosporum tobira* |
| Natal Plum (Boxwood Beauty, Bonsai) | *Carissa grandiflora* |
| Ming Aralia | *Polyscias fruticosa* |
| Podocarpus | *Podocarpus macrophyllus* 'Maki' |
| Rubber Plant | *Ficus elastica* 'Decora' |
| Weeping Fig | *Ficus benjamina* |

Some plants may take several years to develop enough character to be displayed as a pseudo-bonsai, others as the ming aralia look ancient and gnarled in less than 2 years.

Jade plant is an excellent plant for pseudo-bonsai as it requires a minimum of pruning and training to resemble a miniature tree. Once a plant reaches the desired height and spread, maintain these by root and shoot pruning. Roots should be pruned once a year when plants are repotted. The same size container should be used when repotting. Select a decorative container that complements or contrasts the pseudo-bonsai to make the most effective display. Maintain favorable cultural conditions for plant health and appearance. If this method of growing indoor plants appeals to you, there are several books devoted to bonsai. (See Appendix.) You may also want to join the Bonsai Clubs International for the very latest information.

# Decorating with Indoor Plants

One of the pleasures of growing indoor plants is using them to enhance your interior decor. The natural green tones of plants will complement almost all interior designs, but by choosing plants with various color hues you can accent your color scheme. A room done in browns and tans will seem more interesting if plants with bright yellow color are used as *Dracaena surculosa*. The vibrant reds in many of the bromeliads and begonias will enliven a modern room done in black and white. If blue is your favorite color, African violets will accent your room.

Color can also be added by selecting appropriate colored containers. Clay pots can be painted with enamel paint (latex will not adhere) to match room colors. You can purchase ceramic pots in almost any style or color to cover your clay pots. Hanging baskets can be color-keyed to your decor by choosing from the wide selection of macrame cords. These can be bought already made or you can create your own following the designs in craft books.

An aesthetic arrangement of plants makes a room pleasant and inviting.

In addition to adding color to your room, plants can provide a textural balance. A room with smooth surfaces gains texture from an emerald ripple peperomia. If your living room is formal and elegant with satin drapes and a velvet couch, add the delicate accent of a Victorian table fern. Carry out the ruggedness of ranch or country style family room with plantings of cacti. Normally a grouping of cacti looks better than a single large specimen. Several potted specimens can be grouped together in one area of the room and balanced with a cacti dish garden planting in another area. Redwood planters can be used in a rustic setting.

To carry out your decor in the kitchen, get extra saucers for your dish set and place your potted plants on them. Small plants in clay pots can be slipped inside decorative mugs. For larger plants, you might choose an earthenware bean pot or a copper teakettle for an outer container. One of my wife's favorite kitchen plants is a grape ivy growing in a ceramic tea canister in which I drilled drainage holes.

Furniture designers are aware of the widespread use of indoor plants, and you can purchase furniture built to accommodate plants. Dry sinks with a copper-lined well can be placed in a dining room or living room. The storage area can be used for dishes, a stereo system, or a liquor cabinet while the top is a miniature garden. Artificial light manufacturers have progressed from making the early chrome and enamel trays for plants to **etageres, book cases, and tables. Coffee and end tables are designed as terrariums where you can arrange a complete miniature woodland or rain forest scene. Pole supports are available which hold plants in a spiral arrangement. A colorful and attractive plant display can be devised for any room in your home by selecting from the wide variety of prebuilt or self-constructed items. An unusual and attractive plant display I saw was an old folding stepladder painted to match the room. Each step held a plant and on top was a trailing ivy.**

Plants can also be used to accent different periods of furniture. If you have a room done in Victorian style, use the plants that were in vogue during that era. A cascading fern set in a wicker basket planter, aspidistra in a brass spittoon, or a palm in an antique piece rescued from Grandma's attic will provide that touch which takes us back to the late eighteen hundreds.

In rooms with an early American design, a child's wooden rocking cradle filled with pots of ferns and geraniums can add just the right touch. Copper or brass kettles, coal hods, pewter mugs, and cast iron cooking pots all make period containers which convert many indoor plants into "early American plants." African violets seem to blend well with early American furniture especially if the pots are slipped inside hobnail milk glass. Modern decors are softened by the addition of any of the large palm forms.

Although certain indoor plants seem to complement particular furniture styles more than others, the actual choice of indoor plants is truly an individual matter.

Do not overlook the opportunity to introduce your children to plants. For a number of years we did not have plants in our children's rooms but when our son was 3½ he asked if he could have a plant for his room, too. When allowed to pick a plant for his room, he decided on a Norfolk Island pine so he could have a Christmas tree all year. By having plants in their room, children discover the joy of growing things. A sansevieria sprout was pointed out to our three-year-old daughter. A few days later, she rushed from her room to tell us that another one of her plants, a "Florida Beauty" had two "babies."

## Window Treatments

The most noticeable difference between homes and apartments built in the past forty years and Victorian homes is space. The grace and spaciousness of homes built before the turn of the century provided ample room to grow a multitude of plants. To-

Use your imagination to create unusual decorative plant effects.

day's practical utilitarian room arrangements have a minimum of plant growing areas. Today's indoor gardeners must capitalize on the available space to grow indoor plants.

The best areas for plant growing in most homes are poorly used. Maximize your plant growing areas by using window areas effectively to grow plants. Evaluate each of the windows in your home and determine the particular plant growing environment each has to offer.

## EVALUATING WINDOW AREAS

The four corners of the compass can be used as a rough guideline to assess each window in your home as a plant growing area.

*North windows* seldom receive any direct sunlight and are best for foliage plants. Few indoor plants receive enough light to produce flowers in a north window. If the window is well insulated during the winter, north windows provide an area with uniform light and temperature levels throughout the year. Use a maximum-minimum thermometer to determine the temperature range so you may select the best plants for that location.

*East windows* are a favored location among many indoor gardeners because of the almost ideal growing conditions for most indoor plants. The early morning sun is usually not intense enough to burn foliage of light sensitive plants and yet it is strong enough to promote flowering. Temperatures fluctuate more during the day than in north windows but less than in south or west windows.

*South windows* provide an opportunity for indoor gardeners to grow plants requiring high light intensities. Most flowering plants and succulents require a south window to look their best indoors. Along with the higher light intensities there usually is a heat build-up during the day and only plants that will tolerate these higher temperatures should be used in south windows.

*West windows* are similar to east windows in light intensities but usually have a higher daytime temperature and some indoor plants may sunburn in west windows. West windows provide plant environments somewhat between a south and east window.

## USING WINDOWS EFFECTIVELY

One of the most common complaints of indoor gardeners is that window sills are not wide enough to hold anything but the smallest pot. Actually there are several solutions which allow you to

Effective use of windows will allow you to grow a wide variety of plants.

use the area more effectively. Trays that fit on the window sill can be purchased or built and permit 6 or 8 inch containers to be placed on the window ledge. Window boxes can be used inside to provide additional room for plants. Another widely used solution is to install double strength glass shelves across the window to hold your plants. Teacarts or portable stands provide indoor gardeners with another way of effectively and aesthetically using window areas to grow plants. They not only can be wheeled close to the chosen window, they also can be used to move your plants to the sink for their periodic showers. Some dedicated indoor gardeners even build indoor planters next to windows with desired light intensities. Plant stands and tiered tables located close to windows are other possibilities which provide additional room for an expanding plant collection. Try some of these suggestions to increase your plant growing areas in rooms where space may be limited.

Most kitchens have a window by the sink. This is an excellent location for balanced hanging baskets. Make sure they are located so you will not strike them while you are working. To complement the hanging baskets, shelves can be built around the window to accommodate additional plants. Usually plants grow better in kitchens than in any other room in the home because they are noticed at least 3 times a day and receive better than average care. The utility room with windows is another ideal place to grow a variety of indoor plants. The steam from the washing machine will increase the relative humidity and the plants will help alleviate any wash day blues.

● Memo
Window greenhouses are currently enjoying great popularity and range in size from small units that fit basement windows to large units designed for double windows.

● Memo
The light intensity of a north window is ideal for growing most ferns.

# WATER GARDENING

# HYDROPONICS

Plants are amazingly adaptable and can be grown in many unique ways. Their adaptability is clearly demonstrated in the ability of plants to grow and flourish in nutrient solutions. This technique is variously called hydroponics, water gardening or soilless gardening. Essentially, it consists of growing plants by using water containing the required plant nutrients they would otherwise absorb from the soil. Although hydroponics is a new technique for most indoor gardeners, plants have been grown hydroponically for over a century. Initially, hydroponics was developed as a research technique to determine what nutrients and how much of each nutrient were needed to grow healthy plants. These experiments have been very successful and provide much of the information used to determine fertilizer recommendations.

The lush and rapid growth that occurs when plants are supplied with all the water they need and the required nutrients amazed most people. However, few serious attempts to grow plants hydroponically were made until World War II. During the war, hydroponics was used to grow vegetables in areas that would not support plant growth or where soil was contaminated with disease causing bacteria. Because the U.S. military had been so successful growing vegetables during World War II, vegetable and ornamental growers tried to use this method commercially. The initial investment in equipment and other problems made most vegetables and ornamentals too expensive to compete with soil-grown plants and discouraged most commercial growers. However, inflation and the energy crisis have changed many of these considerations and hydroponics may be the way vegetables and many of our indoor plants will be grown in the future.

When plants are grown hydroponically, there is no guesswork to watering or fertilizing. Many indoor gardeners are amazed at how fast plants can grow when they switch from growing in soil mixes to growing hydroponically. Because plants have a constant water and nutrient supply, leaves and flowers are usually larger and the plants are more attractive.

For apartment gardeners, hydroponics may offer the possibility of growing plants without having to repot. There are no soil mixes to store or to prepare. And hydroponics eliminates the need to pasteurize or sterilize anything. All that's needed is a water supply and a small storage area. In most cases, soil insects and diseases are completely eliminated. Hydroponics also makes it easier to use unusual and decorative containers to match or contrast with your interior decor.

## Pick Your Method

There are three different ways to grow plants hydroponically:
(1) The water-culture method
(2) The nutrient-irrigation method
(3) The insert method
Each one of these methods has its own distinct advantages and disadvantages. Which one is best for your plants is something only you can decide.

### THE WATER-CULTURE METHOD

This method has been used for over a hundred years to grow plants hydroponically and is one of the methods employed for scientific experimentation. This illustration shows the simplest water-culture technique. Nutrient solution is poured into a jar, flask, or bottle until it is ¾ to ⅞ full. Some sort of support is used to hold the stem upright and out of the nutrient solution, but the plant roots are completely submerged. Clear glass containers can be used but most roots grow better in opaque or translucent containers. Mason jars with a sheath of black paper around them are entirely satisfactory. This simple yet effective method was used for years to grow a variety of plants, mostly for research purposes. You may wonder why the plants did not die of root rot or lack of oxygen. For many plants, enough oxygen entered the nutrient solution from the surrounding air for adequate root growth, but many plants grew slowly or died. The illustration to the right shows how the problem was eliminated. The air bubbles entering the solution provide enough oxygen to the water so almost any plant can be grown this way. Larger containers that can support two or more plants are often used in research experiments and commercial growers have built facilities to grow hundreds of plants at the same time.

● Memo
Dr. Julius von Sachs was the first scientist to grow plants hydroponically. The results of his experiments were published in 1860.

The simplest water-culture method to grow plants hydroponically.

Air bubbles through the nutrient solution provide additional oxygen for root growth.

Indoor gardeners can use this system to cultivate any plant that will root and grow in plain water. Plants will grow much faster if the solution is aerated several times a week. Expensive equipment isn't necessary; something as simple as a drinking straw can be used to bubble air through the solution.

An aquarium with an aeration pump makes an ideal water-culture tank. The illustration shows how to set it up. The only thing that is needed is a support for the top to hold your plants. A piece of marine plywood with the desired number of holes drilled in it will work fine. Cut pieces of circular sponge rubber and slit them to hold young plants in place. Nonabsorbent cotton, split corks, or similar materials can also be employed. However, if water-absorbing materials are used to hold the plants in place, the stems will start to rot because they will remain wet constantly. Decorative opaque paper can be taped to the sides of the aquarium to exclude light for those plants whose roots require darkness. It is interesting to see how roots grow, so try a few plants whose roots do not require constant darkness.

Aquariums with air pumps make ideal containers.

## THE NUTRIENT-IRRIGATION METHOD

Variations of this method have been used for over a hundred years to grow plants hydroponically. It and the water-culture method are used in scientific experiments to determine nutrient requirements of plants. Many variations of this method exist, and they all have their relative advantages. One illustration shows the simplest nutrient-irrigation technique. In nutrient-irrigation culture, an inert aggregate (that is sand, crushed rock, clay granules) is used so the root system can support the plant much as it does when plants are grown in soil. A nutrient solution is used to moisten the inert aggregate, providing both water and the required nutrients. Modifications of this method have been used by both commercial vegetable and ornamental growers to grow large crops successfully. The nutrient-irrigation method offers two advantages over the water-culture method: (1) No support has to be provided for the plant, and (2) the solid aggregates are selected so they are coarse enough to allow air to diffuse to the root system, thus no pump or other aeration method is needed. Since this method has been widely adopted, several different ways to use the nutrient-irrigation technique have been developed.

The simplest nutrient-irrigation method uses a container without drainage. Solution is changed as necessary.

## VARIATIONS IN THE NUTRIENT-IRRIGATION METHOD

The most widely used method for research purposes is shown to the right. Enough nutrient solution is uniformly distributed over the aggregates so that excess runs out the drainage holes. This is affectionately known as "slop culture" among scientists using this technique. Periodically the aggregates are rinsed with

Solution drains out of holes in "slop culture" technique of nutrient-irrigation method.

plain water to remove excess soluble salts. Because this method is a bit messy, uses a lot of nutrient solution, and requires frequent applications of the nutrient solution to keep plants from wilting, it has never been popular among indoor gardeners. However, plant roots receive adequate oxygen and plants grow almost as fast as in water culture.

If a number of plants are grown in a large container, the excess nutrient solution is collected to be reused. The nutrient solution is uniformly applied to the aggregate surface and the excess drains into a collection tray. This nutrient solution can be reused for the next application.

If the nutrient solution is collected in a bucket or other container, it can be used again. The easiest way is to irrigate from a bucket connected to the container.

Another modification that can be employed involves corks or plugs used to block the drainage holes in the plant container, while a tube or small pipe is inserted through the side of the plant container. A bucket or similar container is connected to the plant container via a flexible hose. The bucket is filled with nutrient solution and raised above the plant container. The nutrient solution flows into the plant container. When the inert aggregates are wet, the bucket is lowered below the level of the plant container and the excess nutrient solution flows back into the bucket for reuse. Some indoor gardeners have mechanized this method by using an airtight container and an aquarium pump, as shown. The nutrient solution is put into the airtight container which is connected to the plant container and the aquarium pump. When the pump is turned on, an increase in air pressure forces the solution into the plant container. When the pump is turned off, the solution flows back into the container. This method can be further automated by using an electric timer to turn the pump on and off, thus watering and fertilizing your plants even when you are not around.

An air pump can be used to force the nutrient solution out of its container into the inert media.

Another system using the nutrient-irrigation method is based on the wick-watering technique. Holes or slits are cut in the bottom of the plant container to hold watering wicks. The plant container with plants and aggregates is supported on top of a tray filled with the nutrient solution. If the aggregates are not too coarse, the wick will keep the aggregates moist and the plants fertilized. Nutrient solution may be added to the lower tray as required; and once every two weeks, the aggregates should be top watered to rinse away excess soluble salts, and the lower tray washed out and fresh nutrient solution put in the tray.

These modifications of the nutrient-irrigation method work well when growing a number of plants in the same container and are very similar to large-scale adaptations used by commercial growers. However, the most popular adaptation of the nutrient-

Use wicks to continuously supply your plants with nutrient solution.

irrigation method is very similar to using water culture. A container without drainage holes or one in which the drainage holes have been blocked with a cork or other plug is used for planting and filled with inert aggregates. Nutrient solution is added to the container until it is about half full. The plant roots are able to absorb enough nutrients and water from the solution, and still secure enough oxygen from the air spaces around the aggregates and the nutrient solution to produce good growth. This modification is simple, and works well with many indoor plants. A listing of plants that grow well in the various hydroponic methods is included at the end of this discussion.

### THE INSERT METHOD

The insert method has become very popular in Europe and several American companies manufacture containers that can be employed. This hydroponic method uses two different containers: an outer, opaque container to hold the nutrient solution and an inner, open-mesh container (called the insert) to hold the inert aggregates and the plant. This inner-mesh container is about half the depth of the outer container and is slipped inside the larger, opaque container. In homemade models some sort of support is used to hold the mesh container about halfway from the bottom of the outer container. Most manufactured models are built with a wide lip or rim on the insert to hold it at the proper level. The insert hydroponic method combines some of the best characteristics of both the water-culture and the nutrient-irrigation method. The roots of the plant will grow through the aggregates and the openings in the mesh container and into the nutrient solution. The level of the nutrient solution is maintained so the bottom level of the aggregates is kept moist.

Many indoor plants grow well with this system and it is easy to take care of plants. Once plants are established, nutrient levels usually only have to be checked once a week, and plants can be left when you go on vacation with a full supply of water and nutrients. The only problem occurs when plants need to be shifted to a larger container. This sometimes necessitates cutting the original open-mesh container away from the aggregates and plant roots.

## Containers for Hydroponic Growing Techniques

One of the major reasons many indoor gardeners have switched to hydroponic growing techniques is the almost limitless selection of containers that can be used. Wood, plastic, clay, glass, and even concrete containers have been employed. They can be homemade or purchased at your plant store or nursery.

● Memo

Even cacti and succulents can be grown for years in nutrient solutions.

The insert method of growing plants hydroponically.

● Memo

Some companies manufacture a series of different sized containers that a single insert will fit. This permits shifting the plant to larger and larger containers without having to reestablish the plant in a new insert.

*Glass.* Glass containers are easy to clean and come in a variety of shapes and sizes. As mentioned previously, bottle cutters can convert many otherwise unsuitable bottles and jugs into hydroponic containers. If clear-glass containers are used for hydroponics, algae will probably grow as well as your plant because the nutrients required by your indoor plant will also promote rapid algae growth. However, this does not mean that they cannot be used, but rather that you will have to clean them more often than translucent or opaque glass containers.

*Ceramic.* Ceramic containers should be large enough to hold the nutrient solution the plants will need for growth. Drainage holes can be drilled in most ceramic containers with a masonay drill if desired. Glazed containers are more suitable than unglazed ones. Unglazed containers are porous and enough water can evaporate through the sides to raise the soluble salt level to toxic levels if nutrient solution is continuously added. They are prefectly safe if the nutrient level is kept constant by adding plain water.

*Plastic.* Plastic containers are as suitable for hydroponics as they are for plants grown in soil mixes. They are almost as easy to clean as glass. Since they are nonporous like glass and glazed ceramic, no water evaporates through their sides. Most plastic containers also offer the advantage of being opaque and will not promote the growth of algae.

*Metal.* Metal containers are not generally suitable for use for hydroponics. Some of the common metals will react with the nutrient solution and may release dangerously high levels of metal ions into the solution. This is particularly true of copper kettles. Others, like iron, may simply be corroded by the nutrient solution.

*Wood.* Wood containers are satisfactory if they do not leak. Because wood will rot unless it is treated, most wood containers will not have a long life. But wood can be cut, drilled, nailed, and made into various shapes and sizes. Plastic trays or liners can be used to preserve wood containers if desired. Some treated woods contain heavy metals like copper or other toxic materials. Most treated lumber is perfectly safe for building containers for soil-grown plants because the soil mix will deactivate these toxic materials.

## CONTAINERS FOR THE INSERT METHOD

Several manufacturers produce containers that are especially designed for this hydroponic method. If you are evaluating different types of containers, select the ones that contain a transparent window in the outer, opaque container or a water-level indicator so it is possible to see when water should be added to the nutrient solution. Also, look for containers that have a tube or hole

A variety of containers can be used to grow plants hydroponically.

237

through which you can add water to the nutrient solution. If you will be using a large container, you can use the tube or hole to siphon off the spent nutrient solution. Otherwise, you will have to remove the insert with the rooted plant to change the solution.

If commercially made insert-method containers are not available, you can make your own. Select almost any container shape except those that narrow toward the base like the standard clay pot. These will not provide enough room for the spreading roots that develop in the nutrient solution. Inserts can easily be made from polyethylene pipe that will just slip inside the container. Cut the pipe so it is about one-half the depth of the outer container. Attach a perforated or mesh disc to the bottom of the pipe with waterproof glue or tape. The disc should have holes large enough for a plant's roots to grow through but smaller than the inert aggregates that will be used to fill it. The disc should be made of an inert material that will not corrode or release toxic materials into the solution. Provide a support inside the container so the tip of the polyethylene pipe will be level with the top of the outer container.

Although you can use almost any size container that is large enough to fit the root system of the plant you will be growing, it is best to use a container that will hold at least a half of a quart of nutrient solution when it is filled to the correct level for a particular hydroponic method. Several manufacturers make a variety of containers if you prefer to buy your containers. A listing of firms selling containers and other equipment for growing plants hydroponically can be found in the Appendix.

## Selecting an Aggregate

Inert aggregates are used in the nutrient-irrigation and insert methods of growing plants hydroponically. They provide support so the roots can hold the plant erect and allow more oxygen to diffuse to the root system. Your plants will grow best if the aggregates you select are chemically inert (so there is no reaction with the nutrient solution) and if they are resistant to decay or other physical changes. Make sure the aggregates you choose do not become too firmly packed in the container when kept continually wet. If they do, the roots may not receive enough oxygen, and root rot may eliminate your favorite plant. Aggregates are available in various grades or sizes; select the best variety for a plant according to the size of its root system. If the aggregates absorb water, plants will grow even better. A wide variety of materials can be used successfully, what you will use will depend on what is readily available and satisfactory. When considering an aggregate do not forget about weight; in large planters a heavy aggre-

• Memo

When growing plants hydroponically and using the insert method, the outer container should be changed to a larger size as the plant increases in size. This maintains aesthetic balance between the container and the plant, and reduces the frequency of adding water to the nutrient solution.

• Memo

The water culture method is often used in high school biology classes to demonstrate the elements plants need for growth.

gate can make it difficult to move the container, but a heavy aggregate may be needed in a small container to keep it stable. The following materials may be used as aggregates when plants are grown hydroponically.

*Clay granules.* These are made from baking small clay particles at extremely high temperatures. They are lightweight and porous, and chemically and physically inert. Best of all they are cheap and readily available as they are manufactured for a variety of purposes. Almost all of the commercial cat litters, as well as several industrial sweeping compounds are clay granules. Most of these contain dust and broken granules that will cause packing if used untreated. Screen the material, saving only those particles over 1/16 inch and then soak them overnight before using. Clay granules may be used in any size container, but may not provide enough weight to keep small containers stable. Their porous nature provides water and nutrients to plant roots and reduces irrigation frequency when used as a part of the nutrient-irrigation method.

*Crushed brick.* Small pieces of crushed brick between 1/16 to 3/4 inch make excellent aggregates. Wash the crushed brick to remove any loose dust. Crushed bricks are chemically and physically inert and provide aeration because of their irregular surfaces. They also retain water and nutrient solution thus helping to maintain healthy root growth. They are not too heavy and can be used in large containers. However, they will support algae growth where exposed to light.

*Crushed rocks.* A variety of crushed rocks have been used very successfully in growing plants hydroponically. Crushed basalt, quartz, and granite make acceptable aggregates. Small particles between 1/16 and 1/2 inch should be used. Rinse the crushed rocks to remove any fine dust before using. Use them in small containers so their weight will keep the containers stable. They do not absorb water or nutrients, and require more frequent irrigation to support plant growth if the nutrient solution is applied to the aggregates and then drained. Crushed rocks all of one color are very attractive in containers, and colors can be selected to complement or contrast with the plant colors.

*Glass marbles.* Small glass marbles have been used successfully with hydroponic growing techniques. Use sizes between 1/4 and 3/4 inch to provide support and aeration; these seem to work best with plants that have fairly large roots, such as aglaonemas, dieffenbachias, philodendrons, and some of the orchids.

*Gravel.* A mixture of various rocks, gravel has many of the same properties of crushed rock. However, it usually is not as heavy as the common crushed rock. Colors vary but frequently

● Memo
An easy way to clean aggregates and eliminate any diseases or insects is to soak them for two hours in a solution of 10% household bleach. Then soak them overnight in tap water to remove the bleach.

● Memo
Plants started hydroponically can later be grown in a soil mix, but it will take a month or so for them to establish a root system that will function effectively. During this time period they should be kept in a shaded area where temperatures will not exceed 80° F and be protected from drafts or breezes.

there is a grayish color due to the color mix of the individual pebbles. The best cheap gravel is the type called pea gravel, which is often used on macadam roads. Use sizes between 1/16 and 1/2 inch. Aquarium gravel is just the right size and is quite attractive in containers. Although the individual aggregates of gravel do not retain any water or nutrient solution, the irregular surface depressions hold enough nutrient solution so frequent irrigation is not required.

*Perlite*. This is a lightweight aggregate which retains ample amounts of the nutrient solution because of its porous structure. It is available in various sizes; use the small-particle size for plants with fine roots and the larger-particle size for plants with coarse roots. Perlite should be soaked overnight in water to remove the water soluble fluorides it contains. Otherwise, fluoride tip burn will occur on cordylines, dracaenas, marantas, and other fluoride-sensitive plants. Because it is lightweight, perlite is more suitable for large rather than small containers. Its white surface makes it an attractive combination with dark-leaved plants. Protect the top surface layer from full sunshine, as algae grow rapidly on nutrient-soaked perlite particles.

*Pumice.* This is a lightweight volcanic rock. Usually the gases trapped during its formation make it very porous. At one time this was a widely used aggregate, but reports suggest that it reacts chemically with the nutrients to create a basic solution. This problem can be alleviated by soaking the pumice overnight in a dilute vinegar solution (1 cup of vinegar to 1 gallon of water) and then by rinsing it. Use particles between 1/16 to 1/2 inch depending on the size of the root system of your plant. Due to its porous structure, pumice retains adequate amounts of nutrient solution and reduces the frequency of nutrient application. Its coarse structure also provides excellent aeration for plant roots if used in the mesh container required with the insert method of hydroponic growing.

*Sand.* Coarse builder's sand has been used for over a hundred years for hydroponic growing. However, it is not as desirable as some of the other materials as it is difficult for most indoor gardeners to get sand coarse enough so it will not pack when wet. Because of this problem, it is only recommended for those plants with a fine root system. Before using builder's sand, wash it to remove the finest particles. Wet sand is quite heavy and should not be used in large containers that have to be moved.

*Vermiculite*. This is a lightweight, porous material that has been widely used in hydroponics. However, it tends to break down over a period of years and loses much of its porous nature. It is readily available and comes in a variety of sizes, but it is best used for plants you will not keep for more than five years.

• Memo

Most of the large citrus tree groves in Florida are actually grown with a modification of the nutrient irrigation method. The coarse sands retain very little water or fertilizer and the trees have to be watered and fertilized frequently to continue growth.

# Nutrient Solutions

Many different formulas for nutrient solutions have been developed through the years. The idea behind all of them was to determine what chemicals plants required for continued growth. Most of the older formulas (those developed before 1910) only included what are termed the macronutrients, that is, those chemical elements required in greatest amounts by plants. As chemical techniques improved and pure chemical salts could be prepared, additional chemicals were shown to be required by plants. Today there is little dispute over what chemicals are required by plants or what fertilizer salts can supply these elements. The section on fertilizers earlier in this book discusses required elements needed by plants and how the plants use these fertilizers.

When plants are grown hydroponically, you have to provide all the required plant nutrients in the nutrient solution. Thus, the various chemical salts have to be correctly weighed and properly mixed for successful plant growth. The formulas given in this section have been used to grow a wide variety of plants under different conditions. Other formulas can be used, and plants will grow just as well if the required nutrients are available in the correct proportions. If too much of any one chemical is used, it creates an imbalance, and some required chemicals will actually kill plants if too much is used. Remember though that plants are adaptable and have survived for millions of years so any minor mistake is not likely to have a serious effect.

Many plant stores or nurseries sell prepackaged fertilizers specifically developed for growing plants hydroponically. These will produce perfectly satisfactory results with almost all indoor plants. If you prefer to purchase hydroponic fertilizers, it is often a good idea to buy more than one brand and alternate between brands when mixing the nutrient solution. This will usually prevent any deficiencies or toxicities from developing. If you prefer to buy the chemicals separately and make your own nutrient solution, use the formulas in Table 1 or Table 2.

Weigh out the chemicals and mix thoroughly. Then store in an airtight container. Use 1 level teaspoon for each gallon of nutrient solution you make. Stir until all the chemicals are dissolved. This nutrient solution will provide the nutrients your plants need except for boron, copper, manganese, and zinc. Copper and zinc are usually present as impurities in your home water supply or are contained in the chemical salts you used. However, boron and manganese should be added to the nutrient solution before using. Dissolve 1 teaspoon of boric acid crystals and 1/3 teaspoon manganese chloride $(M_nCl_2.4H_2O)$ in 1 gallon of hot water. Label

● Memo

Although investigations are still continuing. no new essential elements for nutrient solutions have been shown to be required by plants for over a quarter century.

this 'stock solution'. Add two teaspoons of this stock solution to each gallon of nutrient solution. If you cannot get manganese chloride, substitute manganese sulfate.

With the exception of manganese chloride, it is not necessary to buy chemically pure salts. In fact, the best grade for most hydroponic solutions is technical grade. The few impurities they contain will not harm your plants; in fact, some are required for continued plant growth. Whether you buy a prepackaged fertilizer or make your own, the nutrient solution should provide enough of each required element for optimum plant growth but not such a high concentration that any element becomes toxic to the plant.

## NUTRIENT SOLUTION FERTILIZER FORMULAS

### TABLE 1

| Chemical | Nutrients | Approximate Amounts (In Ounces) |
|---|---|---|
| Calcium nitrate | Calcium Nitrogen | 6 |
| Magnesium sulfate (Epsom salts) | Magnesium Sulfur | 5 |
| Monopotassium phosphate | Potassium Phosphorus | 1 |
| Potassium nitrate | Potassium Nitrogen | 4 |
| Iron chelate | Iron | ¼ |

### TABLE 2

| | | |
|---|---|---|
| Ammonium sulfate | Nitrogen Sulfur | 2 |
| Calcium sulfate | Calcium Sulfur | 2.5 |
| Magnesium sulfate (Epsom salts) | Magnesium Sulfur | 3.5 |
| Monocalcium phosphate | Calcium Phosphorus | 2 |
| Potassium sulfate | Potassium Sulfur | 13 |
| Sodium nitrate | Nitrogen | 6 |
| Iron chelate | Iron | ¼ |

● Memo

If your tap water contains flouride it will cause tip burn on cordylines, dracaenas, marantas, yuccas, and some palms. Use distilled or deionized water to add to the nutrient solution.

### APPLYING AND CHANGING NUTRIENT SOLUTIONS

Nutrient solutions should be changed on a regular basis. How often depends on the plant and how fast it is growing. Even if plants are growing very rapidly, a quart of fresh nutrient solution will sustain growth for at least a week. Most indoor gardeners find that once every 2 to 4 weeks is about right for plants grown in water culture, or in mesh containers.

Remove the cork or plug from containers with drainage holes and drain the old solution. Replace the cork or plug and refill the container to the proper level. If containers do not have drainage holes, remove the plant and pour off the old solution. Then refill to the proper level with fresh nutrient solution. Use the old solution to fertilize your lawn or garden.

If you are using the nutrient-irrigation method, replace the old nutrient solution with fresh solution about every two weeks.

## Starting Plants in Hydroponics

Although plants are versatile and flexible, they require a little extra care and attention when they are transferred from soil to a nutrient solution. Seedlings make the adjustment easily because they are rapidly growing and just developing their root system. However, seedlings are very susceptible to soluble salt damage, and the nutrient solution should be used at half strength until the plant develops 3 or 4 leaves. Until seedlings develop more extensive root systems, the nutrient solution should be maintained at a higher level so the roots are able to absorb water and nutrients. As the roots elongate, the nutrient level can be lowered until it is at the recommended level.

Mature plants can be changed from growing in soil mixes to growing in nutrient solutions with a little extra care and attention. First, wash all the soil from the plant's roots under a gentle stream of water. Then transfer the plant to its new container. Instead of adding full-strength nutrient solution, add a half-strength solution. Plants require an adjustment period when transferred from soil to water. A different type of root system is produced by plants growing in water. Roots produced in water are thicker, less flexible, and have fewer branches than root systems produced in soil. Most plants will take about a month to initiate a functional root system when transferred from soil to water. During this first month, keep the plant in a cool, bright, draft-free room. After a month, use the full-strength nutrient solution.

### MAINTAINING PLANTS IN NUTRIENT SOLUTIONS

In addition to routine maintenance (pruning, inspecting for insects, etc.), hydroponically grown plants have their own specialized routines.

Wash the soil mix off the plant's roots before transferring to a hydroponic solution.

*Checking Nutrient Levels.* Every two or three days the level of the nutrient solution should be checked. If the solution level has dropped, add *plain* water to bring it back up to the desired level. This keeps the fertilizer salts from becoming too concentrated and burning the plant's roots.

*Water.* Almost all water acceptable for drinking can be used to prepare and add to nutrient solutions. However, some dissolved salts in your drinking water can become toxic to plants if concentrated. They become concentrated in the nutrient solution because every time you add water, you are adding a few more to the solution. If nutrient solutions are changed frequently, toxic levels cannot build up.

*pH.* Nutrient solutions should be kept between pH 5.0 and 6.5. Most garden supply stores now sell pH paper that allows for quick checking. If the pH is too high (7.0 and higher), add one or two drops of vinegar and recheck. Add enough vinegar so the nutrient solution pH is between 5.0 and 6.5. If the nutrient solution is acidic (below 5.0), add a few drops of solution made from bicarbonate of soda. If the pH is too high or too low, some of the nutrients will precipitate.

## PLANTS FOR HYDROPONICS

| Botanical Name | Common Name |
| --- | --- |
| Aglaonema commutatum elegans | |
| Aspidistra elatior | Cast Iron Plant |
| Brassaia actinophylla | Schefflera |
| Clorophytum comosum | Spider Plant |
| Cissus antarctica | Kangaroo Vine |
| Coleus blumei | Coleus |
| Cordyline terminalis | Ti Plant |
| Dieffenbachia amoena | Giant Dumb Cane |
| Dieffenbachia 'Exotica Perfection' | Exotica Perfection |
| Dracaena sanderana | |
| Dracaena surculosa | Gold Dust Dracaena |
| Epipremnum aureum | Golden Pothos |
| Fatshedera lizei | Botanical Wonder Plant |
| Hedera helix | English Ivy |
| Philodendron bipennifolium | Fiddle-leaf Philodendron |
| Philodendron hybrids | |
| Philodendron scandens oxycardium | Heart-leaf Philodendron |
| Scindapsus pictus | Silver Pothos |
| Spathiphyllum 'Clevelandii' | Peace Lily |
| Syngonium podophyllum | Nephthytis |
| Zebrina pendula | Wandering Jew |

# CULTURAL CARE SYNOPSIS

The following is a listing of over 300 plants and their cultural requirements. The plants described and illustrated in the book are starred for your reference. To simplify cultural care guidelines, the following abbreviations and coding numbers are used. The cultural care guidelines apply to indoor plants while actively growing.

## L = Light
(1) Sunny light areas: At least 4 hours of direct sun.
(2) High light areas: Over 200 foot candles, but not direct sun.
(3) Medium light areas: 75 to 200 foot candles.
(4) Low light areas: 25 to 75 foot candles.

## T = Temperature
(1) Cool: 50°F night, 65°F day temperatures.
(2) Average: 65°F night, 75°F day temperatures.
(3) Warm: 70°F night, 85°F day temperatures

## H = Relative Humidity
(1) High: 50% or higher.
(2) Average: 25% to 49%.
(3) Low: 5% to 24%.

## W = Watering
(1) Keep soil mix moist.
(2) Surface of soil mix should dry before rewatering.
(3) Soil mix can become moderately dry before rewatering.

## S = Suggested Soil Mix
Specific ingredients are on pages 00 to 00. The soil mixes are keyed as follows:
(1) Flowering house plants
(2) Foliage plants
(3) Bromeliads
(4) Orchids
(5) Succulents and cacti
(6) Ferns
(7) African violets and other gesneriads

| Botanical Name | Common Name | Family Name | L | T | H | W | S |
|---|---|---|---|---|---|---|---|
| *Abutilon hybridium* | Flowering Maple | Malvaceae | 1 | 1 | 2 | 2 | 1 |
| *Acalypha hispida* | Chenile Plant | Euphorbiaceae | 1 | 2 | 2 | 2 | 1 |
| *Achimenes* hybrids | Magic Flower | Gesneriaceae | 2 | 2 | 2 | 1 | 7 |
| Acorus calamus | Sweet Flag | Araceae | 2-3 | 2 | 2 | 1 | 2 |
| Acorus gramineus | Miniature Sweet Flag | Araceae | 2-3 | 2 | 2 | 1 | 2 |
| Adiantum raddianum | Maidenhair Fern | Polypodiaceae | 2-3 | 2 | 1 | 1 | 6 |
| Adromischus cristatus | Crinkle-Leaf Plant | Crassulaceae | 2-3 | 2 | 2 | 2 | 5 |
| Adromischus festivus | Plover Eggs | Crassulaceae | 2-3 | 2 | 2 | 2 | 5 |
| Aechmea chantinii | Amazonian Zebra Plant | Bromeliaceae | 2-3 | 2 | 2 | 2 | 3 |
| *Aechmea fasciata | Silver Vase | Bromeliaceae | 2-3 | 2 | 2 | 2 | 3 |
| Aechmea miniata 'Discolor' | Purplish Coral Berry | Bromeliaceae | 2-3 | 2 | 2 | 2 | 3 |
| *Aechmea 'Royal Wine' | Royal Wine Bromeliad | Bromeliaceae | 2-3 | 2 | 2 | 1 | 3 |
| Aeschynanthus marmoratus | Zebra Basket Vine | Gesneriaceae | 2 | 2 | 2 | 1 | 7 |
| *Aeschynanthus pulcher | Lipstick Vine | Gesneriaceae | 2 | 2 | 2 | 1 | 7 |
| Agave americana 'Marginata' | Variegated Century Plant | Agavaceae | 1 | 2 | 3 | 3 | 5 |
| Agave victoriae-reginae | Queen Agave | Agavaceae | 1 | 2 | 2 | 2 | 5 |
| *Aglaonema commutatum elegans | Commutatum | Araceae | 3-4 | 2 | 2 | 2 | 2 |
| *Aglaonema commutatum 'Pseudo-Bracteatum' | Golden Evergreen | Araceae | 3-4 | 2 | 2 | 2 | 2 |
| Aglaonema commutatum 'Treubii' | Ribbon Aglaonema | Araceae | 3-4 | 2 | 2 | 2 | 2 |
| *Aglaonema costatum | Spotted Evergreen | Araceae | 3-4 | 2 | 1 | 2 | 2 |

| Botanical Name | Common Name | Family Name | Cultural Care | | | | |
|---|---|---|---|---|---|---|---|
| | | | L | T | H | W | S |
| Aglaonema crispum | Pewter Plant | Araceae | 3-4 | 2 | 2 | 2 | 2 |
| Aglaonema 'Fransher' | Fransher | Araceae | 3-4 | 2 | 2 | 2 | 2 |
| Aglaonema modestum | Chinese Evergreen | Araceae | 3-4 | 2 | 2 | 2 | 2 |
| Aglaonema 'Silver King' | Silver King | Araceae | 3-4 | 2 | 2 | 2 | 2 |
| Aglaonema 'Silver Queen' | Silver Queen | Araceae | 3-4 | 2 | 2 | 2 | 2 |
| Aglaonema simplex | Simplex | Araceae | 3-4 | 2 | 2 | 2 | 2 |
| Allamanda cathartica | Allamanda | Apocynaceae | 1 | 2 | 1-2 | 2 | 1 |
| Alloplectus nummularia | Miniature Pouch Flower | Gesneriaceae | 2-3 | 2 | 1-2 | 1 | 7 |
| Alocasia x chantrieri | Chantrieri | Araceae | 2-3 | 2 | 1-2 | 1 | 2 |
| Aloe aborescens | Candelabra Plant | Liliaceae | 1 | 3 | 3 | 3 | 5 |
| Aloe barbadensis | Medicine Plant | Liliaceae | 1 | 3 | 3 | 3 | 5 |
| Aloe brevifolia | Brevifolia Aloe | Liliaceae | 1 | 3 | 3 | 3 | 5 |
| Aloe ciliaris | Climbing Aloe | Liliaceae | 1 | 3 | 3 | 3 | 5 |
| Aloe humilis echinata | Hedgehog Aloe | Liliaceae | 1 | 3 | 3 | 3 | 5 |
| Ananas comosus | Pineapple | Bromeliaceae | 1-2 | 2 | 2 | 1 | 3 |
| Anthurium andraeanum | Oilcloth Flower | Araceae | 2-3 | 2 | 1-2 | 1 | 2 |
| Anthurium clarinervium | Dwarf Crystal Anthurium | Araceae | 2-3 | 2 | 1-2 | 1 | 2 |
| Anthurium hookeri | Birdsnest Anthurium | Araceae | 2-3 | 2 | 1-2 | 1 | 2 |
| Anthurium magnificum | False Crystal Anthurium | Araceae | 2-3 | 2 | 1-2 | 1 | 2 |
| Anthurium scherzeranum | Flamingo Flower | Araceae | 2-3 | 2 | 1-2 | 1 | 6 |
| Aphelandra squarrosa | Zebra Plant | Acanthaceae | 2 | 2 | 2 | 1 | 2 |
| Araucaria heterophylla | Norfolk Island Pine | Araucariaceae | 2-3 | 2 | 2 | 1 | 2 |
| Ardisia crenata | Ardisia | Myrsinaceae | 2-3 | 2 | 2 | 1 | 2 |
| Ascocentrum miniatum | Miniatum | Orchidaceae | 2-3 | 2 | 2 | 2 | 4 |
| Asparagus densiflorus 'Myers' | Plume Asparagus | Liliaceae | 2-3 | 2 | 2 | 2 | 2 |
| Asparagus densiflorus 'Sprengeri' | Sprengeri Fern | Liliaceae | 2-3 | 2 | 2 | 2 | 2 |
| Asparagus falcatus | Sickle Thorn | Liliaceae | 2-3 | 2 | 2 | 2 | 2 |
| Aspidistra elatior | Cast Iron Plant | Liliaceae | 3-4 | 2 | 3 | 2 | 2 |
| Asplenium daucifolium | Mother Fern | Polypodiaceae | 3 | 2 | 2 | 1 | 6 |
| Asplenium nidus | Bird's Nest Fern | Polypodiaceae | 3 | 2 | 2 | 1 | 6 |
| Astrophytum myriostigma | Bishop's Cap | Cactaceae | 2 | 2 | 3 | 3 | 5 |
| Beaucarnea recurvata | Ponytail | Liliaceae | 1 | 2 | 3 | 3 | 5 |
| Begonia cubensis | Cuban Holly | Begoniaceae | 2-3 | 2 | 2 | 2 | 2 |
| Begonia metallica | Metallic Leaf Begonia | Begoniaceae | 2-3 | 2 | 2 | 2 | 2 |
| *Begonia x rex-cultorum | Rex Begonia | Begoniaceae | 2-3 | 2 | 2 | 2 | 2 |
| *Begonia semperflorens | Wax Begonia | Begoniacaea | 1-2 | 1 | 2 | 2 | 1 |

| Botanical Name | Common Name | Family Name | Cultural Care | | | | |
|---|---|---|---|---|---|---|---|
| | | | L | T | H | W | S |
| *Billbergia nutans | Queen's Tears | Bromeliaceae | 2-3 | 2 | 2 | 2 | 3 |
| Billbergia pyramidalis | Urn Plant | Bromeliaceae | 2-3 | 2 | 2 | 2 | 3 |
| *Billbergia zebrina | Zebra Plant | Bromeliaceae | 2-3 | 2 | 2 | 2 | 3 |
| *Bougainvillea spp. | Bougainvillea | Nyctaginaceae | 1 | 2 | 2 | 2 | 1 |
| *Brassaia actinophylla | Schefflera | Araliaceae | 2-3 | 2 | 2 | 2 | 2 |
| *Brassaia arboricola | Dwarf Schefflera | Araliaceae | 2-3 | 2 | 2 | 2 | 2 |
| *Caladium spp. | Caladium | Araceae | 2 | 2 | 1 | 1 | 2 |
| Calathea insignis | Rattlesnake Plant | Marantacea | 2-3 | 2 | 2 | 1 | 2 |
| *Calathea makoyana | Peacock Plant | Marantaceae | 2-3 | 2 | 2 | 1 | 2 |
| Calathea micans | Miniature Maranta | Marantaceae | 2-3 | 2 | 2 | 1 | 2 |
| Calathea roseopicta | Rose Calathea | Marantaceae | 2-3 | 2 | 2 | 1 | 2 |
| *Calceolaria crenatiflora | Slipperwort | Scrophulariaceae | 2 | 1 | 1 | 1 | 1 |
| Callisia elegans | Striped Inch Plant | Commelinaceae | 2-3 | 2 | 2 | 2 | 2 |
| *Camellia japonica | Camellia | Theaceae | 2 | 1-2 | 1 | 1 | 1 |
| *Campanula isophylla | Star of Bethlehem | Campanulaceae | 1-2 | 1 | 2 | 2 | 5 |
| *Carissa grandiflora 'Bonsai' | Bonsai Natal Plum | Apocynaceae | 1-2 | 2-3 | 2 | 2 | 1 |
| *Carissa grandiflora 'Boxwood Beauty' | Boxwood Beauty | Apocynaceae | 1-2 | 2-3 | 2 | 2 | 1 |
| Caryota mitis | Fishtail Palm | Palmae | 2-3 | 2 | 2 | 2 | 2 |
| Catharanthus roseus | Madagascar Periwinkle | Apocynaceae | 1-2 | 2 | 1-2 | 2 | 1 |
| Cereus peruvianus | Peruvian Apple Cactus | Cactaceae | 1 | 2-3 | 3 | 3 | 5 |
| Ceropegia woodii | Rosary Vine | Asclepiadaceae | 2-3 | 2 | 2 | 2 | 5 |
| *Chamaedorea elegans | Parlor Palm | Palmae | 3-4 | 2 | 2 | 2 | 2 |
| *Chamaedorea erumpens | Bamboo Palm | Palmae | 3-4 | 2 | 2 | 2 | 2 |
| Chamaerops humilis | European Fan Palm | Palmae | 2-3 | 2 | 2 | 2 | 2 |
| Chirita lavandulacea | Hindustan Gentian | Gesneriaceae | 2-3 | 2 | 1-2 | 1 | 7 |
| *Chlorophytum comosum 'Variegatum' | Variegated Spider Plant | Liliaceae | 2-3 | 2 | 2 | 1 | 2 |
| *Chlorophytum comosum 'Vittatum' | Spider Plant | Liliaceae | 2-3 | 2 | 2 | 1 | 2 |
| *Chrysalidocarpus lutescens | Areca Palm | Palmae | 2-3 | 2 | 2 | 1 | 2 |
| *Chrysanthemum morifolium | Chrysanthemum | Compositae | 1 | 2 | 2 | 1 | 1 |
| *Cissus antarctica | Kangaroo Vine | Vitaceae | 2-3 | 2 | 2 | 2 | 2 |
| *Cissus rhombifolia | Grape Leaf Ivy | Vitaceae | 2-3 | 2 | 2 | 2 | 2 |
| Cissus rotundifolia | Wax Cissus | Vitaceae | 2 | 2 | 3 | 3 | 2 |
| Cissus striata | Miniature Grape Ivy | Vitaceae | 2-3 | 2 | 2 | 2 | 2 |
| *Citrofortunella mitis | Calamondin Orange | Rutaceae | 1-2 | 1 | 2 | 2 | 1 |
| *Clivia miniata 'Grandiflora' | Kafir Lily | Amaryllidaceae | 2 | 2 | 2 | 2 | 1 |
| *Codiaeum variegatum | Croton | Euphorbiaceae | 1 | 2 | 1 | 1 | 2 |

| Botanical Name | Common Name | Family Name | Cultural Care | | | | |
|---|---|---|---|---|---|---|---|
| | | | L | T | H | W | S |
| *Coffea arabica | Coffee | Rubiaceae | 2 | 2 | 2 | 2 | 1 |
| *Coleus blumei | Coleus | Labiatae | 2-3 | 2 | 2 | 2 | 1 |
| Columnea hybrids | Goldfish Plant | Gesneriaceae | 2-3 | 2 | 1-2 | 1 | 7 |
| *Cordyline terminalis | Ti Plant | Agavaceae | 2 | 1-2 | 2 | 2 | 2 |
| *Crassula argentea | Jade Plant | Crassulaceae | 2-3 | 2 | 2 | 2 | 2 |
| Crassula falcata | Propeller Plant | Crassulaceae | 1-2 | 2 | 2 | 3 | 5 |
| Crassula hemisphaerica | Arab's Turban | Crassulaceae | 1-2 | 2 | 2 | 3 | 5 |
| Crassula lycopodioides | Toy Cypress | Crassulaceae | 1-2 | 2 | 2 | 2 | 5 |
| Crassula schmidtii | Red Flowering Crassula | Crassulaceae | 2-3 | 2 | 2 | 2 | 5 |
| Crassula teres | Rattlesnake Tail | Crassulaceae | 2-3 | 2 | 3 | 3 | 5 |
| *Crocus spp. | Crocus | Iridaceae | 2 | 1 | 2 | 1 | 1 |
| *Crossandra infundibuliformis | Crossandra | Acanthaceae | 2 | 2 | 2 | 1 | 1 |
| *Cryptanthus bivittatus 'Minor' | Dwarf Rose Stripe Star | Bromeliaceae | 2 | 2 | 2 | 2 | 3 |
| Cryptanthus fosteranus | Stiff Pheasant Leaf | Bromeliaceae | 2 | 2 | 2 | 2 | 3 |
| Cryptanthus zonatus | Zebra Plant | Bromeliaceae | 2 | 2 | 2 | 2 | 3 |
| *Cyrtomium falcatum 'Rochfordianum' | House Holly Fern | Polypodiaceae | 2-3 | 2 | 2 | 2 | 6 |
| *Davallia fejeensis | Rabbit's Foot Fern | Polypodiaceae | 2-3 | 2 | 1 | 1 | 3 |
| *Dieffenbachia amoena | Giant Dumb Cane | Araceae | 2-3 | 2 | 2 | 2 | 2 |
| *Dieffenbachia amoena 'Tropic Snow' | Tropic Snow Dumb Cane | Araceae | 2-3 | 2 | 2 | 2 | 2 |
| Dieffenbachia x bausei | Bausei Dumb Cane | Araceae | 3 | 2 | 2 | 2 | 2 |
| *Dieffenbachia 'Exotica Perfection' | Exotica Perfection | Araceae | 2-3 | 2 | 2 | 2 | 2 |
| Dieffenbachia leopoldii | Leopold's Dumb Cane | Araceae | 3 | 2 | 2 | 2 | 2 |
| Dieffenbachia maculata | Spotted Dumb Cane | Araceae | 3 | 2 | 2 | 2 | 2 |
| *Dieffenbachia maculata 'Rudolph Roehrs' | Gold Dieffenbachia | Araceae | 2-3 | 2 | 2 | 2 | 2 |
| *Dizygotheca elegantissima | False Aralia | Araliaceae | 2-3 | 2 | 2 | 2 | 2 |
| *Dracaena angustifolia honoriae | Narrow-Leaved Pleomele | Agavaceae | 2-3 | 2 | 2 | 2 | 2 |
| Dracaena arborea | Tree Dracaena | Agavaceae | 2-3 | 2 | 2 | 2 | 2 |
| *Dracaena deremensis 'Janet Craig' | Janet Craig | Agavaceae | 2-4 | 2 | 2 | 2 | 2 |
| *Dracaena deremensis 'Warneckii' | Warneckii | Agavaceae | 2-4 | 2 | 2 | 2 | 2 |
| *Dracaena fragrans 'Massangeana' | Corn Plant | Agavaceae | 2-3 | 2 | 2 | 2 | 2 |
| Dracaena goldieana | Queen of Dracaenas | Agavaceae | 2-3 | 2 | 1-2 | 2 | 2 |
| Dracaena hookerana | Leather Dracaena | Agavaceae | 3-4 | 2 | 2 | 2 | 2 |
| *Dracaena marginata | Marginata | Agavaceae | 2-4 | 2 | 2 | 2 | 2 |
| *Dracaena sanderana | Ribbon Plant | Agavaceae | 2-4 | 2 | 2 | 2 | 2 |
| *Dracaena surculosa | Gold Dust Dracaena | Agavaceae | 2-4 | 2 | 2 | 2 | 2 |
| *Dracaena surculosa 'Florida Beauty' | Florida Beauty | Agavaceae | 2-4 | 2 | 2 | 2 | 2 |
| *Dyckia brevifolia | Miniature Agave | Bromeliaceae | 1-2 | 2 | 3 | 2-3 | 2 |

| Botanical Name | Common Name | Family Name | Cultural Care | | | | |
|---|---|---|---|---|---|---|---|
| | | | L | T | H | W | S |
| *Dyckia fosterana* | Silver and Gold Dyckia | Bromeliaceae | 1-2 | 2 | 3 | 2-3 | 3 |
| *Echeveria agavoides* | Molded Wax | Crassulaceae | 1-2 | 2 | 3 | 3 | 5 |
| *Echeveria elegans* | Mexican Snowball | Crassulaceae | 1-2 | 2 | 3 | 3 | 5 |
| *Echinocereus reichenbachii* | Lace Cactus | Cactaceae | 1-2 | 2 | 3 | 3 | 5 |
| *Epidendrum atropurpureum* | Spice Orchid | Orchidaceae | 2 | 2 | 1-2 | 1 | 4 |
| *Epiphyllum* hybrids | Orchid Cacti | Cactaceae | 2 | 2 | 2 | 2 | 1 |
| *Epipremnum aureum* | Golden Pothos | Araceae | 2-4 | 2 | 2 | 2 | 2 |
| *Epipremnum aureum* 'Marble Queen' | Marble Queen | Araceae | 2-4 | 2 | 2 | 2 | 2 |
| *Episcia cupreata* | Flame Violet | Gesneriaceae | 2 | 2-3 | 1 | 1 | 7 |
| *Episcia dianthiflora* | Lace-Flower Vine | Gesneriaceae | 2 | 2-3 | 1 | 1 | 7 |
| *Episcia reptans* | Scarlet Violet | Gesneriaceae | 2 | 2-3 | 1 | 1 | 7 |
| *Euphorbia coeralescens* | Blue Euphorbia | Euphorbiaceae | 2-3 | 2 | 2-3 | 2-3 | 5 |
| *Euphorbia mammillaris* | Corncob Cactus | Euphorbiaceae | 1 | 2 | 2-3 | 3 | 5 |
| *Euphorbia milii splendens* | Crown-of-Thorns | Euphorbiaceae | 1 | 2 | 2-3 | 3 | 5 |
| *Euphorbia obesa* | Gingham Golf Ball | Euphorbiaceae | 1 | 2 | 3 | 3 | 5 |
| *Euphorbia pulcherrima* | Poinsettia | Euphorbiaceae | 1-2 | 2 | 2 | 2 | 1 |
| *Euphorbia tirucalli* | Milkbush | Euphorbiaceae | 1-2 | 2 | 2 | 2 | 1 |
| *Fatshedera lizei* | Botanical Wonder Plant | Araliaceae | 2-3 | 1-2 | 2 | 2 | 2 |
| *Fatsia japonica* | Japanese Aralia | Araliaceae | 3-4 | 1-2 | 2 | 2 | 2 |
| *Ficus benjamina* | Benjamina | Moraceae | 1-3 | 2 | 2 | 2 | 2 |
| *Ficus deltoidea* | Mistletoe Ficus | Moraceae | 2-3 | 2 | 2 | 2 | 2 |
| *Ficus elastica* 'Decora' | Rubber Plant | Moraceae | 1-3 | 2 | 2 | 2 | 2 |
| *Ficus lyrata* | Fiddle-Leaf Fig | Moraceae | 1-3 | 2 | 2 | 2 | 2 |
| *Ficus pumila* 'Minima' | Dwarf Creeping Fig | Moraceae | 2-3 | 2 | 2 | 2 | 2 |
| *Ficus retusa* | Cuban Laurel | Moraceae | 2-3 | 2 | 2 | 2 | 2 |
| *Ficus sagittata* | Rooting Fig | Moraceae | 2-3 | 2 | 2 | 2 | 2 |
| *Ficus willdemaniana* | Dwarf Fiddle-Leaf Fig | Moraceae | 2-3 | 2 | 2 | 2 | 2 |
| *Fittonia verschaffeltii* | Red-Nerved Fittonia | Acanthaceae | 2-3 | 2 | 1 | 1 | 2 |
| *Fittonia verschaffeltii argyroneura* | Silver-Nerved Fittonia | Acanthaceae | 2-3 | 2 | 1 | 1 | 2 |
| *Fuchsia hybrida* | Fuchsias | Onagraceae | 2 | 1-2 | 1 | 1 | 1 |
| *Gasteria hybrida* | Ox Tongue | Liliaceae | 2 | 2 | 2 | 3 | 5 |
| *Gastrolea beguinii* | Lizard Tail | Liliaceae | 2 | 2 | 2 | 3 | 5 |
| *Graptopetalum amethystinum* | Jewel Leaf Plant | Crassulaceae | 2-3 | 2 | 2-3 | 3 | 5 |
| *Guzmania lingulata* 'Major' | Scarlet Star | Bromeliaceae | 2 | 2 | 1 | 2 | 3 |
| *Guzmania monostachia* | Striped Torch | Bromeliaceae | 2 | 2 | 1 | 2 | 3 |
| *Gymnocalycium mihanovichii* | Plain Cactus | Cactaceae | 1-2 | 2 | 3 | 3 | 5 |
| *Gynura aurantiaca* 'Purple Passion' | Purple Passion | Compositae | 2-3 | 2 | 2 | 2 | 2 |

| Botanical Name | Common Name | Family Name | Cultural Care | | | | |
|---|---|---|---|---|---|---|---|
| | | | L | T | H | W | S |
| *Haworthia cuspidata* | Star Window Plant | Liliaceae | 1-2 | 2 | 3 | 2-3 | 5 |
| *Haworthia fasciata* | Zebra Haworthia | Liliaceae | 1-2 | 2 | 3 | 2-3 | 5 |
| *Haworthia subfasciata* | Little Zebra Plant | Liliaceae | 2 | 2 | 3 | 2-3 | 5 |
| *Haworthia truncata* | Clipped Window Plant | Liliaceae | 1-2 | 2 | 3 | 3 | 5 |
| *Hedera canariensis* | Algerian Ivy | Araliaceae | 2-3 | 1-2 | 2 | 2 | 1 |
| *Hedera helix* | English Ivy | Araliaceae | 2-3 | 1-2 | 2 | 2 | 1 |
| *Hemigraphis alternata* 'Exotica' | Waffle Plant | Acanthaceae | 2-3 | 2 | 2 | 2 | 2 |
| *Hibiscus rosa-sinensis* | Chinese Hibiscus | Malvaceae | 1 | 2 | 2 | 2 | 1 |
| *Hippeastrum* hybrids | Amaryllis | Amaryllidaceae | 2 | 2 | 2 | 2 | 1 |
| *Howea belmoreana* | Belmore Sentry Palm | Palmae | 3-4 | 2 | 2 | 2 | 2 |
| *Howea forsterana* | Kentia Palm | Palmae | 2-4 | 2 | 2 | 2 | 2 |
| *Hoya carnosa* 'Variegata' | Wax Plant | Asclepiadaceae | 2-3 | 2 | 2-3 | 2 | 2 |
| *Hoya kerrii* | Sweetheart Hoya | Asclepiadaceae | 2 | 2 | 2 | 2 | 2 |
| *Hyacinthus orientalis* | Hyacinth | Liliaceae | 2 | 1-2 | 2 | 1 | 1 |
| *Hydrangea macrophylla* | Hydrangea | Saxifragaceae | 2 | 2 | 2 | 1 | 1 |
| *Hylocereus undatus* | Honolulu Queen | Cactaceae | 2-3 | 2 | 2 | 2 | 5 |
| *Impatiens wallerana* 'Variegata' | Busy Lizzie Impatiens | Balsaminaceae | 2-3 | 2 | 2 | 2 | 1 |
| *Ixora coccinea* | Ixora | Rubiaceae | 1 | 2 | 2 | 2 | 1 |
| *Jatropha integerrima* | Peregrian | Euphorbiaceae | 1 | 2 | 2 | 2 | 1 |
| *Justicia brandegeana* | Shrimp Plant | Acanthaceae | 1-2 | 2 | 2 | 2 | 1 |
| *Kalanchoe blossfeldiana* | Christmas Kalanchoe | Crassulaceae | 1-2 | 2 | 2 | 2 | 1 |
| *Kalanchoe fedtschenkoi* | Purple Scallops | Crassulaceae | 1-2 | 2 | 2-3 | 3 | 5 |
| *Kalanchoe pumila* | Dwarf Purple Kalanchoe | Crassulaceae | 1-2 | 2 | 2-3 | 3 | 5 |
| *Kalanchoe tomentosa* | Panda Plant | Crassulaceae | 1-2 | 2 | 2-3 | 3 | 5 |
| *Lilium longiflorum* | Easter Lily | Liliaceae | 2 | 1-2 | 2 | 1 | 1 |
| *Macropiper excelsum* | Lofty Pepper | Piperaceae | 2-3 | 2 | 2 | 2 | 2 |
| *Malvaviscus arboreus* | Turk's Cap | Malvaceae | 1 | 2 | 2 | 1 | 1 |
| *Mammillaria bocasana* | Powder Puff | Cactaceae | 1-2 | 2 | 3 | 3 | 5 |
| *Mammillaria compressa* | Mother of Hundreds | Cactaceae | 1-2 | 2 | 3 | 3 | 5 |
| *Mammillaria geminispina* | Whitey | Cactaceae | 1-2 | 2 | 3 | 3 | 5 |
| *Manettia inflata* | Firecracker Plant | Rubiaceae | 2 | 2 | 1-2 | 2 | 1 |
| *Maranta leuconeura erythroneura* | Red Nerve Plant | Marantaceae | 2-3 | 2 | 2 | 2 | 2 |
| *Maranta leuconeura kerchoviana* | Prayer Plant | Marantaceae | 2-3 | 2 | 2 | 2 | 2 |
| *Maranta leuconeura leuconeura* | Rabbit's Foot | Marantaceae | 2-3 | 2 | 2 | 2 | 2 |
| *Mazus reptans* | Wart Flower | Scrophulariaceae | 1 | 2 | 1-2 | 2 | 1 |
| *Mikania ternata* | Plush Vine | Compositae | 2-3 | 2 | 2 | 2 | 2 |
| *Monstera deliciosa* | Philodendron Pertusum | Araceae | 2-4 | 2 | 2 | 2 | 2 |

| Botanical Name | Common Name | Family Name | Cultural Care | | | | |
|---|---|---|---|---|---|---|---|
| | | | L | T | H | W | S |
| Monstera obliqua | Window Leaf | Araceae | 3 | 2 | 2 | 2 | 2 |
| Murraya paniculata | Orange Jessamine | Rutaceae | 2-3 | 2 | 2 | 2 | 2 |
| *Narcissus hybrids | Daffodils | Amaryllidaceae | 2 | 1-2 | 2 | 1 | 1 |
| Nautilocalyx lynchii | Black Alloplectus | Gesneriaceae | 2-3 | 2 | 2 | 1 | 7 |
| *Neoregelia carolinae 'Tricolor' | Tricolor Bromeliad | Bromeliaceae | 2-3 | 2 | 2 | 2 | 3 |
| Neoreglia spectabilis | Fingernail Plant | Bromeliaceae | 2-3 | 2 | 2 | 2 | 3 |
| Neoregelia zonata | Zonata | Bromeliaceae | 2-3 | 2 | 2 | 2 | 3 |
| *Nephrolepis exaltata 'Bostoniensis' | Boston Fern | Polypodiaceae | 2-3 | 2 | 1-2 | 2 | 6 |
| *Nephrolepis exaltata 'Fluffy Ruffles' | Fluffy Ruffles | Polypodiaceae | 2-3 | 2 | 1 | 2 | 6 |
| Nephrolepis exaltata 'Whitmanii' | Feather Fern | Polypodiaceae | 2-3 | 2 | 1 | 2 | 6 |
| Nidularium fulgens | Blushing Cup | Bromeliaceae | 2-3 | 2 | 2 | 2 | 3 |
| *Nidularium innocentii nana | Miniature Birdsnest | Bromeliaceae | 2-3 | 2 | 2 | 1 | 3 |
| Notocactus rutilans | Pink Ball | Cactaceae | 1-2 | 2 | 3 | 3 | 5 |
| *Oncidium sphacelatum | Golden Shower | Orchidaceae | 2 | 2 | 2 | 2 | 4 |
| Opuntia vilis | Little Tree Cactus | Cactaceae | 1-2 | 2 | 3 | 3 | 5 |
| Opuntia vulgaris | Irish Mittens | Cactaceae | 1-2 | 2 | 3 | 3 | 5 |
| Oxalis braziliensis | Shamrocks | Oxalidaceae | 2 | 2 | 2 | 2 | 2 |
| *Oxalis deppei | Good Luck Plant | Oxalidaceae | 1-2 | 2 | 2 | 2 | 1 |
| Oxalis flava | Finger Oxalis | Oxalidaceae | 1-2 | 2 | 2 | 2 | 1 |
| Oxalis hirta | Hirta Oxalis | Oxalidaceae | 1-2 | 2 | 2 | 2 | 1 |
| Oxalis megalorrhiza | Carnosa Oxalis | Oxalidaceae | 1-2 | 2 | 2 | 2 | 1 |
| Oxalis rubra | Red Oxalis | Oxalidaceae | 1-2 | 2 | 2 | 2 | 1 |
| Pachyphytum compactum | Thick Plant | Crassulaceae | 1-2 | 2 | 2-3 | 2-3 | 5 |
| Pachyphytum oviferum | Pearly Moonstones | Crassulaceae | 1-2 | 2 | 2-3 | 2-3 | 5 |
| Pachystachys lutea | Yellow Shrimp Plant | Acanthaceae | 2-3 | 2 | 2 | 2 | 1 |
| *Paphiopedilum hybrids | Ladyslipper Orchids | Orchidaceae | 2-3 | 2 | 2 | 1-2 | 4 |
| *Pedilanthus tithymaloides 'Variegatus' | Ribbon Cactus | Euphorbiaceae | 2-3 | 2 | 2 | 2 | 5 |
| Pelargonium x domesticum Geranium | Pansy Flowered | Geraniaceae | 1-2 | 1-2 | 2 | 2 | 1 |
| Pelargonium graveolens | Rose Geranium | Geraniaceae | 1-2 | 1-2 | 2 | 2 | 1 |
| *Pelargonium hortorum | House Geranium | Geraniaceae | 1-2 | 1-2 | 2-3 | 2 | 1 |
| Pelargonium peltatum | Ivy Geranium | Geraniaceae | 1-2 | 1-2 | 2 | 2 | 1 |
| Pellaea rotundifolia | Button Fern | Polypodiaceae | 2-3 | 2 | 2 | 1-2 | 6 |
| Pellionia daveauana | Trailing Watermelon Begonia | Urticaceae | 2-3 | 2 | 2 | 1-2 | 2 |
| Pellionia pulchra | Satin Pellionia | Urticaceae | 2-3 | 2 | 2 | 1-2 | 2 |
| Pentas lanceolata | Egyptian Star Cluster | Rubiaceae | 1 | 2 | 2 | 2 | 1 |

| Botanical Name | Common Name | Family Name | Cultural Care | | | | |
|---|---|---|---|---|---|---|---|
| | | | L | T | H | W | S |
| *Peperomia caperata* | Emerald Ripple | Piperaceae | 2-3 | 2 | 2 | 2 | 2 |
| *Peperomia clusiifolia* | Red-Edged Peperomia | Piperaceae | 2-3 | 2 | 2 | 2 | 2 |
| *Peperomia crassifolia* | Leather Peperomia | Piperaceae | 2-3 | 2 | 2 | 2 | 2 |
| *Peperomia obtusifolia* | Baby Rubber Tree | Piperaceae | 2-3 | 2 | 2 | 2 | 2 |
| *Peperomia obtusifolia* 'Variegata' | Variegated Peperomia | Piperaceae | 2-3 | 2 | 2 | 2 | 2 |
| *Peperomia orba* | Princess Astrid Peperomia | Piperaceae | 2-3 | 2 | 2 | 2 | 2 |
| *Philodendron bipennifolium* | Fiddle-Leaf Philodendron | Araceae | 3-4 | 2 | 2 | 2 | 2 |
| *Philodendron* 'Burgundy' | Burgundy | Araceae | 2-4 | 2 | 2 | 2 | 2 |
| *Philodendron* 'Emerald Queen' | Emerald Queen | Araceae | 2-4 | 2 | 2 | 2 | 2 |
| *Philodendron erubescens* | Blushing Philodendron | Araceae | 2-4 | 2 | 2 | 2 | 2 |
| *Philodendron* 'Florida' | Florida | Araceae | 2-4 | 2 | 2 | 2 | 5 |
| *Philodendron martianum* | Flask Philodendron | Araceae | 3 | 2 | 2 | 2 | 2 |
| *Philodendron* 'Prince Dubonnet' | Prince Dubonnet | Araceae | 2-4 | 2 | 2 | 2 | 2 |
| *Philodendron* 'Red Emerald' | Red Emerald | Araceae | 2-4 | 2 | 2 | 2 | 2 |
| *Philodendron scandens oxycardium* | Heart-Leaf Philodendron | Araceae | 2-4 | 2 | 2 | 2 | 2 |
| *Philodendron selloum* | Selloum | Araceae | 2-4 | 2 | 2 | 2 | 2 |
| *Phoenix roebelenii* | Pigmy Date Palm | Palmae | 2-3 | 2 | 2 | 2 | 2 |
| *Pilea cadierei* | Aluminum Plant | Urticaceae | 2-3 | 2 | 1-2 | 1 | 2 |
| *Pilea microphylla* | Artillery Plant | Urticaceae | 2-3 | 2 | 1 | 1 | 2 |
| *Pittosporum tobira* | Japanese Pittosporum | Pittosporaceae | 1-3 | 2 | 2 | 2 | 1 |
| *Pittosporum tobira* 'Variegata' | Variegated Pittosporum | Pittosporaceae | 2 | 2 | 2 | 2 | 1 |
| *Platycerium bifurcatum* | Staghorn Fern | Polypodiaceae | 2-3 | 2 | 2 | 2 | 6 |
| *Plectranthus australis* | Swedish Ivy | Labiatae | 2-3 | 2 | 2 | 2 | 2 |
| *Plectranthus australis* 'Marginatus' | Candle Plant | Labiatae | 2-3 | 2 | 2 | 2 | 2 |
| *Podocarpus macrophyllus* 'Maki' | Podocarpus | Podocarpaceae | 2-3 | 2 | 2 | 2 | 2 |
| *Polyscias balfouriana* 'Marginata' | Variegated Balfour Aralia | Araliaceae | 2-3 | 2 | 2 | 2 | 2 |
| *Polyscias fruticosa* | Ming Aralia | Araliaceae | 2-3 | 2 | 2 | 2 | 2 |
| *Pteris ensiformis* 'Victoriae' | Victorian Table Fern | Polypodiaceae | 2-3 | 2 | 1 | 2 | 2 |
| *Punica granatum nana* | Dwarf Pomegranate | Punicaceae | 1 | 2 | 2 | 2 | 1 |
| *Rhapis excelsa* | Lady Palm | Palmae | 2-3 | 2 | 2 | 2 | 2 |
| *Rhododendron* hybrids | Azaleas | Ericaceae | 2 | 1-2 | 1 | 1 | 2 |
| *Ruellia graecizans* | Red-Spray Ruellia | Acanthaceae | 1-2 | 2 | 2 | 2 | 1 |
| *Saintpaulia* hybrids | African Violets | Gesneriaceae | 2-3 | 2 | 2 | 1 | 7 |
| *Sansevieria parva* | Parva Sansevieria | Agavaceae | 2-3 | 2 | 3 | 2-3 | 5 |
| *Sansevieria suffruticosa* | Spiral Snake Plant | Agavaceae | 2-3 | 2 | 3 | 2-3 | 5 |

| Botanical Name | Common Name | Family Name | Cultural Care | | | | |
|---|---|---|---|---|---|---|---|
| | | | L | T | H | W | S |
| *Sansevieria trifasciata 'Hahnii' | Birdsnest Sansevieria | Agavaceae | 2-4 | 2 | 3 | 2-3 | 5 |
| *Sansevieria trifasciata 'Laurentii' | Gold-banded Sansevieria | Agavaceae | 2-4 | 2 | 3 | 2-3 | 5 |
| *Sansevieria trifasciata 'Zeylanica' | Zeylanica | Agavaceae | 2-4 | 2 | 3 | 2-3 | 5 |
| Saxifraga stolonifera | Strawberry Geranium | Saxifragaceae | 2-3 | 1-2 | 2 | 2 | 2 |
| Schlumbergera bridgesii | Grandmother's Christmas Cactus | Cactaceae | 2-3 | 2 | 2 | 2 | 2 |
| *Schlumbergera truncata | Christmas Cactus | Cactaceae | 2-3 | 2 | 2 | 2 | 2 |
| *Scindapsus pictus | Silver Pothos | Araceae | 3 | 2 | 2 | 2 | 2 |
| Sedum lucidum | Tortuosum | Crassulaceae | 1-2 | 2 | 2-3 | 2-3 | 5 |
| Sedum multiceps | Pigmy Joshua Tree | Crassulaceae | 1-2 | 2 | 2-3 | 2-3 | 5 |
| Sedum spectabile | Showy Sedum | Crassulaceae | 1-2 | 1-2 | 2-3 | 2-3 | 5 |
| Sedum spectabile | Showy Sedum | Crassulaceae | 1-2 | 1-2 | 2-3 | 2-3 | 5 |
| Sempervivum arachniodeum | Cow Web Houseleek | Crassulaceae | 1-2 | 1-2 | 2-3 | 2-3 | 5 |
| Setcreasea pallida 'Purple Heart' | Purple Heart | Commelinaceae | 1-2 | 2 | 2 | 2 | 2 |
| Sinningia pusilla | Miniature Slipper Plant | Gesneriaceae | 2-3 | 2 | 1 | 1 | 7 |
| *Sinningia speciosa | Gloxinia | Gesneriaceae | 2-3 | 2 | 1-2 | 2 | 7 |
| *Soleirolia soleirolii | Baby Tears | Urticaceae | 2-3 | 2 | 1-2 | 1 | 2 |
| *Spathiphyllum 'Clevelandii' | Peace Lily | Araceae | 2-3 | 2 | 2 | 1 | 2 |
| Spathiphyllum floribundum | Spathe Flower | Araceae | 2-3 | 2 | 2 | 1 | 2 |
| *Spathiphyllum 'Mauna Loa' | Mauna Loa | Araceae | 2-3 | 2 | 2 | 1 | 2 |
| Stapelia nobilis | Carrion Flower | Asclepiadaceae | 1-2 | 2 | 2-3 | 2-3 | 5 |
| Streptocarpus x hybridus | Cape Primrose | Gesneriaceae | 2-3 | 2 | 2 | 2 | 7 |
| Strobilanthes dyeranus | Persian Shield | Acanthaceae | 2-3 | 2 | 2 | 2 | 2 |
| Syngonium hoffmanii | Goose Foot | Araceae | 3 | 2 | 2 | 2 | 2 |
| *Syngonium podophyllum | Nephthytis | Araceae | 2-4 | 2 | 2 | 2 | 2 |
| Syngonium wendlandii | Wendlandii | Araceae | 3 | 2 | 2 | 2 | 2 |
| Tetranema roseum | Mexican Violet | Scrophulariaceae | 2-3 | 2 | 2 | 2 | 1 |
| Tillandsia bulbosa | Dancing Bulb | Bromeliaceae | 2 | 2 | 2 | 2 | 3 |
| Tillandsia lindenii | Blue-Flowered Torch | Bromeliaceae | 2 | 2 | 2 | 2 | 3 |
| Tolmiea menziesii | Piggyback Plant | Saxifragaceae | 2 | 1-2 | 2 | 2 | 2 |
| Tradescantia blossfeldiana | Flowering Inch Plant | Commelinaceae | 2-3 | 2 | 2 | 2 | 2 |
| Tradescantia sillamontana | White Velvet | Commelinaceae | 2-3 | 2 | 2 | 2 | 2 |
| *Tulipa spp. | Tulips | Liliaceae | 2 | 1-2 | 2 | 1 | 2 |
| *Vanilla planifolia | Vanilla | Orchidaceae | 2 | 2 | 2 | 2 | 3 |
| *Vriesea x mariae | Painted Feather | Bromeliaceae | 2 | 2 | 2 | 2 | 3 |
| *Vriesea splendens | Flaming Sword | Bromeliaceae | 2 | 2 | 2 | 2 | 3 |
| Yucca elephantipes | Spineless Yucca | Agavaceae | 2 | 2 | 3 | 2 | 2 |
| *Zebrina pendula | Wandering Jew | Commelinaceae | 2-3 | 2 | 2 | 2 | 2 |

# APPENDIX A

## PLANT SOCIETIES

American Begonia Society, Inc.
139 North Ledoux Road
Beverly Hills, CA 90211

Bonsai Clubs International
445 Blake Street
Menlo Park, CA 94025

Bromeliad Society, Inc.
P.O. Box 3279
Santa Monica, CA 90403

Cactus and Succulent Society
of America, Inc.
Box 167
Reseda, CA 91335

Epiphyllum Society of America
218 East Greystone Avenue
Monrovia, CA 91016

International Geranium Society
11960 Pascal Avenue
Colton, CA 92324

National Fuchsia Society
10954 East Flory Street
Whittier, CA 90606

The American Fuchsia Society
Hall of Flowers
Golden Gate Park
San Francisco, CA 94122

The American Gesneriad Society
11983 Darlington Avenue
Los Angeles, CA 90049

American Fern Society
Biological Sciences Group
University of Connecticut
Storrs, CT 06268

The American Gloxinia/
Gesneriad Society, Inc.
Department AHS
P.O. Box 174
New Milford, CT 06776

The American Hibiscus Society
Box 98
Eagle Lake, FL 33139

American Orchid Society, Inc.
Botanical Museum of Harvard
University
Cambridge, MA 02138

The Indoor Light Gardening
Society of America, Inc.
423 Powell Drive
Bay Village, OH 44140

African Violet Society of
America, Inc.
Box 1326
Knoxville, TN 37901

Saintpaulia International
Box 10604
Knoxville, TN 37919

# APPENDIX B

## GREENHOUSE SUPPLIERS

Aluminum Greenhouses, Inc.
14615 Lorrain Ave.
Cleveland, OH 44111

Janco Greenhouses
10788 Tucker St.
Beltsville, MD 20705

Lord and Burnham
Irvington, NY 10533

National Greenhouse Co.
Pana, IL 62557

Pacific Coast Greenhouse Mfg.Co.
525 East Bayshore Rd.
Redwood City, CA 94063

Redfern's Greenhouses
55 Mt. Hermon Rd.
Scotts Valley, CA 95060

Turner Greenhouses
US 13 S
Goldsboro, NC 27530

Gothic Arch Greenhouses
P.O. Box 1564
Mobile, AL 36601

Sturdi-Built Manufacturing Company
11304 S.W. Boones Ferry Rd.
Portland, OR 97219

# APPENDIX C

## WATER GARDENING
## SUPPLIERS

Eco Enterprises
2821 Northeast 55 Street
Seattle, WA 98105    98105

Environmental Dynamics
Box 996
Sunnymead, CA 92388

Home Grow Products
Tube Craft
1311 West 80th Street
Cleveland, OH 44140

Hydroculture, Inc.
1516 North 7th Avenue
Phoenix, AZ 85007

Hydro-Garden Chem-Gro
P.O. Box 7172
Colorado Springs, CO 80933

Oaklair Hydroponic Plant Food
2140 Waudman Avenue
Stockton, CA 95209

Opus
437 Boylston Street
Boston, MA 02116

Pacific Aqua Culture
3 A Gate 5 Road
Sausalito, CA 94965

Pan American Hydroponics, Inc.
P.O. Box 470
Grapevine, TX 76051

Texas Greenhouse Company
2717 St. Louis Avenue
Fort Worth, TX 76110

Tiffany Industries
Greenhouse Products Division
145 Weldon Parkway
Maryland Heights, MO 63043

Water Works Gardenhouses
Box 905
El Cerrito, CA 94530

# APPENDIX D

Many indoor plants and horticultural supplies can be purchased from local sources, garden centers, hardware stores, florist shops and other retail outlets. If you are interested in obtaining up to date sources for particular plants or plant families, contact individual plant societies. The indoor light society can provide information on equipment for growing plants with artificial light. Most horticultural magazines have advertisements and listings of indoor plants and horticultural supplies.

## PERIODICALS

*American Horticulturist*
published by
The American Horticultural Society
7931 East Boulevard Drive
Alexandria, VA 22308

*Horticulture*
published by
Massachusetts Horticultural Society
300 Massachusetts Avenue
Boston, MA 02115

*Plants Alive*
published by
319 N.E. 45th
Seattle, WA 98105

*Plants and Gardens*
published by
Brooklyn Botanic Gardens
100 Washington Avenue
Brooklyn, NY 11225

The following companies sell seeds of indoor plants, indoor plants, or horticultural supplies along with other gardening supplies. As your interest in indoor plants increases and you communicate with other plant growers, you will probably develop a list of favorite suppliers.

## HORTICULTURAL SUPPLIERS

Ball, George J.
P.O. Box 335
West Chicago, IL 60185

Burpee, W. Atlee, Co.
6876 Burpee Building
Warminster, PA 18974

Park, Geo. W., Seed Co., Inc.
236 Cokesbury Road
Greenwood, SC 29647

Tropical Plant Products, Inc.
Box 7754
Orlando, FL 32804

# GENERAL INDEX

# INDEX